Thailand
A Struggle for the Nation

The **ISEAS – Yusof Ishak Institute** (formerly Institute of Southeast Asian Studies) is an autonomous organization established in 1968. It is a regional centre dedicated to the study of socio-political, security, and economic trends and developments in Southeast Asia and its wider geostrategic and economic environment. The Institute's research programmes are grouped under Regional Economic Studies (RES), Regional Strategic and Political Studies (RSPS), and Regional Social and Cultural Studies (RSCS). The Institute is also home to the ASEAN Studies Centre (ASC), the Singapore APEC Study Centre and the Temasek History Research Centre (THRC).

ISEAS Publishing, an established academic press, has issued more than 2,000 books and journals. It is the largest scholarly publisher of research about Southeast Asia from within the region. ISEAS Publishing works with many other academic and trade publishers and distributors to disseminate important research and analyses from and about Southeast Asia to the rest of the world.

History of Nation-Building Series

Thailand
A Struggle for the Nation

CHARNVIT KASETSIRI

YUSOF ISHAK INSTITUTE

First published in Singapore in 2022 by
ISEAS Publishing
30 Heng Mui Keng Terrace
Singapore 119614
E-mail: publish@iseas.edu.sg
Website: http://bookshop.iseas.edu.sg

All rights reserved. No part of this publication may be reproduced, stored in a retrieval system, or transmitted in any form or by any means, electronic, mechanical, photocopying, recording or otherwise, without the prior permission of the ISEAS – Yusof Ishak Institute.

© 2022 ISEAS – Yusof Ishak Institute, Singapore.

The responsibility for facts and opinions in this publication rests exclusively with the author and his interpretation do not necessarily reflect the views or the policy of the publisher or its supporters.

ISEAS Library Cataloguing-in-Publication Data

Name(s): Charnvit Kasetsiri, 1941–, author.
Title: Thailand : a struggle for the nation / by Charnvit Kasetsiri.
Description: Singapore : ISEAS–Yusof Ishak Institute, 2022. | Series: History of nation-building series | Includes bibliographical references and index.
Identifiers: ISBN 9789815011241 (soft cover) | ISBN 9789815011258 (pdf) | ISBN 9789815011265 (epub)
Subjects: LCSH: Nation-building—Thailand. | Thailand—Politics and government. | Monarchy—Thailand. | Thailand—History.
Classification: LCC DS575 C482

Typeset by Superskill Graphics Pte Ltd
Printed in Singapore by Mainland Press Pte Ltd

Contents

Acknowledgements		vii
Foreword by Wang Gungwu		ix
Prologue by Craig J. Reynolds		xiii
Chapter One	From Dynastic to "National History"	1
Chapter Two	From Siam to Thailand: What's in a Name?	37
Chapter Three	The Monarch and New Monarchy During the Reign of King Bhumibol, Rama IX	69
Chapter Four	The New Monarchy: The Early Years	115
Chapter Five	The Princess Mother and the New Monarchy	155
Chapter Six	Twilight of Two Reigns in Siam and Thailand	197
Epilogue		239
Index		245
The Author		264

Acknowledgements

I wish to thank Professor Wang Gungwu of the National University of Singapore for inviting me to participate in the project on "History of Nation-Building in Southeast Asia". Without his encouragement, understanding and patience this book, *Thailand: A Struggle for the Nation*, would have never been finished. I also thank him for his Foreword to the book.

I would also like to express my sincere thanks to the ISEAS – Yusof Ishak Institute in Singapore for funding the project and the research fellowship at ISEAS. A good number of academics and friends whom I met during many years of research while staying in the island nation have helped to shape my ideas about this book. My gratitude goes to them: Edwin Lee, Taufik Abdullah, Cheah Boon Kheng, Reynaldo Ileto, Patricia Lim Pui Heun, Ch'ng Kim See and the team at the ISEAS Library deserve special recognition, as do the book's editors, Ng Kok Kiong and Rahilah Yusuf.

I am also indebted to my friends in and out of Thailand, who in different ways helped me to write this book: Benedict Anderson and David Boggett read and commented on the first few chapters, and Craig J. Reynolds read the final draft and wrote a fine Prologue. I am grateful for many helping hands from younger colleagues, including Thak Chaloemtiarana, Pasuk Phongpaichit, Chris Baker, Thongchai Winichakul, Kasian Tejapira, Yoko Hayami, Saichol Wannarat, Porphant Ouyyanont, Prajak Kongkirati, Pavin Chachavalpongpun, Sa-nguan Khumrungroj, Serhat Unaldi, Pimpraphai Bisalputra, Jeffery Sng, Mala Rajo Sathien, Rosenun Chesof, Akkraphong Khamkhun, Preecha Phothi, Napisa Wisuttipun, Siriwut Boonchuen, Satthaphum Boonma and Anan Krudphet.

My sincere thanks go to good librarians and libraries with great collections of Thai and Southeast Asian documents at the Kyoto Center for Southeast Asian Studies and Thammasat University, Bangkok. I appreciate very much the assistance of Ono Mikiko, Kanchanaporn Chitsanga, Chaiyasit Angkapunyadech, and finally, Benjamin Ivry.

Foreword

Wang Gungwu

It gives me great pleasure to write this foreword to Charnvit Kasetsiri's volume on the struggle to build the nation called Thailand. Given his long-held view that the country should have retained its name as Siam, he has brought an exceptional perspective to how Thailand approached the idea of modern nationhood—both before and after the age of imperialism. The name change that followed the military coup of 1932 and the end of the historic monarchy had created greater insecurity in a region that was about to be transformed. The uncertainty was compounded by Japanese ambition and the outbreak of the European War that became worldwide. This was followed after the war by a total change in the regional environment when the imperialist powers retreated and new nations gained their independence.

Siam had the difficult experience of remaining sovereign and independent during the nineteenth century when its neighbours were being invaded. The wisdom of its rulers and the skills of its diplomats were the envy of all those who were colonized. Having survived multiple threats with exceptional success, those who were set to build a new kind of nation in 1945 would have assumed that Thailand was free from that particular burden. Indeed, many post-war studies made the process of Thai nationhood appear to be a seamless development that required no special attention. They therefore concentrated on economic, diplomatic and security affairs that enabled the country to play important roles in the region's fresh start as new polities.

It needed someone with Charnvit's historical sensitivity to go behind the country's confident front to discover other dimensions to the special kind of nationhood that the various peoples of Thailand sought to establish. His focus on the long reigns of the royal house as determinants in the country's political architecture is original and illuminating. It does not only emphasize a unique phenomenon but also throws light on how the kings could find the space to strengthen their position under some extremely unstable conditions.

As a historian, he is not satisfied simply to have found an instructive angle from which to explore the mysteries in a modern experimental monarchy. His keen sense of time has filled his narrative with insights that only few people could have identified. To me, that is a mark of one with a fine sense of what the past can mean. I thank him for the chance to see this mature and thoughtful Charnvit at work and commend this book to everyone who wants to understand Thailand better.

I would also like to say why the nation of Thailand has a special significance here. It was at Chulalongkorn University, Bangkok at the 14th International Historians of Asia (IAHA) Conference that I first suggested that it was time for historians to write the history of nation-building in Southeast Asia. I was speaking on the history of nationalism in Southeast Asia and complained that the study of the difficult task of building nation had been largely in the hands of political scientists. I felt that, while that task was still work in progress, there had been enough done over the past fifty years for historians to examine what has been achieved so far.

On my return to Singapore, I asked Chan Heng Chee, then Director of the Institute of Southeast Asian Studies, for her support to plan a modest Nation-Building Series to produce histories of the five original members of the Association of Southeast Asian Nations (ASEAN): Thailand, Philippines, Indonesia, Malaysia and Singapore. She was most encouraging and provided funding for me to invite outstanding historians of the five countries to meet about the project. Her successors also gave me their warm support. I chose five established historians whose work I knew and who each had lived through the nation-building process in their respective countries. I gave an account of this in my introduction to the first volume published, that on Malaysia by Cheah Boon Kheng.[1]

When the historians agreed to join the project, ISEAS invited them to spend time there together and use its extensive library. After a few meetings, we were convinced that each country had a very different story to tell. Each one was building its post-war modern nation under exceptional political conditions that were largely shaped by its distinctive demographic, social and cultural components. As we examined these differences, we were made all the more conscious of the need to identify and explain the backgrounds of each country. We realized that this was a necessary corrective to social science approaches that tend to look for generalities. We concluded that we should not seek to find a common framework for the five volumes but should let the country differences dictate the way each volume should be presented.

We also held a workshop attended by other colleagues who were experts in the history of each of the countries. They were asked, after discussing the project with the five authors, to set down their views in a volume of essays, entitled *Nation-building: Five Southeast Asian Nations*. That way, they could each make a contribution to the project while the five books were being planned. As it happened, Craig Reynolds was the one who drew attention to the ideas of nation and state that applied to Thailand and it is fitting that Charnvit has asked him to provide a Prologue to this volume. It is a gesture of deep friendship and understanding on their parts, something I truly appreciate.

Wang Gungwu
National University of Singapore
14 December 2021

NOTE
1. "Introduction", in *Malaysia: The Making of a Nation*, by Cheah Boon Kheng (Singapore: Institute of Southeast Asian Studies, 2002).

Prologue

Craig J. Reynolds

Charnvit Kasetsiri was born in 1941, the eldest of seven siblings, in Ban Pong on the Maeklong River just outside of Bangkok. Having written numerous history books and articles in Thai and English, he has been a prolific author since his first book in English, *The Rise of Ayutthaya: A History of Siam in the Fourteenth and Fifteenth Centuries* (1976). Through the Social Sciences and Humanities Textbooks Foundation over which he presides, he has fostered the publication of countless works in Thai, many translated from English and other languages. He has passionately advocated the study of Southeast Asia and its languages. His collaborative networking across the region through the Southeast Asia Regional Exchange Program as well as his scholarly accomplishments earned him in 2014 the Distinguished Contributions to Asian Studies Award given by the Association for Asian Studies. In 2012 he won the prestigious Fukuoka Academic Prize for outstanding achievements in the field of Asian Studies.

Charnvit taught history for many years at Thammasat University, founded in 1934 by Pridi Banomyong, one of the architects of the 1932 coup that overthrew the absolute monarchy, and Charnvit has been a tireless campaigner for the integrity of this second-oldest Thai university and for the reputation of Pridi Banomyong who was wronged more than once in the course of Thailand's fractious politics. A Pridi partisan and inveterate international traveller to overseas conferences who has sometimes gone abroad temporarily for strategic reasons, Charnvit does not board a plane without a liberal supply of brochures, pamphlets and T-shirts that advertise new publications by the Textbook Foundations or promote his latest enthusiasms—"Change Thailand to Siam!", "Democracy Walk for Thammasat, Tha Prachan Campus, and Communities on Rattanakosin Island!". On Facebook, Charnvit has supported student protesters in their demands to reform the monarchy.

In recent years Charnvit's team has been organizing historical tours. Its lead guide is able to speak at length on all topics relevant to what the tourists are about to see as they alight from their buses to visit shrines and temples, ancient monuments and public sculptures. A colleague once referred to Charnvit as the Great Disseminator. He has the capacity to turn everything he sees, hears and touches into observations about the past in the present. He cannot help himself.

I mention these details as background to alert the reader about what follows in Charnvit's contemporary history of Thailand's struggle for the nation: expect the unexpected. What transpires in the following pages is not a straightforward account of how this struggle has evolved into the polarized divisions that have paralysed the country for the past two decades. Instead, we find a non-linear narrative that testifies to the dominance of the Thai monarchy, the pole star, "the centre of the universe for everyone's well-being," as one senior Thai historian has put it.[1] Rather than proceeding chronologically from the reform-minded fifth monarch of the dynasty, Chulalongkorn (r. 1868–1910) through the 1932 event, the decline of the institution after the abdication of the seventh monarch in 1935, and the rehabilitation of the institution under King Bhumibol (r. 1946–2016), Charnvit toggles back and forth between the two longest reigns in Thai history.

The structure of the book takes this form to highlight the parallels, the similarities and the differences between what happened when powerful and forward-thinking kings passed from the scene and were succeeded by figures born to reign and rule but who were less able to govern their realms. For those in academic and activist circles familiar with Charnvit's enthusiasms and causes, his treatment of twentieth- and twenty-first-century history may be surprising. Social movements are not a focus of the book; this is not history from below. Nationalism is guided nationalism, the product of elite policies, not the expression of the people's will. At a time when young protestors are being imprisoned for violating the *lèse majesté* law, a statute that criminalizes defamation of the Supreme Institution, it may seem unfashionable to put forward an argument that elite and particularly royal talent, accomplishment and energy have been so beneficial to the kingdom.

The second half of the nineteenth century was the watershed period when the Thai ruling elite was forced to respond to the new world of Western imperialism dominated by *farang*, a Thai loan word for white people. Westerners in Bangkok asked questions of Siamese officials about origins of the Thai, and responses to these questions as well as the technology of printing and cartography gradually transformed the Thai world from religious and dynastic to national as Western models of nationhood took hold in the minds of the elite. King Vajiravudh (r. 1910–25), who was not nearly so interested in governing as his father, articulated in his plays and other writings some of the elite responses to origins and race that have endured in Thai public discourse to the present day.

Vajiravudh's eight years in England epitomizes what had become a hallmark of elite practice: Western education and training. From the middle of the nineteenth century until after the Second World War the world outside Siam was Europe where the first generation of Thais went for their education. Chulalongkorn's travels abroad took him at first to Dutch and British colonies, but in later decades he travelled to Europe where he endeavoured to demonstrate to his hosts in imperial capitals that his ancient kingdom and nascent nation could be as modern as any other. Charnvit describes him as "diminutive and dapper" and through his intuitive grasp of how film and photography could project an international image, as "media-savvy". The social and administrative reforms engineered by Chulalongkorn were as much about lifting Siam's international image in the eyes of Europe as they were about addressing inequities and injustices, although prostration as a sign of subjugation and oppression was a priority reform early in the reign. Left unsaid in Charnvit's account is whether or not prostration was completely abandoned; it returned with a flourish for royal personages in the second half of the twentieth century during the reign of King Bhumibol.[2]

Well into the twentieth century Europe remained the source of the modern. King Bhumibol's father, Mahidol Adulyadej, Prince of Songkhla, went to America for his medical education where he met and married Sangwan Talapat, a commoner. At that time the United States was an unusual destination for Thais to study abroad. Mahidol died in 1929 leaving Sangwan Talapat to raise their daughter, Galyani Vadhana (b. 1923), and two sons, Ananda (b. 1925) and Bhumibol (b. 1927), the elder of whom had become king in 1935 when King Prajadhipok abdicated. The children were brought up in Switzerland until the end of the war when the family was flown back to Bangkok by the British.

Following the mysterious death of Ananda in June 1946, Bhumibol acceded to the throne. By that time the United States, which replaced the French, Dutch and British colonial powers to become the paramount power in the region, had declared itself an ardent foe of the communist-inspired nationalisms in Asia. Thailand found itself in a world divided into "two halves of the same walnut" and was quickly enlisted as an American ally in the Cold War. Many elite children still went to Europe for their education, but middle-class children, hundreds of them, went to the United States courtesy of American funding.

Coups and prime ministers come and go in this history, much of which will be familiar to those knowledgeable about the country's turbulent politics. The longest reign in Thai history from 1946 to 2016 provides a semblance of stability that is both spiritual and political thanks to King Bhumibol's popularity. The military is a constant presence. When the army took over in the late 1930s and changed the name of the country from Siam to Thailand, new lyrics in the national anthem infused Thai identity top-down with race and sacrifice. In 1952 the military government presented King Bhumibol with his own radio station. The king was both announcer and disc jockey and in the daily broadcasts played classical music as well as his own compositions. From 1950 until 1997 he personally attended graduations and awarded degrees to 470,000 students, thus creating a personal rapport between the exalted figure of the monarch and young Thai people who would remember forever the moment they received their degrees from the king's hand.

Charnvit's history throws up all kinds of surprises. An unfamiliar detail about Sino-Thai heritage, so important in commerce, custom, religion, and popular culture, is tucked away in a footnote. After the death of the Princess Mother in 1995 her eldest child, Princess Galyani, and her granddaughter, Princess Sirindhorn, wore mourning clothes of sack and raw cotton in a performance of Kong Tek, the Chinese mourning rite. General Surayud Chulanont was prime minister from 2006 to 2008 after the 2006 coup against an elected caretaker government. Who could imagine that General Surayud's father, Lieutenant Colonel Payom Chulanont, had joined the Communist Party of Thailand in the late 1950s and rose in the ranks of the People's Liberation Army? The twists and turns in Thailand's history can be dizzying.

Charnvit's birth town Ban Pong, once a busy hub of commerce, was on a river route to the west and south. As I turned the pages of Charnvit's history of Thailand's struggle for the nation I wondered if his forebears in Ban Pong during King Chulalongkorn's time had come out to see the king's vessel pass by on the Maeklong River, or later in the early 1900s when the railroad was finished to see the royal rail carriage stop briefly on its journey. With his siblings Charnvit has written lovingly of his upbringing in Ban Pong and Paknam. The two memoirs, dense with details and photographs of family life, include an episode during the Japanese Occupation in 1944–45 when the Japanese used Ban Pong as a base in their construction of the Death Railway in Kanchanaburi.[3]

In 1990 the History Association and the Chulachomklao Royal Military Academy organized an academic conference on "Language and History" at the academy's new campus in Nakorn Nayok where the academy had recently moved. Princess Sirindhorn, known popularly as Phra Thep and patron of the History Association who has given history lectures at the Academy, was in attendance. The most academic of King Bhumibol's four children, she presented a conference paper on an episode at the end of the Second World War when some ten thousand Japanese soldiers were stationed in the area as they were about to be repatriated to Japan.

In the dining room Princess Sirindhorn sat with senior military officers and seemed quite at ease in their company. At lunch one day the kitchen staff prepared *moji*, a chewy red bean desert dusted with coconut, inspired by a Japanese sweet that had made its way into Thai cuisine during the Japanese period. In conversation with conference delegates Charnvit observed that Thailand must be the only country in the world where a princess, patron of an academic association, shared a meal with military officers and the army cooks would serve a Japanese desert reminiscent of the Occupation. Charnvit is always ready with a quip that can turn an otherwise insignificant detail into a historical observation.

His good nature notwithstanding, Charnvit makes clear in the final pages that he is not very sanguine about the country's future. During Thailand's democratic spring in 1974 the Thai constitution was changed to allow female succession. This apparent loosening of male prerogative had no effect on the reign change in 2016 when the designated male heir, Prince Vajiralongkorn, succeeded without challenge to become the tenth Bangkok king. Communism, long gone as the spectre that once haunted Thailand's political order, has been replaced by another. The spectre now haunting Thailand is authoritarianism.

NOTES
1. Nidhi Eoseewong, "The Culture of the Army, *Matichon* Weekly, 28 May 2010", in *Bangkok May 2010: Perspectives on a Divided Thailand*, edited by Michael J. Montesano, Pavin Chachavalpongpun and Aekapol Chongvilaivan (Singapore: Institute of Southeast Asian Studies, 2012), p. 12.
2. Patrick Jory, *A History of Manners and Civility in Thailand* (Cambridge: Cambridge University Press, 2021), Ch. 6.
3. Charnvit Kasetsiri et al., *Mae: klap chak banpong thueng paknam* [Mother: Back from Banpong to Paknam], privately printed, 2010; Charnvit-Nimit Kasetsiri, *Banpong kap pho lae mae: khrang nueng nan ma laew* [Mother and Father in Banpong: Once Upon a Time Long Ago], privately printed, 2014.

CHAPTER ONE

From Dynastic to "National History"

The modern territorial nation and linear history have an intimate relationship. Indeed, one might say that they co-produce each other as the principal mode of belonging in the twentieth century. Individuals learn to identify with nation-states that have supposedly evolved over a long history to reach the self-conscious unity of the two and are thus poised to acquire mastery over the future.[1]

Prasenjit Duara, 1998

Introduction: The Dynastic History of Siam[2]

Few instruments of power are as vital for the modern Thai state as the idea of a bounded nation-state and its corresponding history. To understand nationalism and nation-building in modern Siam, it is therefore crucial to look at how present-day national Thai History was achieved. The official history of Thailand is taught in schools and colleges as a ceaseless forward march of the nation, beginning in ancient times when the Thai people lived in China. The golden age of the mighty Kingdom of Nan Chao (Nanzhao) which they had established in Yunnan, was followed by a mighty fall and swift resurrection.

Driven out by the Mongols, the Thais entered mainland Southeast Asia. By the thirteenth century, they had established their first kingdom after freeing themselves from the yoke of the Khmer of Angkor. The Kingdom of Sukhothai was ruled by the benevolent hero-kings Si Intrathit (?1240s–?1270s) and Ramkhamhaeng (?1279–1298), who brought the Thais another golden age.

In 1351, the second kingdom was founded by King Uthong in the city of Ayutthaya. It remained the main centre of the Thais for more than 400 years, governed by another set of hero-kings (aided by very few women) such as Naresuan (1590–1605) and Narai (1656–88), until, in 1767, Ayutthaya was defeated and sacked by the Burmese. The Thais successfully fought back.

After the defeat of the eternal enemy from the West came the last and present Kingdom of Rattanakosin/Bangkok with ten great King Ramas of the Chakri Dynasty.[3] Siam preserved her independence and became modern during the reign of King Chulalongkorn (1868–1910) who was followed, two generations later, by another great modernizer who steered Thailand through a troublesome time of change, King Bhumibol Adulyadej (1927–2016).

Following this national history of Siam, the story of Siam's geo-body, as Thongchai Winichakul's *Siam Mapped* (1994) deemed it, would appear neatly woven, linear, progressive, and easily traced back through lines of kings, dynasties and kingdoms.[4] Yet, the objective historian recognizes this line of interpretation and presentation as obviously modern and, more importantly, imagined and created. A close look at how the Thai ruling elite has come to view its past in this manner is revealing.

An article written by King Mongkut in the mid-nineteenth century highlights the artificial construction of the history of Siam. It was published in 1851 in Canton, China. That year, Rama III (Nangklao), a half-brother of Mongkut, passed away after reigning for twenty-seven years (1824–51). For all those years, Mongkut had been forced to wear an orange robe as a Buddhist monk. After the death of his half-brother, he immediately disrobed and left his temple, Wat Bowonniwet in Bang Lamphu, to become king. The new ruler's statement was in English, and it is worth quoting in full:

> I am just availing myself of an opportunity for searching into some pages of Siamese ancient history, and beg to state that our ancient capital Ayuthia before the year AD 1350, was but the ruin of an ancient place belonging to Kambuja (now known as Cambodia), formerly called

Lawek ... There were other cities not far remote, also possessed by the Kambujans ... Sometime near the year AD 1300, the former inhabitants were much diminished by frequent wars with the northern Siamese and the Peguans, or Mons, so that these cities were vacated ... and nothing remained but their names.

Former inhabitants declared that the people of Chiang-rai, a province of what is now called Chiang-mai (North Laos), and Kampengpet, being frequently subjected to great annoyance from their enemies, deserted their native country and formed a new establishment at Ch'a-liang in the western part of Siam Proper; and built a city which they called Thepha-maha-na-khon, whence has been preserved, in the national records, as the name of our capital down to the present day, Krung-Thepha-maha-na-khon ... and there five kings of the first dynasty reigned, until the sixth, named U-T'ong Rama-thi-bodi ascended the throne in 1314.

This king, it is said, was the son-in-law of his predecessor, who was named Sirichai Chiang Sen, who was without male issue, and therefore the throne descended to the son-in-law by right of the royal daughter. U-T'ong Rama-thi-bodi was a mightier prince than any of his predecessors, and subsequently conquered and subjected to his sway all Southern Siam, and some provinces in the Malayan Peninsula.

He made Ch'a-liang the seat of his government for six years, and then in consequence of the prevalence of disease of a pestilential character, he caused various researches to be made for some more healthy location, and finally fixed upon the site of Ayuthia, and there founded his new capital in April 1350. This date is an ascertained fact. From this period, our Siamese annals are more exact, and the accounts generally reliable—being accompanied by dates and days, months, and years from 1350 to 1767.[5]

It is very clear from King Mongkut's account that the history of his kingdom did not go back very far into the past. The *time* was around 1300 and the *space* was mostly around Ayutthaya or present-day central Thailand; such *space* was very much more connected with the Angkorian Khmer than with the Chinese.[6]

There was no mention of the Thais in China, nor of Sukhothai and the great King Ramkhamhaeng, both of which were central to later versions of "national" history. Of course, the cities of Chaliang, Chiang Saen, and

Chiang Mai further north were mentioned, but only to establish the dynastic line of King Uthong, the founder of Ayutthaya; and this line went back only five generations.

Even as late as 1904, towards the end of the reign of King Chulalongkorn (1868–1910) who is credited with reforming and modernizing Siam, its history did not much differ from that of King Mongkut. That year, the sizeable volume *The Kingdom of Siam* (1904) was prepared by the Siamese Ministry of Agriculture for distribution at the Louisiana Purchase Exposition in St. Louis, Missouri.

The commission overseeing the volume included Prince Vajiravudh, the future King Rama VI, who had just returned from England by way of America and Japan in early 1903; Prince Devawongse (1858–1923), the minister of foreign affairs; Prince Mahisra (1866–1907), the minister of finance; and Chao Phya Devesra, the minister of agriculture.

It is safe to assume that such a book had royal and governmental approval to present the nation's history to a readership at a prominent international event. In Chapter 5 on "Siam from an Historical Standpoint", the volume states:

> Little is known about the early history of the country, which was first called Siam by the Portuguese and, following them, by the other nations who first came into contact with it … Siemlo, the Chinese name, is of equally doubtful etymology, and by the neighboring countries, such as Burmah and Cambodia, the country was called, after the name of its former capital, Sri Ayuddhya … The Siamese call themselves Thai, probably the equivalent of Franks, the free ones, i.e., free from the foreign (Cambodian) yoke…
>
> The chief source of the earliest history is found in the *Phongsawadan Muang Nua* (The Annals of the North) … Besides these Annals … there are local annals, some written in Pali, some in Siamese or Laosian, which also throw a certain light on pre-Buddhistic times…
>
> In the earliest times, before the capital was established at Ayuthia in 1350, there extended throughout the country a number of small principalities. These extended over what is now called Siam, from the borders of China east and west through the valleys of the Menam Chow

Phya and the Menamkong and down the Malay Peninsula, with Ligor as capital, as far south as Malacca ...

The early history of the race shows a continual migration from the north to the south, seeking an outlet to the sea ... until in 1350 the branch of the Tai race known now as Siamese established their capital at Ayuthia ... The history of the Siamese as a dominant power begins from this date ... From the founding of the capital at Ayuthia in 1350 down to its destruction in 1767 by the Burmese ...[7]

As may be seen from the above, again the *time* was 1350, and the *space* was Ayutthaya. However, since the two sources were written in English, it may be that they were meant for foreign consumption only, reflecting what the Thai elite wanted to present to the outside world, especially to the *farang*, and those who mattered and read or spoke English. A look at the presentation of history intended for local consumption gives a clearer picture of actual historical knowledge and construction at that time.

In 1887, King Chulalongkorn commissioned an important project of ninety-two modern large-format oil paintings, illustrating scenes chosen from among those believed to be core events of the past. Each was to be accompanied by poems describing the historical episode.

They were elaborately framed in gold in a modern Western style. The paintings were exhibited at the cremation ceremony of three of King Chulalongkorn's children who died at early ages, along with one of his concubines. The solemn occasion took place at Sanam Luang, the main ground in front of the Grand Palace, and the public was invited to admire these representations of the past.

Tellingly, the first painting was of the foundation of Ayutthaya by King Uthong. Perhaps more importantly, the poem describing the event was written by King Chulalongkorn himself.

The rest followed in a series according to the Ayutthaya and Bangkok *phongsawadan* (chronicles), focusing on hero-kings, their actions, and battles. Of course, these battles were fought to defend the kingdom against the Burmese. The series ended with painting No. 91 portraying Mongkut's ordination and painting No. 92 showing Henry Burney, a British envoy, at an audience with King Rama III in 1825.[8]

It is again important to note that this history exhibition was of a dynastic, rather than national, nature; and the time went back to 1350, the founding date of Ayutthaya, linking King Chulalongkorn, who commissioned the project, through the early Bangkok kings right back to the founder, King Uthong. Therefore, the Bangkok-Chakri Dynasty was historically linked with that of Ayutthaya and no other.

A glance through lists of turn-of-the-century school history textbooks confirms the conception of time and space and the treatment of history then current. In her study of the Ministry of Education history texts from 1897 to 1969, Suphanni Kanchanatthiti, a senior historian, found that the 1895 official curriculum, probably the oldest, required middle school students to read two history books.

The first was *A Brief Chronicle (Phongsawadan) of Ayutthaya* and the second, *A Chronicle (Phongsawadan) of the Present Dynasty*.[9] She further elaborated that school textbooks from 1897 to 1901 were all about the *phongsawadan* type of history of Ayutthaya and Thonburi-Bangkok.

Suphanni noted that these books were full of detail, "heavy", boring, and required a great deal of memorization, making them unsuitable for young students. She concluded that one can learn from them more about the good, proper and correct forms of Thai court literary style than about history.[10]

Between 1913 and 1931, just before the end of the absolute monarchy, history textbooks were slightly changed in content, and a brief world history was included. More interestingly, a new Thai word coined for history began to appear, though *phongsawadan* was still used.

The new term, found in two textbook titles in 1923 and 1930, was *prawatkan*,[11] eventually to be replaced by earlier coinages—*prawatsat* or *prawatisat*—now popularly used to mean history.

A Step towards "National History"

In his acclaimed study of nationalism,[12] Benedict Anderson pointed out the distinction between Chulalongkorn and Vajiravudh as Kings of Siam. In the chapter "Official Nationalism and Imperialism", Anderson compared Siam to Japan when both dynasties faced the rise of nationalist movements:

> Meiji's contemporary, the long-reigning Chulalongkorn (r. 1868–1910), defended his realm from Western expansion in a style that differed markedly from that of his Japanese opposite number. Squeezed between British Burma and Malaya, and French Indochina, he devoted himself to a shrewd manipulative diplomacy rather than attempting to build up a serious war machine ... Nor was anything much done to push an official nationalism through a modernized educational system ... primary education was not made compulsory till more than a decade after his death, and the country's first university was not set up until 1917, four decades after the founding of the Imperial University of Tokyo ...
>
> Nonetheless, Chulalongkorn regarded himself as a modernizer. But his prime models were neither the United Kingdom nor Germany, but rather the colonial *beamtenstaaten* [official states] of the Dutch East Indies, British Malaya, and the Raj. Following these models meant rationalizing and centralizing royal governments, eliminating traditional semi-autonomous tributary statelets, and promoting economic development somewhat along colonial lines. The most striking example ... was his encouragement of a massive immigration of young single male foreigners to form the disoriented, politically powerless workforce needed to construct port facilities, build railway lines, dig canals, and expand commercial agriculture. This importing of *gastarbeiter* [guest workers] paralleled, indeed was modelled on, the policies of the authorities in Batavia and Singapore. And as in the case of the Netherlands Indies and British Malaya, the great bulk of the labourers imported during the nineteenth century were from southeastern China ... Indeed the policy made good short-term sense for a dynastic state, since it created an impotent working class 'outside' Thai society and left that society largely 'undisturbed'."

For Anderson, Chulalongkorn's Siam was very much a dynastic realm.[13] And as the king's leadership style was organized around the royal centre, it was logical that the past was treated as dynastic history. However, after the turn of the century, things appear to have changed rapidly. Anderson states:

Wachirawut [Vajiravudh], his son and successor (r. 1910–1925), had to pick up the pieces, modelling himself this time on the self-naturalizing dynasts of Europe. Although—and because—he was educated in late Victorian England, he dramatized himself as his country's "first nationalist". The target of this nationalism, however, was neither the United Kingdom, which controlled 90 per cent of Siam's trade, nor France, which had recently made off with easterly segments of the old realm: it was the Chinese whom his father had so recently and blithely imported. The style of his anti-Chinese stance is suggested by the titles of two of his most famous pamphlets: *The Jews of the Orient* (1914), and *Clogs on Our Wheels* (1915).

Anderson concluded:

> Here is a fine example of the character of official nationalism—an anticipatory strategy adopted by dominant groups which are threatened with marginalization or exclusion from an emerging nationally-imagined community. (It goes without saying that Wachirawut also began moving all the policy levers of official nationalism: compulsory state-controlled primary education, state-organized propaganda, official rewriting of history, militarism—here more visible show than the real thing—and endless affirmation of the identity of dynasty and nation).[14]

In short, towards the end of Chulalongkorn's reign and the early years of Vajiravudh's, the Thai dynastic realm was increasingly being threatened and had to come to terms with "Nation-ness". Here are the roots of the shift from dynastic to linear "national" (official) history.

Prince Damrong (1862–1943), a half-brother and right-hand man of King Chulalongkorn who served as his minister of education and the interior, would be labelled as "Father of Thai History".[15] In 1914, Prince Damrong introduced a neatly woven, linear, and progressive interpretation of Thai history. From then on, it was accepted as official and "national" up to the present day.

The prince wrote that the "history of Siam may properly be divided into three periods, namely, (1) when Sukhothai was the capital, (2) when Ayutthaya was the capital, and (3) since Ratanakosin (Bangkok) has been the capital."[16]

This periodization of Thai history became known as *sam krung*, or three capitals (Sukhothai, Ayutthaya, Ratanakosin/Bangkok). It focuses on the time when each capital and its kings were considered the centre of historical events.

This sequence was possibly influenced by the European division of history as classical, medieval and modern. According to these divisions, Sukhothai represented the classical, Ayutthaya medieval, and Ratanakosin/Bangkok modern.

Damrong went back even before classical Sukhothai, adding a lengthy elaboration on eras before the capitals of Sukhothai and Ayutthaya in what was, in his day, central modern Siam. He explained, focusing on territories (space) and races (ethnicities), that the "territory of which Siam is now made up was originally occupied by people of two races, the Khmers (Khom) and the Lao."[17] Since Thais were not the original people of Siam, the Prince had to look elsewhere.

By relying on *nangsu farang* (books written by authors of the white race), Prince Damrong had concluded that the

> Original home of the Thai was in what is now known as Southern China, in a region stretching from the Yangtse River through Szechuan and Yunnan down to the Lao country[18] … the Thai had established several independent states[19] … From about the year B.E. 400, as a result of over-population, these Thais began to emigrate to the South-West and South. Later on, the Chinese, as their power increased, extended their frontiers so as to encroach upon the domain of the Thai who, being thus pressed, were unable to dwell in comfort in the region which they had first occupied. Knowing from their fellows who had emigrated previously that it was easier to support life in the lands to the South-West and South, the Thai thereupon descended into those parts in ever growing numbers.[20]

The Thai southward migration theory advocated by Prince Damrong was convincingly argued. On their long journey southward from Szechuan-Yunnan, the Thais paused to establish the mighty Kingdom of Nan Chao (Nanzhao) in Yunnan, which lasted from the sixth to the mid-thirteenth centuries.

The Prince elaborated at length about Nan Chao (Nanzhao), explaining the hybrid name derivation of the kingdom as from the Chinese (Nan meaning south), whereas Chao (*zhao*) is a Thai word for lord. "For the better understanding of my reader", the historian prince explained, "I shall henceforward refer to Nan Chao (Nanzhao) as *muang Thai doem*, the original country of the Thai."[21]

To illustrate his point, the names of the rulers Meng Hsi-nu-lo /Khun Luang (d. 678), Sheng-luo-pi (712–728), P'i-lo-ko/Pilaoko (728–750), and Ko-lo-feng/Khun Luang Fa (750–778) were cited and their actions regarding the Chinese discussed.[22] Of the Nan Chao (Nanzhao), Damrong concluded that the

> Family of King Hsi-Nu-Lo ruled for thirteen generations, extending over a period of 255 years. The customs of the country became more and more assimilated to those of China, owing to the continual influx of Chinese settlers … In BE 1797 (1254), the Mongols of the Yuan dynasty conquered China, extending their territory to the South-West and subduing the original Thai homeland at the same time as they conquered Burma.[23]

Nan Chao (Nanzhao) was lost, but the link continued. Prince Damrong argued that while the Thais were still powerful in their "original home", many had already migrated to the valleys of the Salween, while some went as far as Arakan and Assam. Large numbers had settled down in northern Vietnam and Laos, and

> about the year BE 1400 (CE 857), a powerful Thai monarch named Phraya Chao Phrom (or King Brahma, the first of the line of King Uthong who founded Ayutthaya) succeeded in wresting territory from the Khmers … [for] the first Thai settlement on the southern bank of the River Mekhong [south of the present-day Golden Triangle].[24]

The last few lines here are crucial to understanding how the Prince established a link between the "original Thai" and their "original home" (*muang Thai doem*) in southern China on the one hand, and on the other, with King Uthong, founder of Ayutthaya at the heart of modern Siam. A linear and progressive history had been completely and satisfactorily created. The time was pushed back from 1350 to around 850.

Damrong's interpretation stretched Thai history back 500 years, if counted from the time of King Phrom, or 800 from Hsi-nu-lo/Khun Luang of Nan Chao (Nanzhao). Meanwhile, the space had been vastly enlarged to cover an area from Sukhothai/Ayutthaya up to the Yangtse and Szechuan-Yunnan.

It included the mainland of Southeast Asia: Shan states in Burma, northern Laos, Vietnam, and Assam in India. The Thais were older and bigger than the Angkorian Empire.

The Thai "nation" suddenly appeared very ancient. It had a good past (Nan Chao [Nanzhao], Sukhothai, and Ayutthaya) and progressed linearly to modern times (1914). This was a history that had, and probably still has, a profound emotional effect on urban educated Thais.

It is unsurprising then to learn that the respected Sino-Thai linguist, anthropologist, and ethnographer Phraya Anuman (1888–1967), is believed to have felt overwhelmed when he stood at the northern tip of modern Siam, in Chiang Rai Province. He imagined a stream of Thais emerging from China into modern Siam on the Southeast Asian mainland.[25]

Farang—King Vajiravudh and the Contestation

Why the change from dynastic to "national history"? Three factors were involved. First was the Thai elite's contact with the West, especially with *farang*, or white people. Second was the impact of Vajiravudh, King Rama VI, and his official nationalist policies. Third was domestic pressures and challenges from a new urban educated social stratum, along with a newly emerging free press.

Doubtless, the linear and progressive version of national history resulted from the elite's contact with the West. As Craig J. Reynolds pointed out,

> [W]e might find that the dominant story types of Western culture have traveled with the global structures of capitalism and the nation-state, a form of the state put in place by elites who had lived and studied in the West. Modern Thai historiography is, to a large extent, a Western import, though it bears some unmistakable features of being a Thai historiography.[26]

Although Thais from the generations of Mongkut and Chulalongkorn-Damrong did not dwell or study in the West, they were highly familiar with its core values and ideas. Mongkut was one of the first Thais to learn how to speak and write English, mainly by teaching himself and associating with missionaries.

The future King Chulalongkorn, his brothers and sisters, as well as ladies of the court were tutored by different foreign teachers.

The best-remembered of these is Anna Leonowens, whose fictionalized memoir later inspired the Broadway musical comedy *The King and I*.[27] A handful of Thai elites followed the same path as the royal children. Some went overseas to get a Western colonial education in British schools in neighbouring Penang and Singapore.

In the 1880s, by the time Chulalongkorn's children were of school-going age, a tradition had started in which princes and other sons of the nobility were sent to elite schools in western Europe, especially England. This was the beginning of a long line of a new breed—the *nakrian nok* (returning students from overseas education).

When these foreign-educated pupils reappeared in Siam, they enjoyed much influence, easily rising in bureaucratic careers. They had huge advantages over their domestically educated counterparts, the *nakrian nai*, and were far more successful materially.

In short, Western education, whether formal or informal, overseas or domestic, had become part of the Thai elite's world since the latter part of the nineteenth century. They knew about the West from classrooms, books, or newspapers, and were also in physical contact with powerful and civilized *farang* at home and overseas: missionaries, merchants, diplomats, teachers, and friends.

It might be useful to visualize the kind of social environment in which the Thai elite encountered *farang*. The experience probably made them more conscious of their own identity. It is easy to imagine that the *farang* often asked about Siam this and that, as well as being Thai or about Thai things.

Phaithūn Phongsabut, a geographer, and Wilatwong Phongsabut, a historian, both at Chulalongkorn University, observed that works by *farang* scholars on the Thai race and the original Thai homeland had a profound impact on the writing of Thai "national history", probably as early as the turn of the nineteenth century.

For example, in his *Cradle of the Shan Race* (1885), Albert Terrien de Lacouperie (1844–94), an orientalist at University College, London, was likely the first to suggest that the Thais originally lived in Central China before migrating south. He came to this conclusion by comparing different Tai dialects of Southeast Asia and those spoken in China. At about the same time, others arrived at similar conclusions.

Archibald Ross Colquhoun (1848–1914), first Administrator of Southern Rhodesia (1890–94), a self-governing British colony in Africa, was among these pioneers. Colquhoun led several exploratory expeditions to Assam, Burma, Indochina and southern China.

In his volume *Across Chrysê: Being the Narrative of a Journey of Exploration Through the South China Border Lands from Canton to Mandalay* (1883), Colquhoun suggested that the Thais were from Yunnan. His proposal was further confirmed by Edward Harper Parker (1849–1926), a British consular official in Hainan, in his essay published in *The Chinese Recorder*, "The Old Thai Empire" (March 1894). This was when Nan Chao (Nanzhao) was first identified as a Thai kingdom.[28]

These are some examples of works in which the Thai ruling elite had to engage with a *farang*-dominated new world. The situation never existed in the early Ratanakosin/Bangkok days of the first two King Ramas (1782–1824). They were never confronted by questions of race or the original Thai homeland.

Their Thai world was religious and dynastic, not national. But by the middle of the nineteenth century, when Western models of nationhood were being emulated, copied and pirated, it became necessary to deal with the issues of race and homeland.

Culture was a crucial mediating force because Siam had abundant religious relics, pagodas, Buddha images, and Hindu statues that were studied and classified by Western scholars from the United Kingdom, France, the Netherlands, Germany and other nations. Identities such as Dvaravati Mon, Angkorian Khmer, and other terms relating to race or kingdom were duly attached to archaeological artefacts.

Consequently, the Thais came to believe that their original homeland was elsewhere. China and Nan Chao (Nanzhao) were proposed as sites of origin upon "scientific" grounds. They seemed appropriate and archeologically (*borankhadi*) correct.[29]

By the start of the twentieth century, Western-style interest in antiquity and a search for the past had become accepted and even fashionable among the Thai ruling elite. Their contacts with—and frequent visits to—Western colonies in Southeast Asia, plus first-hand knowledge of European civilization gave them access to organizations of learning, such as the Royal Asiatic Society, the École française d'Extrême-Orient (EFEO), and many museums, libraries and journals.

One effect was that a series of activities and institutions were established. In 1904, the Siam Society was founded under the patronage of Crown Prince Vajiravudh, who had just returned from his studies in the United Kingdom.

Among the first articles in the *Journal of the Siam Society* was Prince Damrong's "The Foundation of Ayuthia".[30] Thai history was discussed, proposed, and in some way, also created in the journal. In 1905, the Ho Samut Samrap Phra Nakhon, or Bangkok Library,[31] was launched, again with the Crown Prince as president. It was not entirely new, since its predecessor, the Vajirayana Library, had been inaugurated in memory of King Mongkut.

In 1907, the Royal Research Society (*Samakhom subsuan khong buran nai prathet sayam*, later changed to *Borankhadi Samoson* or Antiquarian Society) was also started. These institutions were mechanisms to search for, and learn about, Thainess while promoting official nationalism. From these endeavors grew what is known as Thai studies today. Such studies of antiquity had a particularly acute political and psychological impact upon the Thai ruling elite and the urban educated.

The second point to stress is the impact of Vajiravudh, Rama VI, and his official nationalist policy. As suggested above, the last ten years of King Chulalongkorn's reign were crucial for understanding changes within Thai society in connection with a nation-state's emergence and search for new historiography.

When Vajiravudh returned from England in 1902 at the age of twenty-one, after a nine-year educational sojourn in England, he was poised to become the first king who was a *nakrian nok*. Indeed, he differed from his predecessors on the throne.

As a prince and later king (1910–25), Vajiravudh was considered rather aloof; he isolated himself from his father's large and active palace family, relatives, and the bureaucracy. In the early years of his reign, he often stayed at the newly built Sanam Chandra Palace in Nakhon Pathom Province, 56 kilometres outside Bangkok. He surrounded himself with a male entourage and occupied himself in singular ways. The Bangkok circle likely thought of him as somewhat *plaek* or *pralad* (strange or unusual).

The fifteen years he spent on the throne fell between the long, successful absolutist forty-two-year reign of his father and the relatively weak and unsuccessful effort by the brother who succeeded him, Prajadhipok (Rama VII; 1925–35).

As a highly prolific author, Vajiravudh is now officially remembered as Phra Maha Dhiraratchao, or the Great Scholar King. He signed around 200 travelogues, plays, poetry, songs, articles, and sermons with over 100 pen names. He is also known for his official nationalistic policy which earned him the title of Father of Thai Nationalism.[32]

The reign of Vajiravudh was a time of change. The first work stoppages by Bangkok's Chinese merchants and labourers occurred just before his first coronation on 11 November 1910. The next year, the Celestial Monarchy in Peking abruptly ended.[33]

February 1912 saw an attempted coup, known as *Kabot R.S. 130*, or the 1912 Rebellion, aimed at overthrowing Vajiravudh. It happened only a few months after the thirteen-day extravaganza of his second coronation in November 1911.

Indeed, the 1900s and 1910s differed from previous years. With domestic changes, a new, albeit small, educated middle class emerged, several of whom were Sino-Thai, critical of their absolute monarchy. The time was also marked by the spread of a free press claiming to represent *paksiang* (mouth and voice) of the common people; in addition, print capitalism[34] also made people think of their status in society differently.

And as mentioned before, the rise of nationalism—along with the fall of monarchies in Europe and Asia (the Qing, Ottomans, Romanovs, Habsburgs)—motivated King Vajiravudh to consolidate his rule and compelled him to embark on an individual nationalist policy.

On 1 May 1911, not long after his first coronation, Vajiravudh founded the Wild Tigers Corps (*sue pa*), a royal national paramilitary force intended to "instill the love of the nation" among the Thai. On 1 July, he followed it up by establishing the Boy Scouts (*luk sua*, meaning cubs or male offspring of a tiger).

The Wild Tigers Corps was soon criticized as an unprofessional extension of the king's personal bodyguards. Military leaders did not approve, and the corps was dissolved soon after the reign ended. Yet within the Wild Tigers circle, the king launched his nationalist programmes. He personally lectured them about *chat* (nation), *satsana* (religion), and *phra maha kasat* (great king),[35] which became the three pillars of Siamese modern state ideology; since then, this so-called Holy Trinity has been exploited frequently by right-wing military regimes.

King Vajiravudh used different strategies in historiography and constructing historical narratives to achieve the policy of *pluk chat-pluk chai* or Wake the Nation and the Heart. Doing so, he coined a new Thai term for history, *prawatisat* (from the Pali-Sanskrit: *paravati* + *sastra* or science of recording).

He may have found the established Thai word *phongsawadan* unsuitable in a global context since its direct translation, referring to the reincarnation of a royal family, did not appear sufficiently modern. *Prawatisat* caught on, and by 1917 the word was frequently seen in titles of history texts.[36]

Following the Thai ruling elite's aforementioned interest in antiquity, one important outing for Vajiravudh was to visit the "classical heartland of the Thai". In 1907, the Crown Prince voyaged to Kamphaengphet, Sukhothai, Sawankhalok, Uttaradit and Phitsanulok.

The trip took four months by train, boat and horse. Vajiravudh clearly intended to "discover" the Sukhothai Kingdom. He went very well prepared, taking along copies of translations of King Ramkhamhaeng's *Inscription* (translated into modern Thai by the French scholar of Southeast Asian archaeology and history George Cœdès, not long before this trip).

He also carried a copy of the translation of a Sukhothai inscription, the *Phongsawadan Nua* (Chronicle of the North), and a *Phongsawadan Krung Si Ayutthaya*. These served in some ways as his guidebooks. The Prince examined most of the major ruins in those five cities. He noted details of his observations and added extensive comments, using the inscription and *phongsawadan* as references. He compared them with sites in Egypt.[37]

The outcome of the trip was a sizeable volume entitled *Ruang Thieo Muang Phra Ruang* (A Tour of the Phra Ruang Country 1908) printed with photographs and an appendix consisting of King Ramkhamhaeng's Inscription. In a preface, Vajiravudh expressed the hope that his writings and discoveries would make Thais "aware that Our Thai Nation (*chat Thai*) is not a new nation, and not a nation of barbarians, or what is called in English 'uncivilized'".[38]

In short, Vajiravudh not only "discovered" Sukhothai but gave life to ruins that had been abandoned and covered with trees and vines for over a century since the late 1700s. His observations and comments became part of the plot for a linear history to be developed in full by Prince Damrong in 1914, as mentioned above.

This trip set the stage for what would later become Sukhothai-ism among the Thai ruling class. From then on, the ruins of Sukhothai symbolized the golden age of national Thai history. Sukhothai's stone inscriptions and *phongsawadan* written records would become sources of inspiration, sparking the imaginations of professional and amateur Thai historians.

To them, Sukhothai was an exceptional Buddhist realm of righteous kings "elected" by public consent; it was rich and fertile with "fish in water and rice in the fields".[39]

His upper-class education in Victorian England had familiarized Vajiravudh with Shakespeare, operetta and English language popular theatre. Indeed, the king fell very much in love with English literature and drama. He translated into Thai *Romeo and Juliet*, *The Merchant of Venice*, and *As You Like It*. He also restaged many plays and performances he had seen in England, from *Othello* to Gilbert and Sullivan's *Mikado* for court audiences. He even acted in many of them. These included the 1888 play *My Friend Jarlet* (as *Mittara Teah* or *True Friend*) by Arnold Golsworthy (1865–1939) and E.B. Norman, a work which outside Thailand has been largely forgotten, as well as its authors.

It was in this context that the king began to turn episodes from the *phongsawadan* into plays to "waken" the Nation (*pluk chat*). Of his many plays, two featuring legendary heroes are worth mentioning. They are the stories of *Phra Ruang* and *Thao Saenpom*, illuminating Vajiravudh's type of nationalism and construction of linear history.

Three *Phra Ruang* plays exist: a dance drama from 1912, a modernized version in 1914, and a later musical in the Bangkok style from 1924. The best-remembered today is the 1914 play originally prepared for the king's Wild Tigers entourage.[40] It was formerly included in high school textbooks. Vajiravudh found the plot in the *Phongsawadan Nua* (Chronicle of the North) which he carried along on his 1907 tour, although at the time he commented that the document was unreliable on historical facts.[41]

According to the chronicle, Phra Ruang was Governor of Lopburi (Lavo), just north of Ayutthaya. His duty was to send water as a tribute to the king of Angkor. Using a magic spell, Phra Ruang could command water to remain in bamboo baskets. Upon learning that a man had such powers, the Angkorian king sent a soldier to execute Phra Ruang, who fled to Sukhothai.

The Khmer soldier chased after him by diving into the earth, emerging on the grounds of the Temple of the Great Relics (Wat Phra Si Rattana Mahathat) in Sukhothai, where he eventually found Phra Ruang. Not recognizing him, the soldier asked the governor himself where he might be found. Using magic, Phra Ruang advised the soldier to stay and wait there. The Khmer immediately turned to stone and has stayed put there ever since. Seeing that Phra Ruang had such miraculous powers, the people of Sukhothai "invited/elected" him to be their king. End of story.

By transforming this tale into a play, Vajiravudh modernized and rationalized it to fit a modern nation. For him, Phra Ruang was a Thai king of Lopburi, a vassal of Cambodia. Phra Ruang was ingenious, having invented the basket for carrying water, light enough for long-distance transportation from the central Menam basin to Angkor.

Upon learning of such a clever Thai, the Khmer king sent his commander to eliminate him. The commander went underground (not diving into the earth as in the original version) to find Phra Ruang. He went all the way to Sukhothai, where Phra Ruang was hiding. He met the king, whom he did not recognize, and asked how to find him. Phra Ruang told him to wait, called his men to arrest the Khom, and had chased him back to Cambodia, effectively freeing the Thais from the Cambodian yoke.

In his preface to the play, Vajiravudh said that Phra Ruang was a "*ruang ching*" or true story.[42] After peeling off all the miraculous and fabulous camouflage, he suggested, historical verity remained. He identified Phra Ruang with a figure in the Ramkhamhaeng Inscription.

In his opinion, Phra Ruang was Si Intrathit, the first king of Sukhothai. He made the Thais independent and in return, the local population invited him to be their monarch. By matching the story in the chronicle with information from the inscription and a touch of modern rationalist interpretation, Vajiravudh had constructed the first Thai capital and dynasty, forming a link with previous dynasties in China and with later ones in Ayutthaya and Ratanakosin/Bangkok.

There was a further extravagant attempt to link Sukhothai with Ratanakosin/Bangkok and the Chakri Dynasty. In 1925, preparations were made for an exhibition to showcase the products and culture of Siam at the site now known as Suan Lumpini, on what was then the outskirts of Bangkok. The Bangkok Expo was meant to be a grand event, like those popular in Europe and the United States, which Vajiravudh had experienced while studying in England from 1893 to 1902.

For the fifteenth anniversary of the king's accession to the throne, it was deemed appropriate to have such a grand exhibition to promote Siam as a modern, although unindustrialized, nation. However, the king felt badly ill and passed away on 25 November 1925. The Bangkok Expo never occurred. Yet a commemorative volume entitled *Souvenir of the Siamese Kingdom Exhibition at Lumbini Park B.E. 2468* was prepared for print. Two years later, in 1927, it was published in English and Thai with compelling illustrations.

The section "Historical Sketch of Siam" features a photo of a ruined pagoda. The caption reads *The Seven Rows of Pagodas, Swankaloke, The Middle One Being the Abiding Place of the Relics of the First of the Chakri Dynasty.* This was an attempt to link the Chakri, or probably Vajiravudh himself, with the Sukhothai-Phra Ruang Dynasty, a line some 600 years distant, back to the thirteenth century. It is difficult, almost impossible, to prove any such connection. But nations and nationalism may imagine what is unprovable.

Thin-Skinned

The other play was *Thao Saenpom* or The King Who Had a Hundred Thousand Bumps on His Body. In it, King Vajiravudh again "demythologized the history of the father of the founder of Ayutthaya".[43] As the historian Walter F. Vella pointed out, Thao Saenpom was not turned into a national hero as Phra Ruang had been. Yet by removing the miraculous and fabulous coating around this legendary figure, Vajiravudh again concluded that his hero was real and historical. He established a link between King Uthong's father and branches of ruling Thai families who had migrated across the Mekong into present-day northern Siam.

In 1913, in a handwritten memorandum, the king theorized at length about Thao Saenpom, including where he came from and what he had done. He cited his discussions and arguments on the subject with Prince Damrong and another scholar, Ayutthaya governor Phraya Boran (Phon Tejagupta, 1871–1936), about whether Uthong's city was located south of Kamphaengphet, or Nakhon Pathom, or Suphanburi.

The opinions of these royal-aristocratic historians differed in detail to an extent beyond the scope of this chapter. They shared one vision in common: a linear history of the Thai nation and the steady southward migration of the Thai people.[44]

As is clear from the above account, those involved in the making and writing of history were kings, princes, and other members of the nobility. Modern Thai national history thus appears as a craft of the ruling elite. It was a prerogative of the ruling elite of the dynastic realm.

An Ayutthayan law describes the daily royal routine from 7:00 a.m. until late at night, specifying that at 1:00 a.m., the *Phongsawadan* is to be read to the king before His Majesty retires to bed.[45]

Royal manuscripts were jealously guarded and regarded as sacred. They were kept at the centre of power and were not intended for the public. In the mid-nineteenth century, when one officer got a newfangled bourgeois idea and printed the *kotmai tra sam duang*, or Three Seals Law, for sale, Rama III had the books confiscated and enshrined in a pagoda at Wat Saket in Bangkok.

It took an outsider to break the taboo. By 1863, Rama III was long gone and Mongkut, his half-brother, had become Rama VI (r. 1851–68). Dan Beach Bradley (1804–73), an American Protestant missionary from Marcellus, New York, defied tradition by printing a *Phongsawadan* in two volumes. They were for sale and were allowed to circulate freely. Bradley was a key figure in bringing print capitalism and modern journalism to Siam. He was the first to translate the American Constitution into Thai language, published in his own journal in the late 1860s.

This English language journal, *The Bangkok Recorder*, received subscription requests from seventeen princes, fifty-seven noblemen, seven foreigners (*farang* and Chinese), and nineteen monks and commoners[46] for a total circulation of only 100. The literate circle, mostly male, of Bangkok was still very limited.

This first newspaper of Siam was printed monthly from 1844 to 1845 and again from 1865 to 1867. It did not prosper commercially. Nevertheless, printing had become a competitive business. Another American missionary, Samuel Smith, founded his own printing house, issuing the *Siam Weekly Advertiser* and *Siam Repository*. For a time, King Mongkut likewise had his court announcements printed as *ratchakitchanubeksa*, the Royal Gazette. In 1873, in the era of Chulalongkorn, the Royal Printing House was established.

Nevertheless, the ruling elite began to gradually lose their prerogatives, as David K. Wyatt has noted:

> Late in the Fifth Reign and early in the Sixth, a handful of mavericks, outsiders, trenchantly criticized the existing social, economic, and political order. Noteworthy among them were the turn-of-the-century journalists and essayists K.S.R. Kularb and Thianwan, both commoners.

Craig J. Reynolds called K.S.R. Kularb (1834–1913) a "challenge to royal historical writing" and Walter Vella praised Thianwan as "a man who fought giants".[47] Both became known through print capitalism and belong to the first group of nationalists from humble backgrounds.[48] Kularb became involved with the realm of royal history.

He was born in Bangkok at a time when Western influence, especially the printing press and journalism, first made itself felt. His father was Chinese, while his mother was from the Nakhon Ratchasima (known as Korat) official class. He grew up in a minor princely residence, became a novice and later a monk, thus receiving a traditional Thai education.

But he represented not only old Siam but also the modern West, during the fifteen years that he toiled as a clerk for several *farang* companies. Reportedly he travelled widely to Singapore, Penang, Sumatra, Manila, Batavia, Macao, Hong Kong and Calcutta. Some even claim that he went as far as England which would have outdone some Siamese kings and princes.

By the 1880s, Kularb was known and respected as a learned man in the small-scale educated circle of the Bangkok elite. He stood out because of his background as a commoner, as well as his energetic printing and writing. He had become a bibliophile, with a large personal library. In 1882, on the occasion of the Bangkok-Chakri Centennial, Kularb joined a royal exhibition by showcasing 1,000 books from his private collection.

In the 1890s, he became an editor and published his own journal, *Sayam praphet*. A prolific author, he wrote many works expressing changes that took place during the transitional nineteenth century. He published biographies and genealogies of important individuals and families of Siam, an unusual activity at the time.

Eventually, this practice got him into trouble with the Palace, when he wrote a biography of a Supreme Patriarch. Kularb was accused of *lèse majesté* and fabrication. After the investigation was over, he was sent for a one-month hospital stay to be "cured" of his "madness" (a new notion of punishment in modern Siam).[49]

After that, his reputation was tarnished. The ruling elite, which had no interest in a writer from outside its circles, had successfully associated him with lies, fabrication, invention, shamelessness, and madness.

As Reynolds pointed out, his crime was likely "borrowing" and "pirating" royal documents, which he later edited and published in different versions. This infuriated the ruling elite.

In 1897, Kularb wrote an essay, "On the Independence of a Country". He presented it as a series of questions and answers exchanged by a father and son, including some recondite references from *Phongsawadan* and other ancient texts:

Q: What must one do to remain a civilized and independent country?
A: To remain independent and prosperous, a country must have four qualities. It must:
(1) be a land of the Buddha,
(2) be a Kingdom ruled with law and order,
(3) have a good Government and
(4) have good people.

This was Kularb's idea of the nation, which he formulated long before the triad of nation, religion, and king of Vajiravudh. Notably, he emphasized good leadership and good relations between king and people as mutually dependent masters and servants. As Reynolds put it,

> Evidence exists that [Kularb] had a part in awakening nationalist sentiments, speaking sometimes as a cultural nationalist by criticizing European handkerchiefs, Egyptian cigarettes, Swedish matches, and imported whisky in which faddish residents of Bangkok indulged. But his reaction was not so much one of xenophobia but of dismay at the lack of confidence in the Siamese way.[50]

In his publication *Ayatiwat* (Growth or Progress; 1911)[51] he compiled 136 stories about "changes from old to new customs", offering a vivid picture of what was happening in the top echelons of Thai society at the time. He wanted to inform and alert his public readership, the small urban educated class in Bangkok, about changes taking place. The cover of *Ayatiwat* was decorated with his seal and picture inside a rose (his name Kularb, a word derived from the Persian, means rose).

On it he wrote "*Ayatiwat*: A book for knowledge of the *people*, on the changes of various official customs, from old to new, 136 stories, useful for officials and the *public* to know."[52] Kularb survived until the age of 79, but by the time he died in 1913, he had been reduced to an impoverished, marginalized status.

Kularb's life and work indicate that the rise of nationalism and nationness in Siam was not just hierarchical. This becomes more explicit in a PhD thesis by Matthew Phillip Copeland, *Contested Nationalism and the 1932 Overthrow of the Absolute Monarchy in Siam.*[53]

Copeland convincingly argues that the role of the Chakri kings in the "early history of Thai nationalism has been grossly overstated", that attempts to make monarchy the "focal point of Thai nationalist sentiment met with little success", and that Thai nationalism is a matter of contestation between the "ruling elite and a disenfranchised urban literato".[54]

Copeland observed that many royal nationalist programmes triggered criticism, contestation, and reinterpretations, of the concept of *samakkhi* or unity, patriotism, nationalism, and most controversially, races and the Chinese. From 1912 to 1915, Vajiravudh wrote essays under his penname Asvabahu, promoting his ideas of the nation.

Using strong and sharp language, they invited responses, backlash, and sometimes outright ridicule. Vajiravudh promoted unity, but his critics from among the disenfranchised urban literati countered with diversity.

For example, in his 1915 essay on "True Nationhood", Vajiravudh wrote that there were many interpretations of *chat*, or Nations. Some were held by those who claimed that they were *samai mai*, or modern, but this group was merely following the *farang*, or Westerners. Vajiravudh compared them with Thewathat, the enemy of the Buddha, because following these people would amount to destroying the nation. He went on to elaborate on which words were beneficial to the nation.

He put it simply: words which created unity, yes, but division, no. He concluded that what was national was determined by one's language. To him, nation and language were one.

A further requirement was loyalty. "If he loves and is loyal to the King of Siam, he is, therefore, really Thai (*Thai thae thae*)." On the other hand, if one considered oneself free, with no loyalty to anyone, one must be stateless, since no one person or group can be established as a separate nation.

Such essays triggered heated reactions over who were the "nation's real patriots". There was even an assertion implying that the "false patriots" of the realm were none other than Vajiravudh and his courtiers.[55]

His 1914 essay, "Jews of the Orient" was controversial, suggesting that, according to one academic, the "Anglicized monarch had imbibed the particular racisms of the English ruling class".[56] It also met with mild to extreme approval, but hostile reactions were common, especially from the Sino-Thai community.

Copeland referred to an editorial in *Chino-Sayam Warasap*, Thailand's first daily Chinese newspaper, which urged its readers to oppose such discriminatory views. However, the tone of the editorial was highly restrained. The editor

> also offered a brief explanation of how he conceived of his "duties" as a Sino-Thai, asking readers to judge for themselves whether he posed a threat to the nation. Among other things, he noted that he had a responsibility to promote justice in Siam, to not only love justice as an abstract principle but also to make sure that it was afforded to "people of all races" so that none could claim that the kingdom had no justice to give them... he felt there was nothing right about unjustly maligning "fellow citizens of Chinese descent."[57]

On 22 July 1917, King Vajiravudh declared war against Germany and the Central Powers. The declaration, drafted by the king himself, stated that Siam wished to defend the "peace of the world", "respect for small states", and the "sanctity of International Rights".[58] An expeditionary force of 1,300 soldiers was sent to Europe. They marched under a new three-coloured national flag: red (symbolizing the nation), white (religion), and blue (king). The symbol of Siam had thus been changed from an image of a white elephant before a red background to fall in line with iconographic norms of the civilized West. War became an act of nation-building.

The king's declaration was therefore praised as wise and practical because "first, [Siam] will secure her place as an independent nation.... she will throw off extraterritorial rights which now brand her as a nation of inferior civilization ... (and) relieve her of unequal and unfair tariff agreements."[59]

But the king's policy did not go unchallenged. Narin Phasit (1874–1959),[60] a controversial gadfly, opposed the war declaration, claiming that "Siam should just sit still. Joining the war is like joining a pack of dogs' (*ma mu*, or when dogs gang up to attack others). Narin was jailed for two years.[61] But he had already taken a place among those who joined the "contest for the Nation" like Kularb, Thianwan, and other political journalists.

Narin had served as governor of Nakhon Nayok, but had resigned in 1911, disgusted by bureaucracy. He proceeded to found his own press, propagating ideas about nation, religion, and monarchy. He published pamphlets like *Choie bamrung chat* [Help and Care for the Nation] and launched *Khana yindi kan kadkhan* [Glad to Oppose Party], to help exploited and underprivileged people petition the king.

One of Narin's most important achievements was successfully disputing *ngoen ratchupakan*, a head tax levied upon the population. He managed to eliminate it after the coup of 1932; the new government went along with Narin's long, patient campaign.

In terms of religion, Narin accused the *sangha*, the community of monks, of materialism. He overturned Thai men's monopoly on Buddhist ordination by having his daughter ordained as a monk, a tradition he claimed existed in Buddha's time, but had lapsed in modern Siam. As for the monarchy, Narin campaigned for the rehabilitation of King Taksin, whom he respected for restoring the independence of Siam after the fall of Ayutthaya in 1767.

Taksin was portrayed by early Bangkok *phongsawadan* as having gone insane, a claim that was used to justify his execution by Rama I, a

Siamese general who created a new dynasty, the Chakri, in 1782. Since the mid-nineteenth century, Taksin's Chineseness was exaggerated to weaken his legitimacy as a king of Siam. King Mongkut wrote, "The first king established in Bangkok was an extraordinary man of Chinese origin, named Pin Tat. He was called by the Chinese Tia Sin Tat, or Tuat."[62]

That does not necessarily mean Mongkut was overly concerned about race. It may have been natural for him to state the kind of fact which he had learned.

But by the time of Vajiravudh, race had become an important element in nationalistic programmes. *The Souvenir of the Siamese Kingdom Exhibition at Lumbini Park B.E. 2468*, the 1925 commemorative volume published at the end of Vajiravudh's reign, put it candidly:

> It was reported that the King had become very unpopular owing to at least three causes: his foreign extraction, for he was partly Chinese by birth; his appointment to those high offices which the Siamese considered should have been regarded, so to speak, as an heirloom for themselves ... the King was forced to his mental attitude, and, as a result, the conclusion was come to that it was a matter of absolute necessity that there should be a change ... [and] selected one of their own members as his successor ... Somdet Chao Phya Maha Krasat Seuk [Rama I].[63]

In the early morning of 24 June 1932, a coup took place. The last absolute monarch, King Prajadhipok (Rama VII) and his Queen were at their seaside residence, Klai Kang Won (*Sanssouci*) Palace in Hua Hin, 190 kilometres south of Bangkok. A group of 100 Western-educated military officers, lawyers, and bureaucrats had assembled a People's Party, or Khana Ratsadon.

They called themselves promoters (*phu ko kan*, short for *phu ko kan plian plaeng kan pokkhrong*, literally, initiators of change in government). They took five days, from 24 to 28 June, to finish the task:

June 24: Captured power and held senior princes and ministers hostage.
June 25: Handed an ultimatum to the king to cede power and return to Bangkok.
June 26: Received the king's agreement to sign a royal pardon for the coup's promoters.

June 27: Had the king sign an interim constitution.

June 28: Convened parliament with seventy selected representatives and appointed Phraya Mano, a senior lawyer, as first Prime Minister of post-absolute monarchy Siam. Siam's short-lived absolute monarchy from Rama V to Rama VII (Chulalongkorn to Prajadhipok by way of Vajiravudh) had ended.[64] The nation was transformed by the People's Party, or *Khana ratsadon* into a "constitutional monarchy".[65]

NOTES

1. Prasenjit Duara, "The Regime of Authenticity: Timelessness, Gender and National History in Modern China", *History & Theory* 37, no. 3 (1998), p. 287.
2. The word *Phongsawadan* is generally translated as chronicle. It combines two Pali-Sanskrit words: *vaṃsa* (line, family, king) and *avatāra* (reincarnation). The coining is *vaṃsāvatāra*, pronounced *phongsawadan* in Thai language. They mostly contain dynastic history, with stories of kings who are supposed to be reincarnations of Hindu gods. In the Thai case, the king is a reincarnation of Vishnu. See Charnvit Kasetsiri, "Thai Historiography from Ancient Times to the Modern Period", in *Perceptions of the Past in Southeast Asia*, edited by Anthony Reid and David Marr (Singapore: Asian Studies Association of Australia by Heinemann Educational Books, 1979). See also Chris Baker and Pasuk Phongpaichit, "Thailand in the Longue Durée", and Charnvit, "Thai Historiography", both in *Routledge Handbook of Contemporary Thailand*, edited by Pavin Chachavalpongpun (London and New York: Routledge – Taylor & Francis Group, 2020). See also Craig J. Reynolds, "Nation and State in Histories of Nation-Building, with Special Reference to Thailand", in *Nation-Building Five Southeast Asian Histories*, edited by Wang Gungwu (Singapore: Institute of Southeast Asian Studies, 2005), p. 26.
3. See *Wilatwong Phongsabut, Prawatisat thai chan matayom suksa ton plai* [Thai History for Secondary Schools] (Bangkok: Thaiwatanapanich, 1976).
4. See also Thongchai Winichakul, "The Changing Landscape of the Past: New Histories in Thailand Since 1973", *Journal of Southeast Asian Studies* 26, no. 1 (March 1995): 99–120.
5. See King Mongkut's article "Brief History of Siam, with a detail of the leading events in its Annals", written by the king himself; however, the English was gone over by a certain missionary named W.D. (?). Therefore, it does not have the kind of flavour like most of the king's writings. The article was

published in *The Chinese Repository* XX, No. 7 (July 1851): 315–63. At the end of the article, the editor has included a very favourable report of the king's ascension to the throne, printed from the Singapore Free Press.
6. It is revealing to compare of the position of two Thai kings, Vajiravudh and Narai, who lived 200 years apart. Vajiravudh dated his dynastic state/nation Ratanakosin-Chakri back 700 years to Sukhothai in the thirteenth century, comprising a space within the boundaries of modern Siam. King Narai (1656–88) of the Ayutthya-Prasatthong dynasty went back further, to the eighth century, and extended the nation to Cambodia. For Narai if a golden age existed, it was not in Sukhothai, but Angkor. See Michael Smithies and Dhiravat na Pombejra, "Instructions Given to the Siamese Envoys Sent to Portugal, 1684", *Journal of the Siam Society* 90, no. 1&2 (2002). See rendering into Thai by Michael Wright in *Sinlapa Watthanathem* 26, no. 4 (February 2005); and by Phuthorn Bhumadhon, "Ruang na ru samai somdet phra Narai" [Interesting stories from the time of King Narai], an unpublished paper given at a seminar on King Narai, Lopburi, February 2011.
7. See A. Cecil Carter, *The Kingdom of Siam 1904* (New York: G.P. Putnam's Sons, 1904).
8. See *Khlong Phap Phraratchaphongsawadan* [Poems and Painting from Chronicles], 5th ed. (Bangkok, Amarin Printing, 1983; first printing 1887). I am indebted to Dr Sunait Chutintranond of Chulalongkorn University for pointing this out to me.
9. Suphanni Kanchanatthiti, *Bannanukrom Babb Rien Visha Prawatisat Khong Krasuang Suksatikarn Tang Tae B.E. 2440–2512* [Bibliography of the Ministry of Education's History Textbooks from 1897 to 1969] (Bangkok: Ministry of Education, 1970).
10. Ibid.
11. Ibid.
12. Benedict Anderson, *Imagined Communities: Reflections on the Origin and Spread of Nationalism* (London: Verso, 1991).
13. Ibid., see his section on "Official Nationalism and Imperialism", pp. 99–100.
14. Ibid., p. 101.
15. Ironically, Prince Damrong (1862–1943) is popularly labelled as Phra Bida Haeng Prawatisat Thai, meaning Royal Father of Thai history. The prince never fully accepted the newly coined word *prawatisat*, corresponding to the English "history". He remained committed to Phongsawadan (popularly taken as meaning chronicle) until the end.
16. See translation by Oskar Frankfurter, "The Story of the Records of Siamese History", in *Miscellaneous Articles Written for the Journal of the Siam Society*

by His Royal Highness Prince Damrong (Bangkok: Siam Society, 1962), p. 31.
17. Prince Damrong mistook the word Lao for Lawa. The two are ethnically and linguistically different. Lao belongs to the Tai-Lao family and Lawa is Mon-Khmer. He went on to ask, "Who were the original Khmers and Lāo? To-day we only know that the peoples designated under the names of Kha, Khamu, Cambodians, Mons and Meng all speak languages which are of Khmer stock. We may conclude, therefore, that these peoples are descended from the Khmers. As for the original Lāo, they are to be identified in the people styled today Luǎ or Lawā...". See "History of Siam in the Period Antecedent to the Founding of Ayuddhya by King Phra Chao U Thong", in *Miscellaneous Articles Written for the Journal of the Siam Society by His Royal Highness Prince Damrong*, p. 49.
18. Ibid., p. 50.
19. Ibid., p. 60.
20. Ibid., p. 60.
21. Ibid., p. 61.
22. Strangely, Nan Chao (Nanzhao) names of kings do not sound Thai, and that Nan Chao kings had naming customs different from the Thais. For example, the three names of its famous warrior kings: (A) Sheng-lo-pi; (B) P'i-lo-ko; and (C) Ko-lo-fung. The last word of (A) becomes the first of (B), and the last of (B) becomes first of (C). This is probably a genealogy, signalling succession from father to son. This naming custom was unknown in old or modern Siam. Prince Damrong dismissed this issue with only a casual remark. He stated: "As regards the Chinese rendering of the names of the Thai kings, it is quite impossible to say what were the various equivalents in the Thai language", ibid., p. 65.
23. Ibid., p. 65.
24. Ibid.
25. See Phya Anuman Rajadhon, *Ruang khong chart Thai* [Story of the Thai Nation] (Bangkok: 1940 first printing).
26. Craig J. Reynolds, "Plot of Thai History: Theory and Practice", in *Patterns and Illusions: Thai History and Thought*, edited by Gehan Wijeyewardene and E.C. Chapman (Singapore: Richard Davis Fund and Department of Anthropology, Research School of Pacific Studies, The Australian National University, 1992), p. 314.
27. For details on Hollywood films and plays about Anna Leonowens and King Mongkut, see note 9 in Chapter 3.
28. See Phaithoon and Wilatwong Phongsabut, *Prathet Khong Rao* [Our Country]

(Bangkok: Thai Watthana, 1992), pp. 2–5. As mentioned above, the theory that China was the original homeland of the Thai and their mighty kingdom was Nan Chao, was finally accepted by Prince Damrong in 1914. The idea was further developed by Luang Wichitwathakan in the 1930s and 1940s, especially after the 1932 coup overthrowing the absolute monarchy. It became a monstrous Thai past, attached with nationalistic emotion during the first Phibun regime (1938–43) when even the official name of the country, Siam, was changed to Thailand in 1939. The theory remained unchallenged through the 1950s until in 1964 when Frederick W. Mote, a senior China Historian at Princeton University, criticized its validity in his short, but influential, article "Problems of Thai Prehistory", *Sangkhomsat Parithat* 2, no. 2 (October 1964). The idea of original homeland, however, remained influential within academic circles. See also *Lak Thai* [Thai Pillars], a highly influential text on the Thai original homeland by Khun Wichitmatra (Sa-nga Kanchanakhaphan; 1897–1980). The book was given a literary prize by King Prajadhipok in 1928. See also Charles Backus, *The Nan-chao kingdom and T'ang China's Southern Frontier* (Redwood Burn Ltd., Trowbridge, Wiltshire: Cambridge Studies in Chinese history, Literature, and Institutions, 1981), pp. 47–52. For more discussion on the original homeland of the Thai, see, for example, Chalong Sutharavanich, "Ruang chon chat thai: khamtham thi tong chuy kan top" [The Thai ethnic group: Questions to be answered], an unpublished paper given at the Chulalongkorn University Conference, October 1990. See Chris Baker, "From Yeu to Tai", *Journal of the Siam Society* 90, no. 1&2 (2002) and Grant Evans, "The Ai-Lao and Nan Chao/Thai Kingdom: A Re-orientation", *Journal of the Siam Society* 102 (2014).

29. The word *borankhadi*, which is now taken to mean archaeology, reveals an inherent connection between race and homeland. It means studies or affairs of old things. Since old things were labelled as Mon or Khmer, Thais must originally be from elsewhere.
30. A good account of the early years of the Siam Society is by William Warren, *The Siam Society: A Century* (Bangkok: The Siam Society, 2004).
31. The library's name is usually translated as "National Library". However, in Thai it is the Library for Phra Nakhon (Nagara), meaning for Bangkok and/or for the capital, which further implies that it belongs to the dynastic, rather than the national realm.
32. The best positive account of Vajiravudh in English is by Walter F. Vella, *Chaiyo! King Vajiravudh and the Development of Thai Nationalism* (Honolulu: University Press of Hawaii, 1978). On his official nationalism, see more in Anderson's *Imagined Communities* (cited above) and Kullada Kedboonchoo,

"Official Nationalism under King Chulalongkorn", paper presented at the International Conference on Thai Studies, Canberra, 1987; also see her *The Rise and Decline of Thai Absolutism* (London: RouledgeCurzon, 2004). The book is translated into Thai as *Somburanayasitthirat: Wiwatthakan rat Thai* (Fah diew kan, 2019). See also Stephen L.W. Greene, *Absolute Dreams: Thai Government Under Rama VI, 1910–1925* (Bangkok: White Lotus, 1999), and a provocative new treatment of the inner court life of Vajiravudh by Chanan Yodhongs, *Nai nai nai samai ratchakan thi 6* [Inner Men in the Reign of King Rama VI] (Bangkok: Matichon, 2013).

33. Anderson, *Imagined Communities*.
34. Ibid. See his discussion on "print-capitalism" in Chapter 3, "The Origins of National Consciousness".
35. Benedict Anderson remarks that Vajiravudh's triad echoes the theme of late Tsarist Russia, Autocracy, Orthodoxy and Nationality, but in reverse order. Anderson, *Imagined Communities*, p. 101. Many Thais believe that the king copied the English slogan of God, King, and Country, adapting it in a different order in Thai language.
36. See Krommakhun Phitthayalab, *Huakho prawatisat phak 1* [Headings of History, Part 1], 1917. The author claimed that he first saw this word used by Ramchitti, one of King Vajiravudh's many pen names, published in *Witthayachan*, no. 16, p. 104.
37. Vajiravudh, *Ruang thieo muang phra ruang* [A Tour of the Phra Ruang Country] (first printing 1908; 12th printing 1983), p. 97.
38. Ibid. See the preface by Vajiravudh himself. Here, the prince assumed the pen name: Ram Vajiravudh. One must wonder whether the prince had, by this time, come to identify himself with Rama of the Ramayana as well as King Ramkhamhaeng of Sukhothai. He seems to have merged the present with the past. Vajiravudh also started the traditions of naming Chakri kings Rama and numbering them as Rama I, II, III to Rama X.

    In the heated debate over whether the King Ramkhamhaeng Inscription is genuine, Dr Piriya Krairiksh used the writings of Vajiravudh along with his extensive study of the context of the Inscription, to question the validity of the famous stone, which had become the foundation of the modern Thai state and Sukhothai historiography. See the huge volume by James R. Chamberlain, *The Ram Khamhaeng Controversy* (Bangkok: The Siam Society, 1991).
39. See the discussion of "royal-official-ultra nationalist historiography", in "Constructing the Ideal State: The Idea of Sukhothai in Thai History, 1833–1957", by Bryce Beemer (unpublished MA thesis, University of Hawaii,

Manoa, 1999); see also Mukhom Wongthes, *Intellectual Might and National Myth: A Forensic Investigation of the Ram Khamhaeng Controversy in Thai Society* (Bangkok: Matichon, 2003).
40. See Vella, *Chaiyo!* Ch. 3.
41. See Vajiravudh, *Ruang thieo muang phra ruang*.
42. See *Bot Lakhon Phud Kham Klon Phra Ruang* [The Rhyming Play of Phra Ruang] (Bangkok: Aksornsampan, 1974; first printing 1917).
43. Vella, *Chaiyo!* p. 212.
44. See Vajiravudh, *Ruang thao saenpom* [The king who had a hundred thousand bumps on his body] (Phra Nakhon: Sophonpipatthanakorn, 1925).
45. See Yupa Chumchantra, "Prawatisat nipon thai B.E. 2475–2516" [Thai Historiography, 1932–1973] (unpublished MA thesis, Chulalongkorn University, 1987), p. 23.
46. Ibid., p. 45.
47. For K.S.R. Kularb, see Craig J. Reynolds, "The Case of K.S.R. Kularb: A Challenge to Royal Historical Writing in Late Nineteenth Century Thailand", *Journal of the Siam Society* 61, no. 2 (July 1973): 63–90. For Thianwan, see Walter F. Vella, "Thianwan of Siam: A Man Who Fought Giants", in *Anuson Walter Vella*, edited by Ronald D. Renard (Honolulu: University of Hawaii, 1986), pp. 78–91; see also Yuangrat and Paul Wedel, *Radical Thought, Thai Mind: The Development of Revolutionary Ideas in Thailand* (Bangkok: Assumption Business Administration College, 1987), pp. 23–36. For Thai language sources, see Chai-Anan Samudavanija, *Chiwit lae ngan khong Thianwan lae K.S.R. Kularb* [Lives and Works of Thianwan and K.S.R. Kularb] (Bangkok: Teeranan, 1979); also, Mananya Thanaphum, *K.S.R. Kularb* (Bangkok: Social Science Association of Thailand, 1982).
48. Reynolds, "The Case of K.S.R. Kularb".
49. "Madness" has been conspicuously diagnosed in those who oppose a ruling elite's ideology. During the reign of King Mongkut (Rama IV), Somdet To of Wat Rakhang was one of these "mad" individuals. He was reputed to be critical of the court of King Mongkut and expressed his antagonism by carrying a lamp in the middle of the day, implying that there was darkness in the middle of the day. During the Fifth Reign (Chulalongkorn), it was Kularb and, later, Narin for the Sixth Reign (Vajiravudh); see note 60 below.
50. Reynolds, "The Case of K.S.R. Kularb", p. 87.
51. *Ayatiwat* (Growth or Progress), reprint by the Thai Club of Japan, 1993. See the informative introduction on the life and work of Kularb by Nakharin Mektrirat. See also my "Siam/Civilization—Thailand/Globalization: Things to come?", *Thammasat Review* 5, no. 1 (2000); reprinted in my work, Charnvit

Kasetsiri, *Studies in Thai and Southeast Asian Histories* (Bangkok: The Social Sciences and Humanities Textbooks Foundation, 2015).
52. Ibid.
53. The best treatment on this topic is by Matthew P. Copeland, "Contested Nationalism and the 1932 Overthrow of the Absolute Monarchy in Siam" (unpublished Ph. thesis, Australian National University, 1993). I am indebted to Prani Wongsdes for bringing this to my attention.
54. Ibid., p. 11.
55. Ibid., p. 45.
56. Anderson, *Imagined Communities*, pp. 100–1.
57. Copeland, "Contested Nationalism and the 1932 Overthrow of the Absolute Monarchy in Siam", p. 43.
58. Vella, *Chaiyo!* p. 111.
59. Ibid., p. 113.
60. Sakdina Chatkul na Ayudhya, *Narin Klung khon khwang lok* [Narin: A man against the world] (Bangkok, Matichon, 1993). See a new interpretation of Narin by Peter Koret (1960–2020), *The Man Who Accused the King of Killing a Fish: The Biography of Narin Phasit of Siam, 1874–1950* (Chiang Mai: Silkworm Books, 2012).
61. Yupa Chumchantra, "Prawatisat nipon thai B.E. 2475–2516", p. 52.
62. See note 5 above: "Brief History of Siam, with a detail of the leading events in its Annals", p. 351.
63. *The Souvenir of the Siamese Kingdom Exhibition at Lumbini Park B.E. 2468* (Bangkok: Krungthep Daily Mail, 1927), p. 42. Narin lived until 1950, dying at the age of seventy-six. Many joined him in restoring Taksin to a place in Thai history. Over the course of this effort, the linear royal line had to be adjusted to include the period when Taksin's seat of power was across the river from Rama I's Rattanakosin (present-day Bangkok). The line of kingdoms now comprised Sukhothai, Ayutthyaya, Thonburi, and Rattanakosin. On 17 April 1954, during Phibun's government, a statue of Taksin, galloping on horseback, with a sword-bearing arm raised, was officially inaugurated. His effigy followed statues of the three Chakri kings: Chulalongkorn, Rama I, and Vajiravudh, in that order.
64. See Chapters 6 and 7 of Chaiyan Rajchagool, *The Rise and Fall of the Thai Absolute Monarchy* (Bangkok: White Lotus, 1994). See also a pioneer work by Thawatt Mokarapong, *History of the Thai Revolution: A Study in Political Behaviour* (Bangkok: Chalermnit, 1972). A thorough, sympathetic work of this period is found in Benjamin A. Batson, *The End of Absolute Monarchy in Sia* (Singapore: Oxford University Press, 1984). Batson's book was translated

into Thai language in 2000 and published under the auspices of the Social Sciences and Humanities Textbooks Foundation.

In the 1990s, renewed interest and reinterpretations of the 1932 events showed up among academics. For example, see books by Nakarin Mektrairat, *Kan Patiwat Sayam 2475* [1932 Revolution in Siam] (1992); Charnvit Kasetsiri, *2475 Kan Patiwat Sayam* [1932 Revolution in Siam] (1992); Thamrongsak Phetlertanan, *2475 Lae 1 Pi Lang kanpatiwat* [1932 Revolution and the Aftermath] (2000); Charnvit Kasetsiri and Thamrongsak Phetlertanan, *Patiwat 2475* [1932 Revolution in Siam] (2004); all published by the Social Sciences and Humanities Textbooks Foundation. See a recent debate on when Thailand became a nation-state only after the 1932 Revolution by Somkiat Wanthana et al., *Mua dai chung pen chat Thai* [Becoming a Thai Nation, when?] (Bangkok: Illumination, 2021). See also Phinyaphan Potchanalawan, *Kamnoed prathet Thai phaitai phadetkan* [Birth of Thailand under dictatorship] (Bangkok: Matichon, 2015). See two provoking ideas on Thai historiography by Nidhi Eoseewong, *Prawattisat haeng chat som chabab kao sang chabab mai* [National history: Repair the old version and remake the new] (Bangkok: Ministry of Culture, 2006), and by Somsak Jiemthirasakul, *Prawattosat phueng sang* [Just invented histories] (Bangkok: Fah Diew Kan, 2011).

See also an extremely interesting treatment, a bestseller, on the royalist anti-1932 coup movement by Nutthapon Jaijing, *Kho fanfai fai fan an lua chua* [To dream the unbelievable dream] (Bangkok, 2013).

65. In the 2020–21 protest against the Prayut Chan-o-cha government, a good number of young activists prefer to use the word *ratsadon* instead of *prachachon*, meaning the people. Therefore, they see themselves in line of having the same political desire as the 1932 *khana ratsadon* revolutionary group.

Therefore, the so-called 2020s new young generation Z has become fascinated by the 1932 revolutionary promoters. In their protests against the Prayut Chan-o-cha government and their demand for monarchy reform, they have been referring to examples of those old *khana ratsadon* (The People's Party).

See, for example, Peera Songkünnatham, "The Law Ought to Be King", *Boston Review*, 1 October 2020, http://bostonreview.net/global-justice/peera-songkunnatham-the-law-ought-be-king; Supalak Ganjanakhundee, "Youthquake Evokes the 1932 Revolution and Shakes Thailand's Establishment", *ISEAS Perspective*, no. 2020/127, 6 November 2020, https://www.iseas.edu.sg/wp-content/uploads/2020/10/ISEAS_Perspective_2020_127.pdf; Kanokrat Lertchoosakul, "The White Ribbon Movement: High School Students in the

2020 Thai Youth Protests", *Critical Asian Studies* 53, no. 2 (2021): 206–18; Duncan McCargo, "Disruptors' Dilemma? Thailand's 2020 Gen Z Protests", *Critical Asian Studies* 53, no. 2 (2021): 175–91, https://www.tandfonline.com/doi/full/10.1080/14672715.2021.1876522; Wolfram Schaffar and Praphakorn Wongratanawin, "The Milk Tea Alliance: A New Transnational Pro-Democracy Movement against Chinese-Centered Globalization?", *Austrian Journal of South-East Asian Studies* 14, no. 1 (2021): 5–35; Aim Sinpeng, "Hashtag Activism: Social Media and the #Freeyouth Protests in Thailand", *Critical Asian Studies* 53, no. 2 (2021), https://www.tandfonline.com/doi/full/10.1080/14672715.2021.1882866

CHAPTER TWO

From Siam to Thailand: What's in a Name?

As national leader, Field Marshal Phibunsongkhram was well known for his two main styles of leadership: the Than Phunam/Leader style during the war years; and the beloved Paw Khun/Father-figure style of leadership during his second administration ... It is apparent that throughout his lengthy premiership, Phibun strove to present himself as a national leader, replacing the absolute monarchs of bygone days ...[1]

Kobkua Suwannathat-Pian, 1995

Introduction

As a student of Thai history, I have always been puzzled by the change of the name of my country from Siam to Thailand in 1939. I had no love for the hybrid word *Thai + land* and formerly participated in Back to Siam, a sort of literary movement to revert to the former name. In the late 1960s, while studying in the United States, I joined a group of Thai students who regularly wrote brief articles that were published back in Bangkok.

These were rather well received by the public and eventually collected and printed in two paperback volumes under the curious title *Kid thung muang Thai* (Thinking of the Land of the Thai). In using the term *Muang Thai* (Land of the Thai) in our writings, my friends and I saw no contradiction in continuing to propose a movement Back to Siam. Our proposal went nowhere, in any case. Nevertheless, when I returned home I still cherished the belief that Siam was a more appropriate name. At one point I had a visiting card printed with my address listed as Bangkok, Siam. My visiting card did not advance the Back to Siam movement either.

Since 1973, I have taught history at Thammasat University in Bangkok, where my main assignment has been modern Thai political history. I often asked students about their opinions of choosing between the names Siam and Thailand. To my surprise, they always preferred Thailand; some even looked at me strangely, as if I were impossibly *boran* (old fashion and outdated).

Armed with this experience, from 16 to 18 December 1998, I sought to participate in an international conference on Post-Colonial Society and Culture in Southeast Asia, held in Myanmar, another country whose name had also changed. I felt that it might be timely, at least on a personal basis, to try to understand the case of Thailand and Siam nomenclature. Why had the name changed in the first place, and why had it remained so after 1939, despite several attempts to revert to Siam?

The Siam-to-Thailand name change occurred during the first Phibun government (1939–44) coinciding with the Second World War. At the time, Thailand was dominated by an energetic and aggressive brand of nationalism in domestic and foreign policy. Phibun and his close associates were seen as linked to Fascist and Nazi military dictatorships.[2]

This happened in part because the new Thailand moved into areas of mainland Southeast Asia which had already been satisfactorily partitioned between two European powers: France and the United Kingdom.

It was also a partial result of military action that had humiliated the West in Asia, especially the French and British; even before the Pacific War broke out, Thailand took Siem Reap, Battambang, Champasak, and Saiyabulee from French Indochina.[3] And it ensued from the initiative on 25 January 1942 when Thailand joined the Japanese "enemy" by proclaiming war against the United States and the United Kingdom to eliminate Western influence.

During the war itself, the new Thailand seized portions of the Shan states (Keng Tung and Mong Pan)[4] and four Malay states (Kedah, Perlis, Kelantan and Terengganu) from the British.

Therefore, Phibun, like the Indian nationalist Subhas Chandra Bose (1897–1945), was restrained by links with defeated leaders of major powers such as Hitler, Mussolini and Tojo, not exalted by association with leaders of reborn nations such as Sukarno and Hatta of Indonesia, or Aung San of Burma.

Fortunately, he was not punished and hanged like his Japanese counterpart Premier Tojo (1884–1948). Therefore, we must consider here how the peculiar case of Thailand can be evaluated against the Southeast Asian background of nation and nationalism.[5]

From Siam to Thailand

On 24 June 1939, in a swift and dramatic political move, Phibun, the prime minister of six months' tenure, declared that the name of the country would change from Siam (Prathet Syam) to Thailand (Prathet Thai).

He was forty-two years old, his military rank was still major general, and he bore the feudal title of Luang Phibunsongkhram.[6]

The official announcement read: "Whereas the country's name has been referred to in terms of both 'Thai' and 'Siam'; and whereas, since the Thai people prefer to be called 'Thai,' therefore, the government deems it a *ratthaniyom* [state cultural decree or "statism"] that the name of the country should be in accordance with the racial name and preference [*niyom*] of the Thai people."[7]

As a result, in the Thai language, the names of the country, the people, and the nationality are all Thai, while in English usage they are Thailand and Thai, respectively.

The change from Siam to Thailand was a well-calculated political move. On that same day, the Phibun government took other political initiatives. For example, *wan chat* or National Day was celebrated as well as new treaties signed with foreign countries. June 24 was declared National Day. This was the first official creation of a holiday unrelated to Buddhist or dynastic celebrations.[8]

June 24 was the date of the Siamese revolution of 1932 that ended the absolute monarchy and brought a new elite, consisting of middle-rank officials, many of commoner origins, to power. They included, for example, Prime Minister Phraya Phahon (1887–1947), whom Phibun (1897–1964) succeeded, as well as Pridi Banomyong (1900–83) who in due course followed him.

In addition to celebrating the June 24 event, a foundation stone for the highly symbolic Democracy Monument was installed in the centre of the royal Ratchadamnoen Avenue. This thoroughfare was King Chulalongkorn's version of the Champs-Élysées in Paris, connecting the old Grand Palace and Dusit Palace, the new Western-style court of King Chulalongkorn.

In addition, the Phibun government did away with the unequal treaties which old Siam had to sign with fifteen countries between 1855 and 1899; the Phibun government explained that this was an auspicious time, marking the moment of first full independence (*ekkarat sombun*) from Europe, the United States, and Japan. Previously, Thai kings were required unequivocally to sign away part of the kingdom's sovereignty according to the terms of the Bowring Treaty of 1855.[9]

The previous night, Premier Phibun had presented a 50-minute radio broadcast, mainly about "love of nation". He suggested that the government should introduce what he called *prapheni niyom pracham chat*, or national traditions, and periodically proclaim a *ratthaniyom*, state cultural decree or "statism" to guide the behaviour of the Thai nation and its inhabitants. To him, this *ratthaniyom* would make the Thai people *araya* (civilized) and also validate *amnat mahachon*, or the power of the people, deriving from *mati mahachon*, or popular opinion.[10]

As a member of the People's Party which staged the "democratic" 1932 coup against the monarchy, Phibun had to be aware of "the people" and different democratic forms of expression. Before the actual name change and other nation-creating devices such as National Day, the new national anthem, songs, plays, dresses, monuments, culture and customs, the Government had eagerly elicited support and participation from the general public, especially from the educated middle class in the Bangkok Metropolitan Area.

Speeches were broadcast on radio, increasingly an instrument for governmental propaganda, and printed in pro-government newspapers. Sometimes the public was invited to enter competitions, such as one to write an essay on the importance of National Day.[11]

The nation's name change was summarily discussed and approved by the cabinet sometime in late May 1939. By early June, the Ministry of

Defence took the lead in propagating the use of the new name. The Ministry, or to be precise, Phibun, directed the campaign to ascertain whether the new name would be widely accepted. In his *kham chakchuan* (words of persuasion), Phibun cited five points in favour of the name Thailand:

1. The name Siam does not accord with the name of the race, which is "Thai".
2. The name Siam contradicts the nationality of the Thai people.
3. Siam was a province of the Khom (Khmer), who once ruled over the Thai nation; and when Phra Ruang gained freedom, the name Siam was dropped.
4. Siam has been used in written, not spoken, language.
5. The Thai nation is great, and it is the only appropriate name for the country in accordance with the prestige of the Thai race.[12]

In addition, to appear democratic in the light of a legislative system, the matter was processed through Parliament after the announcement by the Prime Minister's Office. Three months later, on 28 September 1939, 158 members of Parliament (half elected and half appointed), including the Speaker, met. They unanimously voted the first amendment to the 1932 Constitution, that the nation's name be changed to Thailand.[13]

Ever since the outcome of this constitutional process, the country has been named Thailand, and all subsequent constitutions are written one after another, including most recently, numbers 16/1997, 17/2006, 18/2007, 19/2014, and 20/2017 refer to Thailand and not Siam.

In effect, among Phibun's many controversial ethno-nationalist policies, the national name change has proven one of the most enduring.

The name change faced no serious objection or opposition. While nationalism and ethnocentrism were prevalent among the new Thai elite of the 1930s and 1940s, a sort of mild oppositional nationalism appeared in some newspapers. On 13 June 1939, the daily *Pramuanwan* printed an article ridiculing the use and spelling of the word Thai.

The anonymous author asked readers whether they ever considered why the word was romanized as "Thai", which white foreigners (*farang*) would inevitably pronounce as "thigh". The critic proceeded to explain that the word "thigh" signified a part of the body between the knees and the waist. To continue the satirical japes, the article pursued the subject, clearly implied as inconsequential.

Romanizing the Thai term *Prates Thai* (Country of Thailand) as *Prates* or *Prades Thai*, the article next alluded to the Thai rendering of two Pali words, *Pra* and *desa*, meaning land or country. It was recommended that they be pronounced as two separate syllables with a pause between them, *pra* and *tes*.

This advice was needed supposedly because *farang* would otherwise pronounce the term as if to rhyme with the monosyllabic English word "grades".

As a further mock-insight, it was noted that the English verb *to prate* means to babble inconsequentially. Therefore, it was implied, such errors and mispronunciations of the romanization were due to readers, not writers or those who conceived it, possibly a teasing allusion to Phibun and his government.

Writing some thirty years later, Pridi Banomyong, the civilian leader of the People's Party, and one-time Regent and Prime Minister of Thailand, recalled a minority opposition among cabinet members on that decisive day. At the time, Pridi served as Phibun's finance minister. They worked together productively before diverging during the Second World War. Pridi recounted that six months after Phibun became prime minister, Luang Wichit (1898–1962), then a minister without portfolio as well as arts academic, had just returned from a visit to Hanoi.

At one cabinet meeting, Luang Wichit presented a French map showing Thai/Tai-speaking people inhabiting several parts of Indochina (Vietnam, Laos), China (Yunnan, Kwangsi), Burma (Shan states), and India (Assam). According to Pridi, Luang Wichit bewailed and lamented (*ramphan*) this dispersion of the great Thai race.

He then propagated the concept of *maha anachak Thai* (The Great Thai Empire), covering a vast area from eastern India to Burma and from southwest China to Vietnam, Laos, and Thailand. To Pridi, this approach resembled what "Hitler was doing in Europe" with claims about the Aryan race.[14]

Pridi continued that at the cabinet meeting, Luang Wichit observed that the word Syam (Siam) derived from the Sanskrit Syama, or black. Therefore, it was inappropriate as the nation's name, Luang Wichit added in all seriousness, because the Thai race was yellow rather than black. What's more, he claimed, Syam also derived from a Chinese term, Siam-lo, making it even less appropriate for a government that had recently become anti-Chinese and pro-Japanese.

Pridi recalled that he objected to this line of argument, using as supporting evidence some old Thai legislation from the reign of King Rama I (crowned in 1782). Pridi believed that the word Syam derived from the Pali term Sama, or black, yellow and gold.[15] It was therefore a suitable name for the land of gold or Suwannaphum (Suvarnabhumi) as Siam had also come to be known.

Pridi explained further that after the name change, the government had also changed the lyrics of the national anthem. Phrases were added such as "Thailand combined the blood and flesh of the Thai race." Pridi disagreed with such terminology, pointing out that the nation comprised many varied races. Nonetheless, Pridi's opinions remained minority views in the cabinet, and he was obliged to accede to the majority who preferred Thailand to Siam.

Pridi's account of how the country's name changed is complex and, to some extent, a product of hindsight. Although he claimed to defend the minority point of view, he ultimately accepted the change. Later, however, he claimed to agree only insofar as the Thai language was concerned.

At the meeting, he proposed that in English and French terminology, the name should remain Siam, just as Germans referred to their homeland as Deutschland, while English speakers knew it as Germany and the French as Allemagne. The same pattern was repeated in the case of China or la Chine and Japan or le Japon.

Despite Japan's chauvinism, Pridi felt, the Land of the Rising Sun did not baffle the world by insisting upon the Japanese language terms for itself, Nihon and Nippon.[16]

He continued that even if the word Thai was used, it should not be amalgamated with the word "land", Pridi suggested, creating a hybrid reminiscent of names of English and French colonies in Africa. He claimed that when the Irish Free State was a state established in 1922, the Irish term Éire was preferred to the term Ireland, with its suffix of "land".

So Pridi offered an alternate proposal, of calling the nation Muang Thai, without any mention of "land"; that notion was also rejected.[17]

What's in a Name?

After examining procedural aspects of the name-changing process, two questions arise: why did the change occur in the first place and, secondly, why has the name Thailand persisted?

The answers may lie in part with the interaction between two Thai state traditions of a dynastic Siam versus a national one of Thailand, and in part due to the workings of internal politics and modern historiography.

Again, in his celebrated *Imagined Communities: Reflections on the Origin and Spread of Nationalism*, Benedict Anderson hypothesized three types of global polities: religious communities, dynastic realms, and nation-states; the last-mentioned are the most modern. He called them "imagined communities". Anderson demonstrated that nations and nationalism are products of the eighteenth to twentieth centuries; they arose in the New World, moved to Europe, finally spread to Asia and Africa. Thus, by the start of the twentieth century, different nationalist movements and their leaders appeared in colonized Southeast Asia: Boedi Oetomo, Sarekat Islam, Dohbama Asiayone, Sukarno, Hatta, Aung San, and U Nu, among others.

Although Siam was not fully and conventionally colonized, it was also affected by these waves of nation-ness and nationalism. However, Anderson indicated that Thai nationalism was different in type, as an "official" one, by comparing two kings, Chulalongkorn and Vajiravudh.

All through his long reign, from 1868 to 1910, King Chulalongkorn strove to reform his country, borrowing freely from, and emulating British colonial administrations in Singapore-Malaya and India-Burma, and the Dutch in the East Indies. Before this, Thai and foreign scholars agreed that by the turn of the century, Siam had already become a modern nation-state.[18] However, Benedict Anderson, as mentioned earlier in the previous chapter, argued differently; to him, Siam had been reorganized and centralized in such a way that it had become simultaneously a nation and an absolute state or a dynastic realm.[19]

But by 1910 to 1925, when King Chulalongkorn's son Vajirarudh reigned, things had changed. Monarchies around the world were being threatened and abolished, starting with the end of the Qing dynasty in 1912, the House of Romanov in 1917, and those in Germany, Austria-Hungary, and the Ottoman, which soon disappeared in turn. Domestically, King Vajiravudh faced a rise of a previously imported Chinese, Sino-Thai middle class. They were urban educated and comprised his father's bureaucracy, representing a spread of liberalism, democracy, and the parliamentary system. Therefore, the king turned to official nationalism: a "willed merger of nation and dynastic empire".[20] And this is an "endless affirmation of the identity of dynasty and nation".[21]

Vajiravudh died in 1925, leaving behind a problematic law of royal succession forbidding females to inherit the throne (issued 11 November 1924, barely one year before the king's demise).

He had a single daughter, Princess Bejaratana, born on 24 November 1925, just two days before the king's death. Prajadhipok, his younger brother from the same mother, became the final absolute monarch from 1925 to 1932, an ultimately unsuccessful one who had to agree to be "constitutional" before abdicating in 1935.

As mentioned, on 24 June 1932, a group of educated urban middle-class and middle-ranking army and navy officials, numbering over one hundred males, formed a People's Party and staged a bloodless coup against King Prajadhipok. A compromise was eventually arrived at.

The monarchy was preserved, but a constitution was promulgated, and a parliament convened, with power transferred from the Chakri princes to the upper aristocracy and official classes. The first constitutional prime minister was Phraya Mano (1884–1948), a senior lawyer and an aristocrat; he was supposedly seen as a compromise figure.

At first glance, the political changes in Siam appeared rather peaceful and oriented towards compromise, leading to a misconception of the "uniqueness and power of assimilation" of Thai politics. However, a closer look tells a different story. The post-1932 coup was a period of instability and political conflict between the new elite and the old regime. By 1 April 1933, less than a year later, parliament was shut down and some constitutional articles were suspended by the conservative-aristocratic Phraya Mano government. A silent or parliamentary coup had occurred.[22]

On 20 June 1933, the 1932 coup leaders responded by staging another coup. This time Phaya Phahon, the coup leader himself, became prime minister. Ex-Premier Mano was sent into exile in Penang, where he died at the age of sixty-four in 1948. But three months later, in October 1933, a serious armed clash broke out. Prince Boworadet (1878–1953), a former defence minister during the time of the absolute monarchy, led troops from the outer provinces of Ayutthaya and Nakhon Ratchasima-Khorat in an attempt to seize Bangkok. The prince demanded that the Phahon government resign immediately. The Phahon government fought back, and the rebels were badly defeated.[23] Colonel Phraya Si Sitthisongkhram (born Din Tharab; 1891–1933, maternal grandfather of General Surayuth Chulanont, the future Thai Premier 2006–8) was the main rebel leader. The Colonel was shot dead on 23 October.

Prince Boworadet fled into exile in Saigon and Phnom Penh for sixteen years, until 1949. The royalist Boworadet coup attempt severely impacted relations between the government and the throne. After the incident, the king and queen decided to depart for England, on the pretext of seeking ophthalmological treatment. On 2 March 1935, less than three years after the 1932 coup and following unsuccessful negotiations and bargaining with the new government, the king decided to abdicate. He remained in England and died there on 30 May 1941, at age forty-seven.

Conflicts and political infighting between old and new elites continued up to the time that Phibun became prime minister. Feeling threatened by the royalists and the old regime after three separate assassination attempts, Phibun dealt a severe blow to his adversaries. Within one month of assuming office, Phibun arrested around forty people on charges of treason. It was his first major action against the royalists and aristocrats, including some members of parliament as well as personal rivals within the Army. They were tried by a specially appointed military tribunal; eighteen were immediately executed and twenty-six were condemned to life imprisonment. Prince Chai Nat (1885–1951), a son of King Chulalongkorn, was stripped of his princely rank. Many others were exiled. With his first move to consolidate power crushing the old hostile political elements, Phibun soon shifted his main energies to the more positive task of building popular support for his regime among the masses.

To Phibun and his nationalist colleagues, the best way to gain mass support was to "awaken, focus and mobilize a national consciousness". The people were often reminded by the government that they were now living in a "new society" and a "new time" which were in the process of renaissance and reconstruction. Indeed, Phibun was responsible for introducing into the Thai language the term and activity *sang chat* or nation-building.

This marks a clear distinction between Phibun and King Vajiravudh, Rama VI, although the former borrowed heavily from the latter. Vajiravudh spoke of *pluk* or cultivating the *chat* (nation), Phibun emphasized the word *sang*, or constructing. The phrase was first used officially on 21 March 1940 on the occasion of his *ratthaniyom* (R. No. 7), a state cultural decree on "Persuading the Thais to Build their Nation".

From 24 June 1939, after changing the country's name to Thailand to early 1940, Phibun brought issues of nation and nationalism to the heart of Thai politics, and they became his main policy focus. His *ratthaniyom* declared that everyone in Thailand should now be Thai, with no more separation into northern, Isan (Lao), southern, or Islamic Thai (*khaek malayu*). At 8:00 a.m. the tricolour (blue, white, red) Thai flag was raised and lowered again at 6:00 p.m., accompanied to the strains of the national anthem, lately revised to mention Thailand instead of Siam, during which anyone in the vicinity was required to rise and salute. Standing for the national flag and anthem remains obligatory in Thailand.

Sansoen Phra Barami, the royal anthem and de facto national anthem of Siam from 1888 to 1932, was retained.[24] Yet its lyrics were abbreviated and altered to fit the new national identity. Thailand is likely the sole monarchy with two major anthems, one for the nation and another for the king, whereas *God Save the Queen* suffices for the British, as does

Kimigayo for the Japanese. Meanwhile, along with economic nationalism mainly directed against local Chinese people,[25] Thais were encouraged by Phibun to use the Thai language and buy Thai products.

Note that the word *ratthaniyom*, or state cultural decree, derives from two Pali words: *rattha* (state) and *niyom* (to admire, favour, prefer, like, desire, popularly accept, or esteem). Attached to any word reflecting ideas or belief, *ratthaniyom* becomes akin to an "ism". For example, *sangkhom* (social or society) plus *niyom* becomes *sangkhomniyom* or socialism. Therefore, *ratthaniyom* may also be translated as statism, a subtle or blatant alternative implied for royalism or *ratchaniyom* (with *ratha* or state contrasting with *ratcha* or *racha/raja*, royal).

Thus, whereas in the time of the absolute monarchy, *ratchaniyom* or royalism was supreme, it was eventually replaced by *ratthaniyom* or statism. The centre now shifted from the palace to the military and Phibun himself. In some ways, the nation became separated from the monarchy, which was no longer identical. How this trend was reversed will be seen in the forthcoming chapters.

Nevertheless, Phibun's versions of nation and nationalism borrowed much from Vajiravudh's official nationalism. Indeed, he admired the king's nationalistic policies. With time, Phibun would have a monument to Vajiravudh designed and built in 1942, outside the king's Lumpini Park, Bangkok.

Phibun's nationalism, though remaining an official one, marked a divorce from nationalism dominated by the monarchy and the hybrid form resulting from the dynastic realm plus nation-state. It was more a military-bureaucratic entity than a royal nationalism. For Phibun, the monarchy and nation were two separate things. The heart of the nation was defined as "the people" (*khon Thai* or *chua chat Thai*, the latter meaning the Thai race).

Therefore, ethno-nationalism dictated that the name of the country had to be Thailand, the land of the Thai, rather than Siam.

Phibun and his collaborators argued repeatedly that the word Siam had been used by "others", not by Thais themselves. These foreigners were Chinese, Khmer, Malay, Portuguese, and all *farang*.

This argument is not far-fetched historically, insofar as traditional Thai states were defined by their centres, rather than territorial boundaries. As we would say now, Ayutthaya was simultaneously the name of the capital and the country. As late as 1828, in a stone inscription of a text by Rama III (1824–51), the king still referred to his nation as Krung Thep Maha Nakhon Sri Ayutthaya.

If foreigners called the country Siam, the Thai ruling class in premodern times was unconcerned. But by the mid-nineteenth century, at the height of colonialism and the spread of Western ideas, things had changed. King Mongkut began to conceive of himself as the King of Siam; he signed his name as SPPM Mongkut Rex Siamensium in letters to foreign friends and diplomats, including the celebrated Sir John Bowring and European monarchs.[26] Since the unequal 1855 treaty with Great Britain that "opened" Siam, Mongkut's proclamations noticeably used the word Syam (Siam) often, this time in the Thai language, to refer to himself and the country.[27]

In 1859, Mongkut even created an image which he named Phra Sayam Thewathirat (a Pali rendering of *Siam deva-dhiraja* or Siam god-king of kings). This was meant to be a guarding spirit protecting the land of Siam. Thereafter, Mongkut's successor King Chulalongkorn signed his name in Thai as Syamin, a coinage from Syam (Siam) and Indra (the god Indra who is heavenly king); hence he was the Indra, or king, of Siam.

By the reign of Mongkut's grandson King Vajiravudh, Syam (Siam) and Thai were used interchangeably, especially in the king's literary writings. Interestingly, Vajiravudh used this dualism in his poetry, but for his prose and nationalistic essays, mainly used the word Thai to describe his nation and people.

By then, the use of the name Siam by colonial powers had finally been accepted by the Thai ruling elite, who saw themselves and their country from the Western point of view as Siamese and Siam, respectively. Yet ironically, popular trends may have moved in a different direction.

In his pioneering *Dictionnaire Siamois Français Anglais* (Siamese French English dictionary; 1896), Bishop Jean-Baptiste Pallegoix (1805–62), vicar apostolic of Eastern Siam and a personal "friend" of King Mongkut, listed the two words *Thai* and *Siem* (Siam) this way:

Thai	*libre*	free
Thai	*les Thai, les Siamois*	the Thai, the Siamese
Siem	*Siam, les Siamois*	Siam, the Siamese
	(mot hors d'usage)	(obsolete term)

To Bishop Pallegoix, who had sustained contacts with local people, the word Siam had become *hors d'usage* or obsolete. If we accept Pallegoix's assertion, Siam was already antiquated by the late nineteenth century, but still associated with the monarchy and dynastic realm.

This accords with the aforementioned instability of internal politics, in which the new elite, especially in the Phibun government, pursued nationalist policies in terms of former leadership, especially by changing the country's name. In short, it may be said that Phibun clarified that the word Siam was a relic of past days of absolute monarchy, whereas Thailand was part of the new "democratic" regime of the present and future. A second question arises: why the name Thailand was accepted and why it persisted?

In hindsight, we can see that Bishop Pallegoix was both right and wrong about the term's archaism. The two words *Thai* and *Siem* (Siam) coexisted in usage throughout the second half of the nineteenth century. The choice of which to employ depended on in what context, when, and for whom it was being cited.

Kings, the nobility, and a modest number of educated Thais in Bangkok used both words. They preferred Siem/Siam when dealing with external *farang* and sometimes in poetry. Siem/Siam was not yet a *mot hors d'usage*. But amongst themselves or for the general public's consumption, an inner utilization of the word Thai for the people and the term *muang Thai* for the nation became current.

As for the people themselves, we have firm evidence that at least in the central Menam Chao Phraya plain, although not in the northeast Khorat Plateau or northern Lanna, the word Thai was widely accepted.

The word *Thai* for the nation (with the prefix *muang*) and the people (with the prefix *khon*) had been used as far back as the seventeenth century, as reported by the French envoy Simon de la Loubère who visited Ayutthaya in 1687.[28]

The printing press arrived in the nineteenth century (with the first publications produced in Thai being religious booklets printed in June 1836 by an American missionary and publisher Dr Dan Beach Bradley and a modern printing press brought to Chiang Mai in 1892 by the American Presbyterian Mission.)

Concomitantly, modern educational guidelines appeared with compulsory primary education first enforced in 1921 in the Bangkok area and other major cities for children aged seven to fourteen, and Chulalongkorn University, the first institution of higher learning, was founded in 1917.

This produced increased mass readership by the first quarter of the twentieth century, along with a sizeable number of writers emphasizing the word *Thai*, rather than *Siam*. In effect, inhabitants of Bangkok and central Thailand learned to think of themselves and their country as *khon Thai* and *muang Thai*, not Siamese or Siam, respectively.[29]

As mentioned in the previous chapter, by the 1920s and 1930s, the construction of the Thai past in symbiosis with race became even more intensified, especially after the Siamese revolution of 1932. The reasons for this were shared between Vajiravudh's official nationalistic campaign, the growing number of educated middle and official classes, and influential British colonial and missionary publications.

We might note that the new emerging educated middle class, especially those of Thai Chinese origin, emphasized the race issue to the point of almost making it the central theme in their personalized version of Thai history. This dynastic-turned-nationalist historiography was linear, with an intimate relationship to the modern territorial nation.[30]

Here we see the history of the Thai race as a long march, a sort of exodus, migrating from the north of China, where it borders Mongolia and Russia. From the Altai Mountains in Central and East Asia, over 5,000 years they migrated through southwest China into Suwannaphum (Suvarnabhumi), or the golden land of Southeast Asia.

They had established centres called Mung, Lung, Pa, and Ai-Lao from central China to Yunnan. Their last great kingdom was Nan Chao/Nanzhao, established in 738 CE in present-day Dali City, Yunnan. After greater Nanzhao was destroyed by Kublai Khan in 1253, Thai centres were shifted successively southward to Sukhothai, Ayutthaya and Bangkok (Thonburi and Ratanakosin/present-day Bangkok).[31]

Theories about the Thais' supposed origin in the Altai Mountains, with a final great kingdom of Nanzhao, have been seriously challenged since the 1960s. Stories to this effect have been partially removed from textbooks, but their impact lingered.

Hypotheses devised by Western colonial orientalists from fieldwork observations by late-nineteenth-century Christian missionaries stationed along the border between mainland Southeast Asia and China were adopted and reproduced by the revered intelligentsia, including Prince Damrong, Phraya Prachakit,[32] Phraya Anuman, Khun Wichit[33] and Luang Wichit.

One of the first treatments on this topic by Phraya Prachakit (Chaem Bunnag, 1864–1907), an intelligentsia (lawyer and writer) who is eleven years younger than King Chulalongkorn, Rama V. He serialized his articles, a kind of *tamnan-phongsawadan* presentation which had a strong impact on modern Thai linear history. They were put together, in 1907, as a book called *Phongsawadan Yonok* (Chronicle of the North); it portrays the movement and migration of the Thai from Yunnan (Rachakrue) into the Shan state and crossed the Mekong into Chiang Saen (Chiang Rai). The Thai encountered and drove away the Khom (old Khmer) to Kampaengphet. After some generations, the Thai took over the whole area of north-central Thailand down to Lopburi and Ayutthaya which eventually became Siam-Thailand.

After Phraya Prachakit, a proliferation of articles and books appeared on the Thai linear and racial past. Probably the three most influential ones along this historiographical line were, in order of importance, *Lak Thai* (Thai Pillars), 1928 by Sanga Kanchanakkhaphan (better known as Khun Wichit Matra, 1897–1980); *Prawattisat sakon* (International History), 1929 by Luang Wichit Wathakan (1898–1962); and *Ruang khong chat Thai* (Story of the Thai Nation), 1940 by Phraya Anuman (Yong Sathiankoset; 1888–1964).

All of these three authors were of Sino-Thai backgrounds and officially belonged to the intelligentsia. At the time of the Siamese revolution of 1932, Luang Wichit Wathakan was thirty-four years old, Khun Wichit Matra was thirty-five, and Phraya Anuman was forty-four. They went along with the new wave of the new regime but maintained good relations with the *ancien*.

The first-mentioned, Luang Wichit Wathakan, became Director of the Fine Arts Department (1934–40). The second, Khun Wichit Matra, rose to be a senior official in the Ministry of Commerce but was better known as a freelance writer and producer-director of silent and talking films during the 1930s and 1940s. This Khun Wichit Matra also wrote lyrics for the new national anthem (used from 1932 to 1939 when the country was still called Siam). He also wrote the lyrics of the alma mater (*phleng pracham mahawitthayalai*) in 1934 for the newly established Mahawitthayalai wicha Thammasat lae kanmuang (University of Moral and Political Sciences), now known as Thammasat University.[34]

In 1928, the aforementioned *Lak Thai* by Khun Wichit Matra elicited an award from King Prajadhipok. The book immediately became a bestseller, going into the second printing of 1,000 copies the following year. The author stated candidly that his linear southern march history of the Thai race was primarily intended to encourage Thai patriotism (*Lak Thai* was published before the Siamese revolution of 1932). Its second purpose was to encourage faith in the Buddhist religion, and thirdly, loyalty to the Crown. Of these three pillars, the author was significantly more interested in the first. The book concluded with an envoi emphasizing the love of nation and the *rao-Thai*, We-the-Thai.

As for Luang Wichit Wathakan, he was one of the most prolific writers of Thailand. He produced an enormous number of historical works, novels, plays, songs and poems. Almost all were intended to infuse the concept of love of nation and the Thai race, worthy of sacrificing one's life, into the hearts and minds of the Thai people. Because of his "modern" middle-class taste and linguistic talent (in Thai, Pali, French and English), Luang Wichit emulated, borrowed, and translated whatever he found suitable from many cultures, turning it successfully into Thai.[35]

He was instrumental in the Thai perception of the exodus from the Nan Chao/Nanzhao Kingdom, Southern China, into present-day Thailand. Indeed, he titled one of his many "*lakhon luang wichit*" musical plays (1939) Nan Chao/Nanzhao.[36] And because of this, he rose to the rank of minister of foreign affairs, and towards the end of the Second World War, and was sent by Phibun as ambassador to Japan.

In September 1945, he was arrested by General MacArthur's occupied forces, and was sent to Bangkok to be charged with war crimes but was set free by March 1946. Luang Wichit Wathakan demonstrated outstanding ability in cooperating with whatever government happened to be in power. He became an influential Permanent Secretary of the Office of the Prime Minister during Sarit's absolutist years, until his death in 1963 at the age of sixty-four. Some labelled him unflatteringly as the Talleyrand of Thailand, referring to the French diplomat who was notorious for his crafty, cynical diplomacy.

As for the voluminous *Prawattisat sakon*, it is more like what would today be termed a world history, focusing on major Eastern and Western civilizations. Interestingly, Luang Wichit managed to include Thai history to demonstrate that the Thai race was among the greatest. The chapter about the Thai began with a discourse on the centrality of the race.

To further press the point, it is worth noticing that books with similar ideology were emphatically encouraged and distributed. They appeared regularly, sponsored by government agencies, published and distributed free of charge during the Tod Kathin Ceremony, an annual religious event where Buddhists present monks with new yellow robes and make merit, as well as at cremations. Praphasiri's *wikhroa ruang Muang Tai doem* (Analysis of the Ancient Tai Nation; 1935), is one illustrative example; another is *Naeo son prawattisat* (History Instruction Guidelines), a Military Academy text from the same year by Major Phra Wisetphotchanakit (Thongdi).

Along with Thailand's new elite and middle-class writings, we again see Western works initiating linear racial ideas and helping to perpetuate and consolidate them to a certain degree. Of all Western texts of the era, the most well-known and popular one is by an American missionary William Clifton Dodd (1857–1919). His extremely inspiring and interesting book is *The Tai Race: Elder Brother of the Chinese* (1923);[37] note the words *Tai* not *Thai* and "elder brother of the Chinese" (!?). It was probably the most influential since writings by E.H. Parker, the Victorian British consular to Hainan.

Edward Harper Parker (1849–1926) was an English barrister and sinologist who wrote several books on the First and Second Opium Wars and other Chinese topics, including influential studies on historical linguistics. His works included *China's Relations with Foreigners* (1888), *Up the Yangtsze* (1892), and *Life, Labours and Doctrines of Confucius* (1897), *A Thousand Years of the Tartars* (1926).

In 1886, Dr Dodd arrived in Chiang Mai, an area which missionaries still referred to as their Laos Mission. He and his wife Isabella Eakin founded mission stations in Lamphun, Chiang Rai, Kengtung and Chiang Rung. Until 1918, he would travel widely, mostly on horseback, to the Shan states, Yunnan, and northern regions of Laos and Vietnam. On one of his many trips, he reached Canton.

In his varied accounts, later compiled, edited, and published by his wife, he met all kinds of Tai-speaking people (*Tai*, but not *Thai*), literate and illiterate, Buddhist and animistic. He was highly impressed by their hospitality.

Dr Dodd died in Chiang Rung (Xishuangbanna, Yunnan) in 1919 at the age of sixty-two, after thirty-three years spent among different ethnic groups on the border of southern China and the Southeast Asian mainland. With an exotic title and full of data from fieldwork, his book became an immediate bestseller among the Bangkok Thai elite. It was translated into the Thai language, at first serialized, and later published at least three times (in 1935, 1939, 1940).

His experiences made the linear racial Thai past exceptionally real and convincing. *The Tai Race* clearly followed in the footsteps of such pioneers as A.R. Colquhoun (1883) about the Tai of Yunnan, Albert Terrien de Lacouperie (1885) for central China, and E.H. Parker (1894) on Nanzhao.

Like these three writers, Dr Dodd made no mention of any original homeland of the Thai in the Altai Mountain bordering China, Mongolia and Russia. But he presented the Tai as belonging to the Mongol race. And because of this, it became possible for Thai thinkers and writers such as Prince Damrong (1914) to conceptually push the origins back to the Altai Mountains.

As for Dodd, his subject matter was confined to the borderlines of southern China as well as Burma, Siam, Laos, and Vietnam. Naturally, his thesis found its way into the highly centralized Ministry of Education, before, and especially after, the era of absolute monarchy, and was enduringly inscribed in all Thai school textbooks. Thai students learned to memorize strange-sounding names of Nanzhao kings of whom their ancestors during the early Bangkok and Ayutthaya periods had probably never heard.

At first, race, original homeland, and successive kingdoms were likely worked out unconsciously. But slowly, the emphasis on the past shifted from palaces and kings. Eventually, Thais, especially those benefiting from the modern educational system, considered themselves Thais inhabiting within the territorial boundaries of Muang Thai, the country of the Thai.

Here, again, we can see that a new society of a greater horizontal, rather than hierarchical, structure or relationship, was taking form. Although race is an abstract and general matter, difficult to identify intellectually, it was easily linked to that same vague idea of "the people".

In terms of the distinction between dynastic realm and imagined communities, race was likely a basis for the transformation from dynasty to nation-state. Phibun's Thailand was suited to his time, because it was modern, indigenous, popular, and national, whereas Siam was old-fashioned, foreign, hierarchical, and monarchic.

Conclusion

Over three-quarters of a century has passed since Siam's name was changed to Thailand, and much has happened to the Thai nation. When the Second World War ended, Phibun and his men were charged with war crimes. They would be acquitted on all counts.

During this brief post-war period, from 1945 to 1948, the name Siam made a recurrence. However, it was only used in English and other foreign languages, whereas in Thai, Prathet Thai or Thailand persisted. Liberal and royalist prime ministers, such as Thawi, Khuang, and Pridi, make no effort to change the name back as used in the Thai language. As discussed, Pridi's version of the 1946 Constitution, which he countersigned on behalf of King Ananda, Rama VIII, was officially termed the Constitution of the Kingdom of Thailand (*ratchanachak Thai*), not of Syam or Siam.

In 1948, Phibun staged a comeback and ruled as prime minister for a further nine years. The country's name under his regime was Prathet Thai in Thai and Thailand in English. At the time of the drafting of the 1949 Constitution, the names Siam or Thailand were officially reconsidered and voted by a committee appointed by the National Assembly.

Thailand narrowly won the polling and was used throughout the anti-Communist Cold War period. In 1957, Phibun was overthrown by a military coup led by his defence minister, Field Marshal Sarit Thanarat; Phibun fled into exile and died in Japan.

At the start of the long military regime of Sarit-Thanom, from 1958 to 1973, and the long constitutional drafting process from 1958 to 1968, the question of Thailand or Siam was again reconsidered and discussed at length by the Constitution Drafting Assembly of Thailand. The Assembly met three times (on 22 June, 6 July, and 20 August 1961).

The well-known leaders Luang Wichit Wathakan, Phin Choonhavan, and Kukrit Pramoj, took turns in debating the two names. Finally, votes were counted; Thailand won over Siam by a count of 134 to 5.[38] This should have been enough to put Siam to rest permanently. Yet the 1960s saw still another attempt to bring back Siam; the intellectual circle led by Sulak Sivaraksa and his respected journal *Sangkhomsat Parithat* took the lead, along with some academics. But the movement met little success, despite the monarchy's renewed prominence during the 1960s.

King Bhumibol, Rama IX restored the power and prestige of the monarchy to unprecedented heights. But obviously, Rama IX saw himself as king of the new Thailand, not old Siam. However, in 1987, when he promoted his daughter Princess Maha Chakri Sirindhorn to a higher rank, the word Sayam (Siam) appeared as part of her new title. She became Grand Princess of Siam (*Sayam borom ratcha kumari*). This somewhat echoed King Chulalongkorn's appointment of his son Prince Vajirunhis as Crown Prince in 1886 to the title of Crown Prince of Siam (*Sayam makut ratcha kumar*).

With the military returned to power, the national name of Thailand persisted. This was so under the wartime regime of Field Marshal Phibun from 1948 to 1957. The appellation was carried forward by Field Marshal Sarit Thanarat from 1958 onwards. Sarit had a better working relationship with the young King Bhumibol, who apparently preferred the name Thailand to Siam, although he sometimes used both names interchangeably.

In this way, the linear theory of the Thai people, from China into Southeast Asia, remained unchallenged through the 1950s and early 1960s, until Frederick W. Mote (1922–2005), an American sinologist and long-time Princeton University history professor, raised doubts by rejecting Nan Chao (Nanzhao) as a Thai/Tai kingdom.[39]

For two decades, Mote's provocative antithetical argument was limited to Thai academics and the Ministry of Education until Sujit Wongthes, an outspoken historical journalist, visited Yunnan and delivered persuasive and humorous arguments against the Nan Chao (Nanzhao) and migration theory. Sujit's major works include *Thais Do Not Come from Anywhere* (*Khon Thai Mai Dai Ma Chak Nai*; 1984); *The Thais Are Here* (*Khon Thai Yu Thini*; 1986); and *The Thais are in Southeast Asia* (*Khon Thai yu nai usakhane*; 1994).

So, in diverse ways, the theories of an original homeland and especially Nan Chao (Nanzhao) as a Thai kingdom were damaged and partially rejected. It is impossible to say if this will eventually affect the name Thailand. But the word Thai is likely to endure with a different connotation and much broader significance. One of Sujit's anti-racial writings was especially appreciated. In 1987, Sujit returned from a visit to Laos and wrote another half-serious, half-ironic travelogue entitled *Chinese Mixed with Lao* (*Jek Pon Lao*). The title was likely an allusion to himself, as Sujit was of Chinese and Lao Phuan heritage. In effect, Sujit was indicating that Thai people are a mixed bunch.

Last but not least, a more constructive analysis is thoroughly done by Grant Evans (1948–2014), an Australian anthropologist-historian who was a long-time lecturer at the University of Hong Kong. In one of his last works he not only questioned that the Ai-lao and Nan Chao were ancestors of the Thai (and the Lao) but presented the southern kingdom as belonging to Southeast Asian Buddhists than closely related to China proper.[40]

After the popular student uprising of 14 October 1973 which overthrew the Thanom-Prapas military regime, the question of Siam or Thailand was once again reconsidered by the 1975 Constitution Drafting Committee. However, this time, it received scant attention. Debating over Siam or Thailand seemed futile. In the late 1980s, when the Thai economic bubble was at its height, the Thai rock band Carabao played guitar chords and intoned the smash hit song, *Made in Thailand*.

Thailand remains the firmly established appellation, even if no one can be sure that the eternal debate will not arise again someday.[41]

NOTES

1. Kobkua Suwannathat-Pian, *Thailand's Durable Premier, Phibun through Three Decades, 1932–1957* (Kuala Lumpur: Oxford University Press, 1995), p. 81.
2. Men like Phra Ratchathamnithet (Phian Taitilanond, 1891–1965), Luang Wichit Wathakan (Kimliang Watthanaprida-Wichit Wichitwathakan 1898–1962, instrumental for the name-change), Luang Yutthasatkoson (1893–1975), Luang Phromyothi (1896–1966 commanding troops against French Indochina in 1940), Luang Wichianphaettayakom (1898–1977), Luang Saranupraphan (1896–1954 who composed nationalistic lyrics for the National Anthem, still in use), Sang Phatthanothai (1915–86 responsible for the nationalist radio-talk programme Nai Man and Nai Khong), among others. See also Thaemsook Numnonda et al., *The Status of Research in History in Thailand 1960–1992* (Bangkok: Odian Store, 2001), Ch. I.
3. Territories taken from French Indochina were renamed after Phibun and his associates. Siem Reap, meaning Siam defeated or flattened in the Khmer language, was gloriously renamed Changwat Phibunsongkhram or Phibunsongkhram Province; Saiyabulee became Lan Chang, or a million elephants, and name originating in the thirteenth-century Lao Kingdom.

    See Charnvit Kasetsiri, *Pramuan sonthisanya anusanya khwam toklong ...* [Collected Treaties-Conventions-Agreements-Memorandum of Understanding and Maps Between Siam/Thailand-Cambodia-Laos-Burma-Malaysia] (Bangkok: The Social Sciences and Humanities Textbooks Foundation, 2011. Also, by the same editor, *Pramuan phaenthi: prawattisat-phumusat-kanmuang*

... [Collected Maps: History-Geography-Politics and Colonialism in Southeast Asia] (Bangkok: The Social Sciences and Humanities Textbooks Foundation, 2012.
4. Ibid., again, this portion of the Shan states was renamed nationalistically as Saha rath Thai doem, or United State of Ancient Thai.
5. See my work, "The First Phibun Government and Its Involvement in World War II", *Journal of the Siam Society* 62, no. 2 (July 1974): 25–88; also, Benjamin A. Batson, "The Fall of the Phibun Government, 1944", in the same volume of *JSS*, pp. 89–120.
6. On 28 July 1941, with his successful nationalistic and territory campaign against French Indochina, Premier Major General Phibun was promoted to the rank of a Field Marshal. Interestingly, on 15 May 1942 Phibun went ahead by officially abolishing feudal bureaucratic ranks (*bandasak*) granted by the royal court: khun-luang-phraya-chaophraya. See Charnvit Kasetsiri, "The First Phibun Government and Its Involvement in World War II".
7. *Ratthaniyom* derives from two Pali words: *rattha* meaning state and *niyom* is supposed to equal to "ism". Therefore, *ratthaniyom* is state cultural decree or "statism". Its implication is that it is from the State or the Government (of new Thailand) not from the *ratchaniyom* or from the royal place or the court of absolute kings (of old Siam).
8. 24 June remained *wan chat* or National Day from 1939 until the early 1960s, when it was changed, 1960, by the Sarit Government to 5 December; the new date corresponds with King Bhumibol's birthday. This is one of the first measure by the military government to erase the legacy of the 1932 revolutionary promoters.
9. *Phleng wan chat* or the 24 June national song was composed to celebrate the occasion and broadcast on the Radio of Thailand and officially promoted among young students throughout Thailand from 1939 to 1960.
10. During the first Phibun Government (1938–44), a series of *Ratthaniyom* ("statism") announcements were issued by the Office of the Prime Minister:
    i. On the Use of Names for the Country, People, and Nationality (24 June 1939)
    ii. On Preventing Danger to the Nation (3 July 1939)
    iii. On Further Use of the Name of the Thai People (2 September 1939)
    iv. On Saluting the National Flag, the National Anthem, and the Royal Anthem (8 September 1939)
    v. On Exhorting Thai People to Consume Products which are produced in Thailand (1 November 1939)
    vi. On the Melody and Lyrics of the National Anthem (10 December 1939)

vii. On Persuading the Thai People to Build their Nation (21 March 1940)
viii. On Changing the Word Siam to Thailand in the Royal Anthem (1 April 1940)
ix. On the Use of the Thai Language and Duties of Good Citizens (24 June 1940)
x. On the Costume of the Thai People (15 January 1941)
xi. On Daily Activity of the Thai People (8 September 1942)
xii. On Treatment of Children, the Aged, and the Handicapped (28 January 1942).

11. See award-winning articles on the topic *Khwam samkhan khong wan chat* [The Importance of National Day] published on the occasion of the National Day Celebration, 1940.
12. See Phonphirom Iamtham, *Botbat thang kanmuang khong nangsuephim thai tangtae kanplianplaeng kanpokkhrong 2475 thung sinsud songkhram lok khrang thi song* [Political role of Thai newspapers from the change of regime in 1932 to the end of World War II], Ch. 2.
13. Chulla Ngonrot, *Kamnoed lae khwam penma khong latthi chatniyom nai prathet Thai* [The Origin and Development of Nationalism in Thailand] (unpublished MA thesis, Chulalongkorn University, 1970), p. 68.
14. Pridi Banomyong, *Khwam penma khong chue prathet sayam kap Prathet Thai* [The Development of the Names Siam and Thailand], 1974, pp. 4–5. See also his *Ma Vie Mouvementee et mes 21 ans d'exil en Chine Populaire* (Paris, 1972).
15. See also Lawrence Palmer Briggs, "The Appearance and Historical Usage of the Terms Tai, Thai, Siamese and Lao", *Journal of the American Oriental Society* 69 (1949): 60–73; partly translated by Yupa Chumchan and published in *Chulasan Khrongkan Tamra* 3, no. 4 (July–September 1976). The best academic treatment of the use of all these terms is done by Jit Phoumisak (1930–66), a young radical left-wing writer in his *magnum opus: Khwampenma khong kham sayam thai lao lae laksana thang sangkhom khong chu chonchat* [Etymology of the terms Siam, Thai, Lao and Khom, and the Social Characteristics of Nationalities].

Jit probably wrote it while in prison from 1958 to 1964. He handed the manuscript to a friend and left for the jungle to join the Communist Party of Thailand in the Northeast. He was shot dead on 5 May 1966. Jit's work was first published in 1976 by the Social Sciences and Humanities Textbooks Foundation. And for the best account in English on Jit Phoumisak and his radical thinking, see Craig J. Reynolds, *Thai Radical Discourse: The Real*

Face of Thai Feudalism Today (Ithaca: Cornell University Southeast Asia Program, 1987).

16. Pridi Banomyong, *Khwam penma khong chue prathet sayam kap Prathet Thai*, p. 7.
17. However, Pridi's version of the name change was rather eccentric. At the end of the Second World War, he had emerged as one of the most powerful Thais, as Regent of Thailand insofar as King Rama VIII was still residing in Switzerland. Pridi's regency enabled him to lead the Free Thai underground movement against the Japanese. On 16 August 1945, when Japan surrendered, Pridi as Regent issued the Royal Proclamation Issued by the Regent of Thailand in the name of King Ananda Mahidol. He wrote, "The Regent, in the name of His Majesty the King, thereby, openly proclaims on behalf of the Thai people that the declaration of war [by Phibun] on the United States of America and the United Kingdom is null and void ..." The proclamation served as a basis for Thailand to negotiate peace treaties with the victorious Allies without being punished for joining the Axis forces during wartime. Note that Pridi used the word Thailand, instead of Siam. Again, in 1946, Pridi had a new constitution proclaimed to replace the 1932 version. He himself countersigned the new version. On this occasion again, the name Thailand, rather than Siam, was used.
18. See David K. Wyatt, *Thailand: A Short History* (New Haven: Yale University Press, 1995), Ch. 7. See also Chaiyan Rajchagool, *The Rise and Fall of the Thai Absolute Monarchy* (Bangkok: White Lotus Press, 1994).
19. Benedict Anderson, *Imagined Communities: Reflections on the Origin and Spread of Nationalism* (London: Verso, 1991), see Ch. 6 on "Official Nationalism and Imperialism".
20. Ibid., pp. 94–95.
21. Ibid., p. 101.
22. See Thamrongsak Phetlertanan, *2475 lae 1 pi lang kanpatiwat* [1932 Revolution and the Aftermath] (Bangkok: The Social Sciences and Humanities Textbooks Foundation, 2000).
23. The Boworadet Rebellion took place between 13 and 23 October 1933. Government troops led by Phibun used heavy artillery to suppress the rebels. Fighting broke out in the area between Bangkok and the Don Mueang Airport and continued on through the railway up to the Northeast. The government lost seventeen soldiers and police including a friend of Phibun, a member of the People's Party. There were fifty-four casualties. On the opposite side, Colonel Phraya Sisitthisongkhram (Din Tharap; 1891–1933) the rebel commander was killed. The last fighting was at Hin Lap Railway Station, Sraburi Province close to the Khorat Plateau. Din Tharap is the maternal grandfather of the future

Premier and President of the Privy Council General Surayuth Chulanond. See Natthapoll Chaiching, *Kabot Boworadet: Buangraed patipak patiwat sayam 2475* [Boworadet Rebellion: Up against the 1932 revolution of Siam] (Bangkok: Matichon, 2016).

24. An interesting outcome of Siam's meeting with the West is the invention of Western-style royal anthem. King Mongkut used to borrow the melody of *God Save the Queen* from his contemporary Queen Victoria of the UK. However, there had been many versions of melody and lyrics for the royal anthem. By the time of King Chulalongkorn, in 1888, a Russian musician by the name of Pyotr Schurovsky was assigned to write up a melody. It has been in use till today. But the lyrics are by Thais.

25. Here is the origin of the ubiquitous *kueteo phad Thai* or Thai fried noodles, a popular snack for tourists as well as Thais. Obviously, noodles are of Chinese origin. To make them Thai, they must be fried with cheap dried shrimp instead of relatively expensive pork in the Chinese style. Generous helpings of vegetables are added, including bean sprouts, green onion leaves, and banana flowers, as well as lime juice and chili. The folkloric circle dance *ramvong* is another of Phibun's nationalist inventions, whose popularity still survives across the nation in many versions. As part of his policy of Thaification, Phibun hoped to replace popular Western dances such as the foxtrot or waltz by promoting *ramvong*.

26. SPPM Mongkut Rex Siamensium = Somdet Phra Poroamenthra Maha Mongkut King of Siam. This is King Mongkut's Siamese-Latin signature to Sir John Bowring and reproduced in his book *The Kingdom and People of Siam: With a Narrative of the Mission to That Country in 1855* (J.W. Parker, 1857; reprinted by Oxford University Press, 1969; and Cambridge University Press, 2013).

See a Thai translation version by Charnvit Kasetsiri and Kanthika Sriudom, eds., *Ratchanachak lae ratsadon sayam* [The Kingdom and People of Siam], (Bangkok), and our article on "lok khong phrachao krung sayam" [The World according to the King of Siam] in *Phracao krung sayam and Sir John Bowring* [The King of Siam and Sir John Bowring] (Bangkok, The Social Sciences and Humanities Textbooks Foundation, 2005). Also see https://commons.wikimedia.org/wiki/File:King_Mongkut_(Rama_IV)_of_Siam_Signature_(English).svg.

27. See Charnvit Kasetsiri, ed., *Prachum prakat ratchakan thi 4* [Collected Proclamations of the Fourth Reign: King Mongkut], 2 vols. (Bangkok: The Social Sciences and Humanities Textbooks Foundation, 2004).

28. Simon de la Loubère (1642–1729), *Du royaume de Siam* (A. Wolfgang, 1691).

29. The same process would continue with others who were not called, nor

did they think of themselves as Thai, such as the people of Lanna, who rejected the word Lao and called themselves *khon muang* (people of the city) and speaking *kham muang* (language of the city). Whereas people in the Northeast who formerly preferred the term Lao, but after Isan was applied to their region, eventually admitted it as an appellation for the people and the language. See David Streckfuss, *Creating "Thai-ness": The Emergence of Indigenous Nationalism in Non-Colonial Siam 1850–1980* (unpublished MA thesis, University of Wisconsin, 1987).
30. See my "Preliminary Observation on Thai Historiography", in *Studies in Thai and Southeast Asian Histories*, (Bangkok: The Social Sciences and Humanities Textbooks Foundation, 2015).
31. This linear history had already been developed by the turn of the twentieth century, mainly through the works of Vajiravudh and Prince Damrong, and various writers with modern education. See "The Story of the Records of Siamese History", translated by Oscar Frankfurter, *Journal of the Siam Society* 11, no. 2, "Translation of the Historical Records" (1914): 1–20. See W.A.R. Wood, *A History of Siam from the Earliest Time to the Year A.D. 1781* (Bangkok: Siam Barnakich, 1933).

For one of the best summaries of the turn of the century theory on origins of the Thai-Tai, see Rong Syamananda, a well-known Professor Emeritus at the History Department of Chulalongkorn University, Bangkok, *A History of Thailand* (Bangkok: Thai Watana Panich, 1973), Ch. 1–3 and his abbreviated version in Thai written on "Books Initiated by King Bhumibol", number 23, *Ruang prawattisat thai* [On Thai history] (Bangkok: Saksopha, 1984).
32. Phraya Prachakit (Chaem Bunnag, 1864–1913), a historian-lawyer who is eleven years younger than King Chulalongkorn, Rama V. He wrote a kind of *tamnan-phongsawadan* manuscript which had a strong impact on modern Thai linear history. His *Phongsawadan Yonok* (Chronicle of the North), 1907, portrays the Thai moving down from Yunnan (Rachakrue) into the Shan state and crossed the Mekong into Chiang Saen (Chiang Rai). They encountered and then drove away the Khom (old Khmer) who fled further south to Kampaengphet. After some generations the Thai took over the whole area of north-central Thailand down to Lopburi and Ayutthaya which eventually became Siam-Thailand.

Another good example along this line of interpretation of this linear historiography is by Praya Borihan Boriraksa (Phueg Xuto, 1862–1923). The Praya was an intelligentsia and a court official during the absolute monarchy time. He was sent and stayed to Great Britain for two years between 1884 and 1886, acquiring good knowledge in metropolitan London. In 1892 he became Permanent Secretary of Agriculture, moving to the Ministry of

Justice before dying in 1923. Few years before his death in 1921 he wrote a manuscript entitled *"Tamnan thai sangkheb"* [Short historical story of the Thai]. The book has a long title added as *"thai ton nua, thai ton klang, lae thai ton tai nai sayam prathet pen lamdap talod ma chon sin ratchakan somdet phra ramathibodi"*, which can be translated as (of) northern Thai, central Thai, and southern Thai in the country of Siam accordingly to the end of the reign of King Ramathibodi-Uthong (the founder of Ayutthaya in 1351). See this rare book here: http://adminebook.car.chula.ac.th/viewer/ 119100484868657610152908811088110501145611767103113656161/1/2/0/ viewer.html?url=%0D%0Ahttp%3A%2F%2Fadminebook.car.chula.ac.th%3 A80%2Fviewer%2F11910048486865761015290881108811050114561176710 3113656161%2F1%2F2%2F0%2Fviewer.html

33. Khun Wichit Matra (Sanga Kanchanakpan, 1897–1980), a lawyer-writer-film producer, he is of the same generation of Phibun and Pridi. As mentioned earlier his manuscript: *Lak Thai* [Thai pillars] won a literature award from Rama VII in 1928, four years before the 1932 revolution. The book became one of the bestsellers in Thai publishing history and most influential for Thai linear history. Here, Khun Wichit claimed that the Mongols were the oldest homo sapiens, older than the Egyptians, Babylonians, and the Aryans. The Thai are a branch of the Mongols, and their original homeland was along the Altai Mountains, the range along Mongolia, China, Russia, and present-day Kazakhstan. They had move down to the areas between the Yellow and Yangtze Rivers before establishing a powerful kingdom of Nan Chao (Nanzhao).*ff*

    From there the Thai moved down to form four kingdoms respectively: Sukhothai, Ayutthaya, Thonburi, and Krungthep (Bangkok). See Khun Wichit Matra, *Lak Thai* [Thai pillars] (Bangkok: Odeon Store, 1963).

34. Charnvit Kasetsiri, Sunthari Asawai, Suphaphon Charanpat, Songyote Waeohongsa, Suwimot Rungcharoen, Nakharin Mektrairat, and Damrong Khraikrual, *Samnak nan thammasat lae kanmuang* [That institution thammasat and politics] (Bangkok: Dokya Publishing House, 1992), Chs 1 and 5.

35. Craig J. Reynolds, "Nation and State in Histories of Nation-Building, with Special Reference to Thailand", in *Nation-Building: Five Southeast Asian Histories*, edited by Wang Gungwu (Singapore: Institute of Southeast Asian Studies, 2005), pp. 27–33.

36. The so-called *"lakhon luang wichit"* musical plays were invented by Luang Wichit Wathakan as director of the newly renovated Krom Sinlapakon or Fine Arts Department. The Department originated in different arts, dramatic, crafts, museum, and library offices from the era of absolute monarchy. They were reorganized to fit new mores after the Siamese revolution of 1932.

From 1934 to 1940, Luang Wichit served as its first director before being appointed foreign affairs minister and later, wartime ambassador to Tokyo. He hyperactively produced a new type of *lakhon* that may be termed hybrid, as it mixed classical music, singing, and dance with modern drama borrowed from the West. The stories were historical and imaginative evocations of patriotism and love for the Thai people. Notably, most of the plays required at least three hours for performance. Luang's *Lakhon* can be divided into two phases, before and after the Second World War. They were produced and funded by the first and second Phibun governments. see more in *Wichit Wathakan Anuson* [In memory of Wichit Wathakan, 1898–1962], V, II (Bangkok: Mongkol Karn Pim, 1962), p. 294.

Examining the first phase, from 1936 to 1940, provides a clear picture of the Thai government campaign for official nationalism's aims. Nine plays were written in four years:

i. *Luad Suphan* (Suphan Blood) 1936. A story of late eighteenth century villagers, just before the fall of Ayutthaya in 1767. They fight bravely against Burmese invaders, and all die heroically. The *lakhon* was so popular that the Fine Arts Department was able to build a new theatre on the profits from tickets sold. The play script and sheet music were sent to all government schools, so that students could perform it for local audiences nationwide. In addition, the Ministry of Defense required all Armed Forces cadets to see the play.

ii. *Ratmanu* (Rajamanu), 1936. About a leading warrior in sixteenth-century Ayutthaya, based on *phongsawadan*, a history of Siam and Cambodia in which the latter was conquered and reduced to the vassal state of Ayutthaya/Siam. This second *lakhon* was not as successful as the first.

iii. *Phrachao Krung Thon* (King of Thonburi), 1937. The story of King Taksin, who restored the country after it was destroyed by the Burmese in 1767. The play could be interpreted as having a twofold purpose. At first glance, it was a conventional story of Siam fighting for independence but can also be seen as challenging the Chakri Dynasty, whose founder, Rama I, reached power after a coup against Taksin, who was beheaded.

iv. *Suk Thalang* (Battle of Thalang), 1937. When the Burmese invaded southern Siam at the start of the nineteenth century, two sisters were reported in the *phongsawadan* history as leading the resistance in the town of Thalang (Junkceylon or modern-day Phuket). The sisters, Thao Thepsatri and Thao Srisunthon, were later deemed heroines by the Chakri Dynasty. This play was not a hit.

v. *Chaoying Saenwi* (Princess of Hsenwi), 1938. A story about two Tai principalities in the Shan States of Burma during the twelfth and thirteenth centuries. The plot has nothing to do with fighting external invaders but emphasizes the Tai/Thai race and its patriotism. This play was highly successful, and many of its songs were used by military governments from the 1940s through the 1960s. But by the mid-1970s, songs composed by King Bhumibol himself or written for him have replaced those of Luang Wichit to a degree.

vi. *Maha Thewi* (The Great Queen), 1938. The protagonist is a female ruler in sixteenth- century Chiang Mai. The historical figure fought for her kingdom against the Burmese as well as Thai domination. However, for dramatic purposes, literal history was revised, and she was depicted as helping to unify Siam into one great nation. This play was not popular nor successful.

vii. *Nan Chao* (Nanzhao) 1939. One of the landmark plays of the era, a highly influential story of how the kingdom of Nan Chao (Nanzhao) in Yunnan was destroyed by Kublai Khan in 1253. As we have seen, by the end of the nineteenth century, European philologists had discovered Nan Chao and designated it as a Thai kingdom. By the second decade of the twentieth century, the Thai elite of the era of absolute monarchy had come to accept this Western discovery and include it in their historiography. Luang Wichit coopted this inclusion in *lakhon* format. The play is certainly an ultra-nationalistic saga of how the Thai race was driven out of their homeland. It created powerful political effects by astutely mixing fact and fiction. The results are an official version of linear history of the Thai nation from China into Suwannaphum (Suvarnabhumi) or the golden land of Southeast Asia. The plot coincided with the old Thai elite's adhesion to the West during the second half of the nineteenth century and again when the new military-bureaucratic ruling class collaborated with the Japanese during the 1930s and 1940s.

viii. *Anusawari Thai* (Thai Monument), 1939. This was the sole play not historically based. Instead, it tells of nation-building and repelling threats from an unidentified external enemy. The result was a most unpopular play.

ix. *Pho Khun Phamuang* (Lord Phamuang), 1940. This is the last political play just before the outbreak of the Pacific War. Luang Wichit the playwriter and the director of the Fine Arts Department, was promoted to the position of minister of foreign affairs. This was after Premier Phibun signed a military pact with Japan (21 December 1941). The tale is about a thirteenth-century Thai prince who overthrew his Cambodian overlord. Subsequently, the Thais established Sukhothai, their first historical kingdom, on the Southeast Asian mainland.

37. William Clifton Dodd (1857–1919), *The Tai Race: Elder Brother of the Chinese* (Iowa: The Torch Press, Cedar Rapids, 1923). This book like many other interesting ones is compiled and edited postmortem by his wife. The gigantic manuscript was a result of experiences, exploration, and research of the missionary over thirty years among the Tai people in Siam (not yet Thailand), Burma and China. The book used here is a reprint published by White Lotus Press, Bangkok, 1966 with a foreword by B.J. Terwiel.

38. See *Syam rue Thai chak kan aphiprai nai sapha rang ratthathammanun* [Siam or Thailand, from debates by the Constitution Drafting Commission] (Bangkok: 1960).

39. Frederick W. Mote, "Problem of Thai Prehistory", *Social Science Research* 2, no. 2 (Bangkok) (October 1964).

40. Grant Evans, "The Ai-Lao and Nan Chao/Tali Kingdom: A Re-orientation", *Journal of the Siam Society* 102 (2014). See also Chris Baker, "From Yue to Tai", *Journal of the Siam Society* 90, no. 1 & 2 (2002).

41. Intriguingly, despite Thailand's notoriety as a land of recurrent coups and constitutional rewrites, the name Thailand was readily accepted with almost no public debate. In the final two events associated with the most recent two constitutional drafts and proclamation in 2007 and 2017, respectively, almost no serious debate was heard over the respective merits of the names Siam or Thailand.

Even more decisively, since the 1998 emergence of the Thai Rak Thai (Thai love Thai, or TRT) party led by Thaksin Shinawatra, the word Thai has become increasingly popular for use in naming political parties. In 2007, after TRT was banned, Thaksin's sister Yingluck headed a new party named Pheu Thai (for the Thai-PT). In 2011, like her brother, Yingluck won a landslide election; she became the first female prime minister of Thailand before the 2014 coup during which, again like her brother, she was expelled from office.

Currently in 2021, sixty-nine political parties are officially registered, twenty-three of which contain the word Thai in their names, with not a single mention of the alternate name, Siam. It would appear that the word Siam or Sayam is considered more appropriate for the arts and commerce. The biggest shopping and entertainment area in Bangkok is Siam Square, constructed in the mid-1960s next to Chulalongkorn University. A gigantic new shopping mall cropped up in 2018 on the other side of the Chao Phraya River, named Iconsiam. One of the most popular gay Thai films in recent years, released in 2007, was entitled *Love of Siam* (*Rak haeng sayam*).

CHAPTER THREE

The Monarch and New Monarchy During the Reign of King Bhumibol, Rama IX

In October 1973 ... demands were made for a permanent constitution and an end to government by martial law. Arrests of student leaders provoked a massive popular demonstration, which unfortunately led to the killing of a number of student activists and innocent bystanders. The situation was threatening to erupt into a destructive national confrontation. The government had lost control. The King, sensing the suffering of the people, intervened in a dramatic television appearance. His Majesty was able to reassure the people that the crisis had subsided and that key military figures had decided to leave the country ...

Anand Panyarachun, 1996

Two Views of the Monarchy in 1996

The year 1996 was a landmark year for Thailand, the modern Siam, during which King Bhumibol Adulyadej, Rama IX of the Chakri Dynasty, became the world's longest-reigning monarch. At age sixty-nine, the king had reigned for fifty years. In hindsight, this was probably the apogee of his reign.

Throughout the year, celebrations were held across the kingdom, accompanied by torrents of praise and acclaim. One such was the opening ceremony of the 14th Conference of the International Association of Historians of Asia (IAHA) at Bangkok's Chulalongkorn University on 20 May, barely a year before the 2 July 1997 Thai baht devaluation.

At the ceremony, Anand Panyarachun, who had been appointed as prime minister in 1991 and again in 1992, made a keynote speech of glorification entitled "His Majesty's Role in the Making of Thai History". Anand told the international gathering of around one hundred participants:

> I am sure that all of you here are aware of this historic event in our country. The entire nation joins hands in the national celebrations of His Majesty's Golden Jubilee this year. The outpourings of joy, gratification, and pride have no parallel in over 700 years of our nation's history.[1]
>
> It has indeed been a remarkable reign of a Thai king who succeeded to the throne after the abdication of his uncle, King Prajadhipok, Rama VII, in 1935, and the untimely demise of his elder brother, King Ananda Mahidol, Rama VIII, in 1946.

Anand mentioned that Bhumibol became king "by accident" at age nineteen. Without further mentioning the tragic death of King Ananda on 9 June 1946, Anand quickly proceeded to explain unacademically that the Thai monarchy could be traced back 700 years to the golden age of the Sukhothai Kingdom and that the Thai people then chose to "elevate the wisest and most capable among them to be king", to "rule the country with righteousness".

Such a king was a *dharma raja* (righteous ruler) and *pho khun* (patriarch). The king also followed the royal code of conduct according to Buddhist precepts of the tenfold duties of kingship (*thotsaphit ratchatham*): charity, morality, altruism, honesty, gentleness, self-control, calmness, nonviolence, forbearance, and uprightness.

Since Rama IX possessed all these supreme qualities, Anand quickly concluded, he had been chosen to reign in 1946 following ancient Sukhothai tradition. But Anand omitted to mention that then Prime Minister Pridi Banomyong was the one who, on the evening of the tragic day, had nominated Bhumibol for the National Assembly's approval.

Since King Ananda, Rama VIII, had no descendants, Pridi apparently just followed the 1924 Palace Law of Succession, written under the supervision of King Vajiravudh, Rama VI. This modern law of succession, still in effect today, was based on the principle of male primogeniture and ruled out women as heirs to the throne. Pridi followed this statute while also observing the European tradition of proclaiming, "The king is dead, long live the king." Clearly, this was no Sukhothai-style election based on the monarch's superior qualities.

Anand continued his speech of glorification, arguing that during his fifty-year reign, Bhumibol had never deviated from the pledge, made in his oath of accession, that he would "reign with righteousness for the benefit and happiness of the Siamese people".[2] Besides reigning as a traditional Buddhist *dharma raja* (righteous ruler), the king was a modern "working monarch" with three contemporary qualities, defending: (1) his subjects' well-being; (2) state security and stability; and (3) national unity, Anand told the audience.

To help his subjects, the king began a series of development programmes now known as *khrongkan phra rathcha damri* (royally initiated projects, or RIP), numbering at that time about 3,000. They covered wide-ranging areas, including irrigation, water-resource management, forest and fishery conservation, soil improvement, crop substitution, reforestation, land development, rural and community development, primary healthcare, leprosy eradication, education, flood control, reservoirs, urban traffic and environmental protection.

Anand elaborated further on Bhumibol's role by referring to the model of the British monarchy, quoting the economist Walter Bagehot's phrase that, as constitutional monarchs, kings possessed the "rights to be consulted, to encourage and to warn".[3] But King Bhumibol also benefited from less legalistic sources of power and influence. Throughout his long reign, he had gained what Anand called *barami*. This Theravada Buddhist term can be defined as accumulated merit or goodness, which the king translated into action whenever circumstances required. When "extraordinary political situations" demanded an intervention, Anand recalled, the king drew "on his reserve power to defuse national crises". Examples can be seen during the cases of the 1973 Thai popular uprising and Bloody May in 1992.

These political crises became signposts of Bhumibol's reign. Anand recalled the 1973 crisis:

> In October 1973 ... demands were made for a permanent constitution and an end to government by martial law. Arrests of student leaders provoked

a massive popular demonstration, which unfortunately led to the killing of a number of student activists and innocent bystanders. The situation was threatening to erupt into a destructive national confrontation. The government had lost control. The king, sensing the suffering of the people, intervened in a dramatic television appearance. His Majesty was able to reassure the people that the crisis had subsided and that key military figures had decided to leave the country ...

Anand then proceeded to praise the king's similar role in 1992, arguing that he had defused a crisis and prevented further bloodshed. That time, Anand said, the royal intervention was even more extraordinary and televised live. The two main contenders for power at the time were the temporary prime minister, General Suchinda Kraprayoon, and Major General Chamlong Srimuang, leader of the popular revolt against the military dictatorship. After a bloody crackdown on protestors, the two were eventually invited to an audience with the king. Both crawled and prostrated themselves on the floor while the king sat on a sofa chair, telling them to behave properly and stop fighting. They listened quietly like good children. Evoking the scene, Anand asserted:

The May 1992 tragedy was a classic case of a government out of touch with the times and feelings of the people. The attempts by demonstrators to topple the government gained momentum outside parliamentary confines. There again, senseless shootings precipitated an outburst of mob mentality, resulting in a horrifying showdown.

The king, closely following the increasingly tragic developments and accurately assessing the country's mood, summoned the two antagonistic leaders to the palace in a nationally televised audience. He quietly, but sternly, admonished them for the dire consequences of their actions. The entire kingdom, as well as CNN and BBC viewers around the world, witnessed how a national crisis had been resolved by His Majesty's reserve power ... The bloodshed stopped immediately. The prime minister [General Suchinda Kraprayoon] resigned. Two weeks later, a new civilian prime minister [Anand himself] not a member of the House of Representatives, was nominated ..."

Notably, in citing Bhumibol's political interventions, Anand only referred to events of 1973 and 1992, keeping mum about the bloodshed and the coup leading up to the 6 October 1976 massacre.

In 1976, Field Marshal Thanom Kittikachorn, after almost three years in exile, returned from Boston to Bangkok. He immediately donned the yellow robe of a Buddhist novice and was rushed to the royal temple of Wat Bowonniwet. There Thanom was promptly ordained by the temple's abbot, Phra Yannasangwon, who would serve as Supreme Patriarch of Thailand from 1989 to 2013. Phra Yan had also been the *phra phi liang* (guardian and adviser) of Bhumibol when he entered a fifteen-day monkhood in late 1956.

Students opposed Thanom's return and rallied at Thammasat University. On 24 September, Chumporn Thummai and Wichai Ketsriphongsa, two electrical company officials who had been part of protests to oust Thanom, were tortured and killed, reportedly by police, with their bodies hanged on display at the Red Gate in the main city district of Nakhon Pathom.

To protest these deaths, students at Thammasat staged a mock lynching, photos of which were published in different newspapers, especially the ultra-rightist *Dao Siam*. Some pictures were retouched to make it appear that the face of the student actor in the mock hanging resembled that of Crown Prince Vajiralongkorn.

Charges of *lèse majesté* were broadcast by a huge and influential network of military and state media. The national mood was tense. Eventually, right-wing groups aided by police officers, mainly from the Border Patrol Police, stormed Thammasat's Tha Prachan campus, using heavy artillery against the young protesters. Students were brutally and publicly murdered.[4]

Official reports state that 46 were killed and 167 were wounded, while unofficial reports state that over 100 demonstrators were killed. Several hundred arrests were made, and many resistance fighters fled into the jungle to join the Communist Party of Thailand (CPT). The massacre shocked the Thai public and the international media. Given the magnitude of the 6 October 1976 massacre, it was even more surprising that Anand managed to ignore it, instead of concluding his hagiographic keynote address in this way:

> Without His Majesty's guiding hand, we would not be where we are today—a nation which has consistently demonstrated its inner strength, political resilience, social harmony and economic dynamism—a trait which has enabled Thais to survive many a threat and misfortune during their long history ...
>
> His Majesty the King personifies positive elements of our national characteristics and is the embodiment of the common character of Thai people of all ethnic groups, religion, and culture. He is our inspiration towards a stronger, more secure, and prosperous destiny. He has deservedly earned the respect and trust of his people to the point that his *barami* will overcome all adversaries.
>
> He is the soul of the Thai nation. Long Live His Majesty.

Similarly, M.R. Sukhumbhand Paribatra noted in an academic essay of glorification that the May 1992 event showed King Bhumibol at the height of his reign, with full command of his Buddhist accumulated merit, or *barami*. A notable academic, politician, and royal family member, Sukhumbhand served as deputy foreign affairs minister from 1997 to 2001 and had been governor of Bangkok from 2009 to 2016, only to be removed by special order of Premier Prayut Chan-o-cha. From his position as a privileged member of Thai society, Sukhumbhand wrote about May 1992:

> The situation seemed hopeless. More and more people began to pray for the kind of political miracle that had occurred nearly two decades before, during the 1973 student uprising against military rule ...
>
> Eventually, their prayers were answered. The main protagonists, Prime Minister General Suchinda Kraprayoon and Major Chamlong Srimuang, the de facto leader of the anti-government protest movement, were summoned to the palace ... The crisis was instantly diffused. The two powerful protagonists backed down. Battle-ready military units returned to the barracks. Demonstrators dispersed. A few days later, Suchinda resigned, and power was peacefully transferred to an interim government ...

Judging from the accounts of Anand and Sukhumbhand the long reign of King Bhumibol had been unanimously remarkable, particularly when measured against a backdrop of significant domestic and international turmoil, globalization, and the advent of new media. The Thai monarch steered the country through the Cold War and an eventful American Era in Thailand. He watched several coups and coup attempts unfold. A total of nineteen new constitutions succeeded one another after 1932, including seventeen after Bhumibol's coronation. In the eyes of many, the king had become the main pillar of Thai society and politics. King Bhumibol was neither an absolute monarch nor a constitutional one. He was a wholly new monarch, with powers that went beyond legal prescriptions as prescribed in successive Thai constitutions. There were none like him in old Siam and there would never be one like him in the future.

In 1986, Derek Davies, editor of the *Far Eastern Economic Review*, analysed the complexity of challenges faced by Bhumibol:

> The king bears many heavy burdens. Even on a straightforward trip to a tiny village, he is operating on many levels—as a modernizer, as a technocrat, as an initiator, as a coordinator, as a catalyst, as an example and as a caring monarch. Beyond that, as the villagers kneel and prostrate themselves before him, the king is at once a Brahmanical God-king and the incarnation of a Buddhist righteous ruler …
>
> On top of all his kingly duties, the monarch is also a husband and a father. In none of his roles can he afford to stumble. He strides on, the ninth monarch of the Chakri Dynasty, with the full weight of the past, present and future role of the monarchy in Thailand on his shoulders.[5]

Unlike Davies, Anand and Sukhumbhand might be termed royalist public intellectuals who spoke for, represented, and reinterpreted—to the point of propagating—the monarch and monarchy. We will see that this sort of glorification has accelerated over many years from the late 1950s onwards until recently. One of the masters of this glorification, who helped construct a positive royal image, was M.R. Kukrit Pramoj, the late prime minister.[6]

M.R. Kukrit Pramoj (1911–95): A Royal Public Intellectual

Kukrit was one of the most multitalented all-rounders produced by modern Siam; he was a prolific writer, eloquent lecturer, thinker, novelist, actor, traditional *khon* dancer, radio guest, and politician.

He also founded the once-influential *Siam Rath* (State of Siam), in daily and weekly editions catering to Bangkok middle-class readers. *Siam Rath Daily* and *Siam Rath Weekly* became political organs for the revival and invention of traditional Thai values and the modern monarchy.

The prefix M.R. (*mom rachawong*) of his name indicates that Kukrit was a fourth-generation descendant from a king. In his case, Kukrit descended from the line of King Rama II (Phra Phutthaloetla Naphalai, who reigned from 1809 to 1824).[7] By the time he became prime minister briefly from March 1975 to January 1976, Kukrit had had already been a prominent royal public intellectual for two decades. Born in 1911, he was the son of Brigadier General Prince Khamrob (1871–1939), the first Thai Police Director-General.

Khamrob fathered nine children with three wives. Kukrit was the youngest son of the principal wife, Mom Daeng (Bunnag). His older brother from the same mother, M.R. Seni (1905–97), would become prime minister briefly three times, from late 1945 to early 1946, again in early 1975 and a final time in mid-1976.

Like most offspring of prosperous Thai elite families, Kukrit was sent to a British boarding school, in his case Trent College in Derbyshire, after finishing his Suankularb College secondary school education. Founded in Bangkok by King Chulalongkorn to educate the children of the nobility and the royal household, Suankularb College is also known as Suankularb Wittayalai School.

In 1933, Kukrit received a BA in philosophy, politics, and economics from Oxford University, and returned home to work briefly at the Ministry of Finance. In 1936, he married M.R. Pakpring Thongyai, a woman of his social class and circle. They had one son and one daughter, but later divorced.

During the territorial Franco-Thai War of 1940 and 1941, known to the Thais as the Indochina War, Kukrit was drafted as a corporal in the Thai army at age twenty-nine. After the war was over, he decided to enter politics. He established his own party, Phak Kaona (Progressive Party), later merged with the conservative Democrats led by Khuang Aphaiwong.[8]

Kukrit was first elected to the National Assembly in 1946 and became Deputy Minister of Finance in the last Khuang government. He then turned to writing books and journalism, remaining a prolific political author from the 1950s to the 1970s. His writings established an image of an engaged public intellectual which still endures today.

During the turmoil of the early 1970s, Kukrit became a vocal opponent of the Thanom-Prapas-Narong dictatorship and a source of inspiration for young students, especially at Thammasat University. When the military was eventually removed from politics, albeit only temporarily, after the 1973 Thai popular uprising, Kukrit founded his Social Action Party.

In 1975, this party only managed to win eighteen seats in the House of Representatives. Yet, he eventually became prime minister by defeating and replacing his brother Seni, by then head of the Democrats, which had won seventy-two seats. This was Kukrit's first and last prime ministership.

Despite a brief stint in office, he managed to leave an impression on the political memory of progressive Thais. They supported him because of his vanguard populist policies of financial subsidies for agricultural workers, free transport, and free medical service for the poor.

One of his foreign policy successes was opening relations with China. He travelled to meet Mao Zedong and Zhou Enlai in July 1975, effectively ending twenty-six years of Cold War hostility between the two countries. Despite his association with progressive social policies, Kukrit was a staunch royalist who believed that the pen was mightier than the sword. He wrote passionately, especially when he believed the monarchy was under attack.

In 1946, soon after the war, Hollywood distributed the first instalment of a series of screen adaptations of the lives of King Mongkut and the English teacher Anna Leonowens. *Anna and the King of Siam* (USA; 1946), a Twentieth Century Fox picture directed by John Cromwell, starring Irene Dunne and Rex Harrison.[9]

Unsurprisingly, most Thai elites appeared to despise the movie's plot, in which a clever British teacher enlightens an irrational Oriental ruler about morals and civility. They felt it was an insult to their king. However, in the liberal postwar atmosphere, the film was publicly screened in Bangkok. But Kukrit and his brother Seni fought back by compiling authentic historical documents about the king. The compilation was published in book form with the title, *The King of Siam Speaks* (1948).

Two years later, the Thai political climate had changed. The government was once again dominated by the military, led by Phibun and Phin. Field Marshal Plaek Phibunsongkhram, known as Phibun (1897–1964), was a military officer and politician who served as prime minister and dictator from 1938 to 1944 and 1948 to 1957. Field Marshal Phin Choonhavan (1891–1973) was a military leader and deputy prime minister.

By then, Kukrit had founded his daily *Siam Rath* and was already an ardent contributor. He became one of the nation's most influential writers of the 1950s and 1960s and continued to publish for the rest of his life.

His literary career started with brief poetic lines (*sakrawa*) and a daily advice column in question-and-answer format. He eventually progressed to short stories, criticism, historical novels, and travel accounts.

Kukrit published over one hundred books, among them *Phuean non* (Bedfellow, 1952), *Lai chiwit* (Many Lives, 1954), *Thok khamen* (Khmer Discussed, 1953), *Susi thaihao* (Empress Dowager Cixi, 1957), *Muang maya* (City of Illusion/Hollywood, 1965), and *Phama sia muang* (The Burmese Lost Their Country, 1969).

He even embarked on a screen acting career, playing a small role as a prime minister in the film *The Ugly American* (USA, 1963), a Universal Pictures production directed by George Englund and starring Marlon Brando.

But his magnum opus and most remembered work was the novel *Si Phaendin* (Four Reigns), which originated as a newspaper serial in *Siam Rath* daily.[10] An expansive romantic account of the life of Phloi, a courtier born in 1882, *Si Phaendin* begins in the early 1890s.

Its action takes place within and beyond palace walls. From the reign of King Chulalongkorn (Rama V) until the mid-1940s with the death of his grandson, King Ananda Mahidol (Rama VIII), four reigns are evoked.

The lives of minor courtiers are described in the context of Thailand's social and political evolution from an absolute, to a constitutional, monarchy. The Japanese occupation of Thailand is also dramatized, in its effect on the lives and relationships of Phloi and her family.

At first, when King Chulalongkorn consolidated his dynastic power, Phloi came to live in the inner part of the Grand Palace. Here she solemnly observed changes unfolding from the fifth to eight reigns of the Chakri dynasty until in 1946, when King Ananda Mahidol died suddenly and unexpectedly.

Presented as a perfect Thai female courtier in her beauty, observance of traditions, calmness, politeness, and loyalty to the monarchy, Phloi was also a caring wife and mother to three children and a stepson. Her viewpoint on history reflects the progress of events with detail and sensitivity, so it is worth looking at the novel's plot in some detail.

Phloi's husband, a bureaucrat, rose through the ranks and was especially active during the sixth reign, from 1910 to 1925, of Vajiravudh, King Rama VI. Yet her family became divided in the time of Prajadhipok, King Rama VII, from 1925 to 1935, the last absolute monarch and first constitutional monarch of Thailand. Phloi's eldest son sides with a leader of the People's Party which overthrew absolute monarchy in 1932. Then her adopted son turned against the new government, and her second son became discouraged by the fraternal discord in his family.

As for Phloi's daughter, she playfully accepted new changes from the era of transition from Siam to Thailand. When Rama VII abdicated in the wake of the Siamese revolution of 1932, Phloi appeared to be downhearted. But she was encouraged by the return of the new boy king Ananda Mahidol (Rama VIII) to Bangkok for a short visit from his residence in Switzerland.

During the Second World War, Phloi's home in Bangkok was damaged by Allied bombing, and she took refuge at her original family house across the river. On 5 December 1945, after the war ended, King Ananda was escorted by British forces from Switzerland to Siam. At age twenty, the king was young, handsome and charming, as Kukrit describes, capturing a romantic view of modern Thai history.

Yet on 9 June 1946, King Ananda met a tragic and premature death in the Grand Palace. On the same day, Phloi's heart also stopped beating and she floated away in the low tide of the Chao Phraya River.

This assimilation of Thai history into the scope of popular fiction was highly successful. Before it appeared in book form in 1953, Kukrit's *Si Phaendin* was already a sensation in its serialized form. Enthused readers among Bangkok's upper and middle classes were devoted to it, dramatizing history by showing its effects on average people in a way comparable to the US author Margaret Mitchell's novel *Gone with the Wind* (1936), which gripped generations of readers from the American South.

In 1996, Witayakorn Chiengkul, director of Rangsit University's Social Research Institute, began to compile a list of 100 Must-Read Thai books, in a study sponsored by the Thailand Research Fund. A report in the 14 March 1998 issue of the *Bangkok Post* noted that among these unmissable volumes was *Si Phaendin*, suggesting that its powerful resonance was still alluring to Thai readers.

It has been filmed four times as TV miniseries since 1961 and was frequently dramatized in the theatre and even adapted to the musical stage in a singing version.

By the mid-1950s, *Si Phaendin* had turned Kukrit into one of the major promoters of the new monarchy. During this time, King Bhumibol and Queen Sirikit, aged twenty-four and nineteen, respectively, had returned to reside permanently in Bangkok together with their first daughter. Courtiers surrounding them started to shape the style of King Bhumibol's reign. Kukrit had a role in this process.

As a part-time lecturer at two leading universities, Chulalongkorn and Thammasat, one of Kukrit's achievements was to link the royal couple with university students who comprised a rising educated middle class. In the 1960s he became even more socially and politically engaged with the young generation, especially at Thammasat University.

A little background information about that institution of higher learning helps us better understand Kukrit's remarkably influential academic career and trajectory as an inspirer of Thai youth.

Originally named the University of Moral and Political Sciences, Thammasat was established in 1934, shortly after the Siamese revolution of 1932. Pridi Banomyong, the civilian leader of the revolution, became its founder and first president, with the goal of educating Thai people about democracy.

Pridi declared in a speech delivered on the opening of Thammasat University:

> A university is, figuratively, an oasis that quenches the thirst of those who are in pursuit of knowledge. The opportunity to acquire higher education rightly belongs to every citizen under the principle of freedom of education … Now that our country is governed by a democratic constitution, it is particularly essential to establish a university which will allow the people, and hence the public, to develop to their utmost capability. It will open up an opportunity for ordinary citizens to conveniently and freely acquire higher education for their own benefits and for development of our country.

Thammasat was an open university with low enrolment fees, which immediately became popular among young men and women among Pridi's followers. From the late 1940s through the 1950s, the university experienced difficulties after military dictatorship seized power again and Phibun replaced Pridi as rector.

In the following years, successive rectors and administrators from the military exerted an ever-stronger influence on Thammasat. By the 1960s, the university had become a far more exclusive institution since a national entrance exam was introduced in 1960 for prospective students. Tuition fees were raised, and student uniforms were required. Thammasat University was transformed to increasingly resemble more the royalist and conservative Chulalongkorn University.[11]

Another major change in 1962 was the establishment of the Faculty of Liberal Arts. University Secretary-General Adul Wichiencharoen, who had been appointed by the dictator Thanom, became its founder and dean for twelve years, from 1962 to 1974. The new faculty became a focus of controversy, as it required all incoming students to enrol in liberal arts courses ranging from East-West civilization to philosophy for two years before being eligible to study law, political science, and economics.[12]

Intriguingly, one of the most energetic student opponents to Dean Adul's policies was Samak Sundaravej, another future Thai prime minister who served in that function from 29 January to 9 September 2008. A well-known television chef in addition to being a politician, Samak had hosted a cooking show called *Tasting, Ranting* on the Thailand ITV television network and Royal Thai Army Radio and Television before the military coup of September 2006.

When Samak became prime minister, he announced that he would resume his career as a TV chef, despite the illegality of any government minister holding another paying job. On 9 September 2008, the Constitutional Court ruled that it was unconstitutional for Samak to work for a private company (Thailand ITV), and he was forced to relinquish public office.

Samak had entered Thammasat as a student in its open admission days, but even so, it took him six years, from 1958 to 1964, to graduate with a law degree. He was much engaged in extracurricular activities, from public speaking to writing short articles for Kukrit's *Siam Rath*. Samak so vehemently opposed the liberal arts requirement that he was almost expelled from the university. Eventually, a compromise was reached, and the compulsory liberal arts training was reduced to one year.

But Adul's faculty retained its oversight of first-year students for more than one decade, well into the 1970s. Then, in 1974, Dean Adul was passed over in favour of Puey Ungphakorn in the competition for the post of university rector. The vacancy was caused when Sanya Dharmasakti, former president of the Supreme Court and member of the Privy Council, was appointed by royal command as prime minister from 1973 to 1975. At that point, Adul was transferred to serve as rector of Silapakorn University.[13]

Yet amidst these academic rivalries, Kukrit became immensely involved with Thammasat University lecturers and students at Adul's Faculty of Liberal Arts. Far from eschewing introductory courses, Kukrit energetically taught all first-year students in the fields of religion, philosophy, and culture for over a decade from 1962 to 1973.

His best-remembered course was on Thai civilization, in which Kukrit memorably defined Thainess and the concept of the Thai monarchy deriving from *Devaraja* (divine king), *Buddharaja* (Buddhist king) and *Dhammaraja* (righteous king) worship.[14]

In 1971, Kukrit helped to establish an area studies centre known as the Thai Khadi Research Institute. Kukrit, along with young academics and students influenced by him, would become agents of the revival and reinvention of royal traditionalism, playing vital roles in the construction of the new monarchy.

This was not done merely by research and published writings. As mentioned, Kukrit's activities spanned many fields of endeavour, including the performing arts.

In 1966, in line with his beliefs and theatrical leanings, Kukrit established a troupe of *khon* performers comprised of students from amateur dramatic and Buddhism clubs. *Khon* is a courtly masked dance-drama performance with male dancers. Its stories, based on the Ramayana epic, were once a familiar part of Siamese state ceremonies associated with the Hindu *Devaraja* ritual.[15]

Kukrit sought to revive *khon* by training male students and occasionally played the part of the demon king Ravana himself. He allowed female students to participate as well, but only in supporting roles in dances of welcome or good augur. Following performances in front of the king and queen, the troupe became popular enough to be occasionally invited to play overseas.

The aristocratic and royal identity of *khon* performances directly expressed Kukrit's ambition to renew ancient Thai court traditions for the postwar world. Inevitably, when Kukrit's students reached a certain level of skill in the dance rituals, they would present their achievements in homage to the royal couple, who as in earlier times, were seen as the ultimate focus and ideal audience for all activities embracing Thainess.

The relationship between Thammasat and Bhumibol was reciprocal at that time, with the king initiating outreach with undergraduates. In 1962, Thammasat students were invited for the first time to a private audience with the king and queen. In the royal gardens, King Bhumibol, an accomplished and expressive saxophone player and composer of lightly swinging jazz music, performed for the students with his jazz band.

The following year, the royal couple visited Thammasat and performed the melody of a new Thammasat anthem (*pleng phra ratcha niphon yung thong*) composed by the king himself. The song replaced the former alma mater from Pridi's era (*mon du dao/phleng pracham maha witthayalai*). On that occasion, the king and queen also planted a new university tree, the *yung thong* (flame tree or *delonix regia*).

Bhumibol's actions corresponded to gestures he had earlier made towards Chulalongkorn University students in 1949. But Thammasat was less of an ultra-traditionalist venue than Chulalongkorn, despite Kukrit's successful efforts to find new ways to interpret and approach the monarchic tradition for Thais of the present and future.

Kukrit maintained this public role, especially as an author, as well as close relations with university lecturers and students throughout the 1980s and 1990s. He died on 9 October 1995 at the age of eighty-four, in the middle of celebrations of Bhumibol's golden jubilee, festivities surrounding which ran from the beginning of 1995 to the end of 1996.

The loss of Kukrit left conservative royalists and Bangkok's urban middle class without their foremost spokesperson. Royalists like Anand and Sukhumbhand came close to his impact, but they lacked some of Kukrit's eloquent and magnetic qualities. And perhaps their role was not as vital as Kukrit's, whose services as a promoter of royalism were more crucial at a time when the monarch and the monarchy had ceased in some ways to be pillars of the nation in the decades after the Siamese revolution of 1932.

In this way, we see that Kukrit's talents in the cultural domain and powerful personality allowed for unsurpassed influence in the ever-evolving Thai modern symbiosis with royalty.

Royal Public Intellectuals after Kukrit: Anand and Sukhumbhand

Despite the diminished importance of royalist intellectuals following the groundwork laid by Kukrit, their role in continuing the construction of a positive royal image should not be underestimated.

Anand Panyarachun is a case in point. He was born on 9 August 1932, the same historic year as Queen Sirikit, which was also by entire coincidence the year of the Siamese revolution against absolute monarchy. The Panyarachun family were of Hakka, a Han Chinese subgroup, and Mon (a Southeast Asian ethnic group) ancestry. The wealthy Panyarachuns were among the elite of Bangkok. His father Sern was a Phraya, a title of nobility accorded to officers who are the permanent secretary of a minister, director-general, governor, commander-in-chief, or royal office chancellor.

Sern Panyarachun was a one-time permanent secretary of education during the reign of King Rama VII. Anand's mother was a Khun Ying, another title of nobility granted to wives of Phrayas. After his father left the civil service, he became the publisher of newspapers in Thai, Chinese, and English, including *Sayam Nikon* (Siamese People), *Suphapsatri* (Lady), *Thai Hua Siang Po* (Sino-Thai Business), and *Bangkok Chronicle*.

Anand's parents had twelve children—seven girls and five boys. All married within the circle of Bangkok's royally connected elite families. One of Anand's brothers married a daughter of Phibun. Anand himself took M.R. Sodsri Chakrabandhu as his wife.

Anand was educated at Bangkok Christian College and Dulwich College, the latter a venerable boarding school for boys in Dulwich, London, England before reading law at Trinity College, Cambridge, from which he graduated with honours in 1955. He became a career diplomat, spending twenty-three years in the foreign service and serving as the Ambassador of Thailand to the United Nations, Canada, the United States and West Germany.

In 1976, he returned to Bangkok and was named Permanent Secretary of the Ministry of Foreign Affairs. In this post, he played an important role in normalizing diplomatic relations between Kukrit's government and the People's Republic of China in 1975.

This initiative soon proved politically costly, as, in the wake of the October 1976 military coup, Anand was branded a Communist by the royalist right-wing government of Thanin Kraivichien, a staunchly anti-Communist Supreme Court judge. Until the civil service panel investigating the allegations cleared him of wrongdoing in making diplomatic overtures to Mao's China, Anand was suspended from the civil service. When the controversy had settled, he was appointed Ambassador to Germany from 1977 to 1978.

Even so, he soon decided to leave the public sector and join the business world instead. In 1979, he left the Ministry of Foreign Affairs to run Saha Union Group, one of the largest textiles and garment corporations in Thailand.

Because of family and personal connections,[16] Anand was twice chosen to be what might be termed an accidental prime minister in 1991 and again in 1992. His first stint was from 2 March 1991 to 7 April 1992, following General Suchinda's coup against General Chatichai Choonhavan.

The military relied on his credentials and reputation as a face-saving strategy while his duty was to carry out elections. His second appointment as prime minister, from 10 June to 23 September 1992, was triggered by the Bloody May event, a name given to the 17–20 May 1992 popular protest in Bangkok against the government of General Suchinda.

Despite the brevity of his rule, Anand's cabinet, consisting of technocrats with a reform agenda, and his comprehensive nationwide HIV/AIDS prevention programme, a pioneering effort in Asia, were praised in retrospect by UNICEF in a 2004 online tribute.

Given Anand's image as a royalist white knight, his name is still mentioned whenever Thailand seems on the brink of political collapse. This duly occurred during extended political crises, including the *coup d'état* of 19 September 2006 by the Royal Thai Army against the elected caretaker government of Prime Minister Thaksin Shinawatra and again on 22 May 2014, when the Royal Thai Armed Forces launched a *coup d'état* against the caretaker government of Prime Minister Yingluck Shinawatra.

Although unsurprisingly, Anand's name was floated as a candidate for prime ministership on both occasions, a third appointment never occurred for him.

Sukhumbhand Paribatra, the third royal intellectual discussed so far, is a respected academic and politician for the conservative-royalist Democrat Party. He was born in 1953 in Bangkok to Prince Sukhumabhinan and his aristocratic wife, Mom Dusadi Na Thalang. Prince Sukhumabhinan was himself a son of Prince Paribatra Sukhumbandhu, the Prince of Nakhon Sawan, a son of King Chulalongkorn (Rama V) with his Queen Consort Sukumalmarsri.

Sukumalmarsri, a daughter of King Mongkut and one of the four consorts of her half-brother King Chulalongkorn (Rama V), gave birth to two children, Princess Suddha Dibyaratana (later the Princess of Ratanakosin) and Prince Paribatra Sukhumbandhu (later Prince of Nakhon Sawan.) During her husband's reign, Sukumalmarsri served as the king's secretary and was referred to as the Princess Consort.

Prince Paribatra later became Minister of the Interior under Rama VII, King Prajadhipok. Prince Paribatra was one of the most powerful men in the kingdom before the Siamese Revolution of 1932. As a result, Prince Paribatra's influence was considered a potential threat by the Khana Ratsadon (People's Party) which organized the 1932 coup ending the absolute monarchy in Siam. So, he was exiled to Bandung, Dutch East Indies, then under Dutch administration. There Prince Paribatra died in exile in 1944, in Japanese-occupied Indonesia.

With the sombre backdrop of his family namesake looming over him, like many children of the Thai elite, Sukhumbhand was educated in England from his primary school days onward.

He attended Cheam School, an ancient mixed preparatory institution in the English county of Hampshire, as well as the famous and even more ancient Rugby School in Warwickshire, England. At Pembroke College of Oxford University, he studied philosophy, politics, and economics (PPE), graduating with a bachelor's degree in 1977. He earned a master's degree in international relations from Georgetown University in Washington, DC.

From 1980 to 1996, he taught international relations at Chulalongkorn University, moving to become a deputy foreign minister from 1997 to 2000 under Chuan Leekpai. In 1999, as deputy foreign minister, he volunteered with two other Thai officials to take the place of eighty-two hostages taken at the Myanmar Embassy in Bangkok by gunmen from the Virulent Burmese Student Warriors, an armed opposition group in Myanmar. All the hostages were released unharmed, it was considered because Sukhumbhand had bravely travelled in a helicopter with the gunmen to convince them to release all the hostages.

In 2008, Sukhumbhand was elected as governor of Bangkok for a four-year term. Despite the city's political turmoil, he managed to conclude his first term and was re-elected in 2013 in a fierce battle against Yingluck's Pheu Thai Party candidate, Police General Pongsapat Pongcharoen. On 24 August 2016, he was suspended indefinitely from his governorship by Thai Prime Minister Prayut Chan-o-cha because of an ongoing investigation into alleged irregularities, according to *The Nation* newspaper of 26 August of that year.

These three royal intellectuals provided a public and political background for modern Thai appreciation of the monarchy and its traditions. Due to their firm loyalties and belief in nurturing traditions, they gave a fresh perspective to time-honoured standards of conduct, as exemplified by the king and the royal family. How their devotion was justified by the comportment of the king himself is part of the latter-day history of Thailand.

Monarch and Monarchy under King Bhumibol from 1946

On 9 June 1946, at the age of nineteen, Bhumibol became king after the sudden and still unexplained death of his brother, King Ananda, Rama VIII. Ananda died from a bullet wound to the forehead around nine o'clock that morning. By the evening, Prime Minister Pridi Banomyong had proposed Bhumibol to the National Assembly as the next king. Bhumibol was duly confirmed as Rama IX.

An updated and clarified form of traditional royal succession was followed, imitating the formula "The King is dead, long live the King" which had been first declared in France at the death of King Charles VI in 1422.

In 1946, Prime Minister Pridi simply followed the Palace Law of Succession, Buddhist Era 2467 (1924). Since Ananda was unmarried and had no descendants, the throne automatically went to his younger brother. This was the third time that a Thai king reigned because of these administrative rules of succession.

The first accession to occur with this new clarity was in 1910, when Vajiravudh became Rama VI, succeeding his father, and the second was in 1925 when Prajadhipok became Rama VII, following his brother. Matters of primogeniture were decided less systematically in the Sukhothai, Ayutthaya, and Thonburi eras, as well as the early Bangkok period.

The new king and his mother stayed on in Bangkok to perform the initial ceremonial rites for the dead king. Two months later, on 15 August, they left for Switzerland, explaining that the new king had to return to his studies.[17] Meanwhile, back in Bangkok, rumours abounded about what had happened to young Ananda. Was it regicide, suicide, or an accident by the king or with someone else's intervention?

From the beginning, the Pridi government unambiguously and officially declared that it was an accident caused by the king himself. But conservative royalists and the military mounted an attack, publicly and behind the scenes, against Pridi and his followers. They insisted that he was accountable for the tragedy.

Rumours that Pridi was somehow culpable of regicide spread around Bangkok. Shouts were heard at the Sala Chalermkrung Royal Theatre, owned by the Crown Property Bureau: *Pridi kha nai luang* (Pridi killed the king).[18] This unsubstantiated gossip had an effect. On 23 August, barely two months after Ananda's death and one week after King Bhumibol had left for Europe, Pridi resigned.

He was succeeded by Thawan Thamrongnawasawat (1901–88), known by his title of nobility, Luang Thamrong. But the new government was unable to produce a satisfactory explanation for Ananda's death, at least not in the eyes of the military or Bangkok conservative royalists. By then, the incident had become highly politicized.

One year later, on 8 November 1947, the military staged a coup in collaboration with the Democrat Party. The Army was led by General Phin Choonhawan (1891–1973). Phin had been the commander of the Thai Army which occupied British Burma's Kengtung State and Mongpan State during the Second World War.

After the war, Phin was dismissed from the army but returned to active duty after the November 1947 coup. Khuang Aphaiwaong, head of the Democrat Party, was awarded the prime ministership for five months from 10 November 1947 to 8 April 1948, before being ejected by still another coup.

With help from British and American diplomats, on 20 November 1947, Pridi had been whisked away to Singapore. As part of the Palace Rebellion, a 1949 coup attempt, Pridi secretly returned to Thailand in February 1949.

He planned to engineer a coup with assistance from former associates, former Free Thai movement members, and the Navy. But as it turned out, Pridi's February 1949 coup attempt was a disaster.

The government had anticipated his actions, and Phibun even made a radio broadcast calling Pridi his "friend" and offering him a governmental post. When Pridi rejected this gesture, an anticipatory state of emergency was declared. On 26 February, a Royal Thai Army officer loyal to Pridi and some supporters seized a radio station, and Free Thai elements and Thammasat University teachers and students occupied the Grand Palace. The occupied radio station announced on the air the formation of a new government headed by Direk Chaiyanam, a Pridi ally.

Major-General Sarit Thanarat moved troops to remove Pridi from the palace grounds, while the Royal Thai Navy and the Royal Thai Marine Corps readied for further violence. The rebels managed to escape in naval vessels across the Chao Phraya River, and after some hours of fighting, a ceasefire was declared.

After this harshly suppressed failure, Pridi was forced into exile in Mao's China for twenty-one years, from 1949 to 1970. Four years after Mao's murderous Cultural Revolution, formally known as the Great Proletarian Cultural Revolution, a violent sociopolitical purge movement that began in 1966, Pridi found it prudent to flee yet again.

This time his destination turned out to be a permanent refuge, the modest working-class Paris suburb of Antony. There he died in 1983 at age eighty-two, to the last denied the civil service pension he was legally entitled to after years of government work. Back in Thailand, his followers experienced far more deadly sanctions; some participants in the Palace

Rebellion were executed and others were silenced by expulsion from public life.

The death of King Ananda and the 1947 coup turned Thailand into a land of political turmoil for fully a decade; it may be said that the impact of these violent events has been felt in Thailand ever since.

From 1948 to 1957, there were two more coups and two countercoups, with Phibun returning to power as prime minister for almost another decade.[19] Thailand—or modern Siam—of the 1950s was a country where the military was in charge.

Bangkok's conservative-royalists busily organized King Bhumibol's first nationwide tours, while Phibun made gestures to leftists by imitating Western-style freedom of speech he had admired at Hyde Park in London, to the point of establishing a so-called Speakers' Corner at Sanam Luang in Bangkok.

Despite these superficial developments, liberals and left-wing activists continued to be suppressed or forced to go underground. Meanwhile, King Bhumibol stayed away from his chaotic nation for almost four years. In early 1950, he returned for a short visit to preside over the elaborate cremation of his brother Ananda in March 1950. The new king also wed M.R. Sirikit Kittiyakorn on 28 April and was crowned on 5 May. Then the king and the new queen returned to Switzerland, where the course of the king's educational plans shifted.

A graduate in literature studies from the Gymnase Classique Cantonal of Lausanne, Bhumibol had enrolled in the University of Lausanne to study science, but the death of his brother made it essential, in his view, to master governmental expertise, so he changed his major subjects to political science and law.

Meanwhile, the Ananda case dragged on, still unresolved, for years. It went through three courts of justice, with officials of the Office of the Attorney General at the Ministry of Interior acting as plaintiffs. Phibun, who also held the interior portfolio from 1954 to 1957, and his right-hand man, Police General Phao Siyanon, who was Minister of the Interior for half a year in 1957, ordered Police General Phra Phinit to resolve the case and its ensuing investigations.

Phra Phinit Chon Khadi (Phinit/Seng Itharathut, 1891–1970) was the brother-in-law of Seni and Kukrit Pramoj. He was a bright young man, gifted with languages who spoke Mandarin, Hainan, Teochew, Thai and English. He became an essential aide for the Police Department in dealing with *angyi*, numerous secrets or illegal organizations run by Chinese migrants.

By marrying the police director's daughter, Phinit was eventually promoted to the rank of police lieutenant. Before the end of the absolute monarchy, his aristocratic rank was high, qualifying him as a *Phra* level of nobility. His descendants became influential in such enterprises as Bangkok Commercial Bank and Serm Suk PLC, former bottler of Pepsi Cola in Thailand.[20]

Phinit had arrested three defendants, charged with regicide. They were Chaleo Pratumros, Chit Singhaseni and But Patthamasarin. Chaleo had been one of the promoters of the Siamese revolution of 1932 and was serving as Royal Secretary-General at the time of Ananda's death. The other two were bed-chamber pages in attendance to the king on the tragic morning.

On 12 October 1954, the five judges of the Supreme Court sentenced them to death. They appealed for a royal pardon, which was refused. All three were executed by firing squad on 17 February 1955.[21]

From a broad perspective, the Thai monarch and the monarchy faced a difficult situation with the unsolved death of Ananda and postwar turmoil. The monarchy had been in decline since the death of King Chulalongkorn in 1910. His son Vajiravudh reigned at a time when monarchies were disappearing around the globe. During the next two decades, the Thai monarchy was challenged as pillar of the nation and contested by an emerging new elite, mainly drawn from the military, civil service, Bangkok lower middle class, and a politicized press.

The Siamese revolution of 1932 eventually ended the so-called Thai absolute monarchy. During most of the subsequent two decades of internal turmoil, from 1935 to 1951, the two new kings, Ananda and Bhumibol, were in Switzerland with their mother. This absence may have shielded them in some ways from ongoing political controversies in the kingdom.

But although like most modern Thai monarchs, King Bhumibol's early life and years of education were spent overseas, eventually his royal duties would summon him home to Thailand, under dramatic circumstances. The degree to which King Bhumibol managed to assume his royal responsibilities while using the training and world view, he had acquired abroad was an example of how internationalized schooling can benefit a modern monarch.

A King with International Perspectives

Bhumibol was born at Mount Auburn Hospital in Cambridge, Massachusetts on 5 December 1927, five years before the Siamese revolution of 1932. His father, formerly Mahidol Adulyadej, Prince of Songkla (1892–1929), was a son of King Chulalongkorn and his second queen, Savang Vadhana. Prince Mahidol would receive an MD degree cum laude from the Harvard Medical School University six months after the birth of his youngest son Bhumibol, a name of Sanskrit origin meaning strength of the land.

The name Bhumibol was bestowed upon him by his half-uncle Prajadhipok, King Rama VII. Bhumibol was born as a *phra ong chao*, or second-rank prince, and never expected to become king. He had one older sister, Galyani Vadhana (1923–2008), born in London, and his brother Ananda (1925–46) was born in Heidelberg, Germany.

In the twilight years of the absolute monarchy, the Mahidol family returned to Siam at the end of 1928 but stayed there only four years. His father died in 1929 when Bhumibol was less than two years old, and his mother was not yet thirty.

On 24 June 1932, when Bhumibol was attending kindergarten at Mater Dei School, a private Catholic School run by the sisters of the Ursuline Order, the absolute monarchy was overthrown by the People's Party and Siam entered a period of constitutional monarchy.

Although the Siamese revolution of 1932 was comparatively nonviolent and King Prajadhipok yielded to most of the opposition's demands, the period after the coup was a different story.

The revolution's organizers chose Phraya Mano (1884–1948), a senior conservative lawyer of the former establishment, to head the new government. They concentrated on controlling the army and the newly appointed National Assembly. During the following months, a power struggle was waged between the new Mano government and the 1932 revolutionary leaders on the one hand, and the king and the new bureaucratic and military elite on the other.

This resulted in a second silent coup of 20 June 1933, during which Mano was removed from power. Phraya Phahon (1887–1947), a senior leader of the Siamese revolution of 1932, became the second prime minister under the constitutional regime. In October of the same year, Prince Boworadet (1877–1947), former defence minister of King Prajadhipok, staged an unsuccessful coup. Heavy fighting between the government and royalist rebel troops erupted in the outskirts of Bangkok and continued along the railway line up to the Khorat Plateau in the northeastern region of Isan.

Because of this political turbulence, several high-ranking princes and royal family members went into exile; sometimes it was self-imposed, and sometimes they were directly forced to leave. Of these high princes, Damrong (1862–1943), once an all-powerful minister and half-brother of King Chulalongkorn, went to live in Penang, Malaysia.

Prince Paribatra (1881–1944), the pre-1932 interior minister and a son of King Chulalongkorn, probably the most powerful prince in the outgoing Cabinet, went to Bogor, Java, where he died. In 1934, King Prajadhipok and his Queen, Rambai Barni, went to England, as mentioned above, on the pretext of needing ophthalmological treatment. The king abdicated the following year and died in England in 1941, aged forty-seven.

Princess Bejaratna (1925–2011), the only child of King Vajiravudh, and her mother Princess Suvadhana (1906–85) also left Bangkok for England in 1938 and did not return until 1957.

As early as 8 April 1933, before Boworadet's attempted coup, the Mahidol family had also left Siam. They went to live in neutral Switzerland, not monarchic England which had long been a favoured dwelling place for

Thai royalty. The Mahidols continued to live in Lausanne for the next two decades and their three children were educated there. In 1948, Princess Galyani earned a Bachelor of Science degree in chemistry at the University of Lausanne. She also studied social science and education.

The future King Ananda studied law but tragically died before completing his university education, while Bhumibol, as described, switched from science to subjects considered more directly pertinent to ruling over a nation.[22] Nevertheless, as all Thais know, as Rama IX, the king remained fascinated with science and innovated with many technological approaches from irrigation to flood control.

Likewise, in addition to Princess Galyani's official subjects of study, she became known in later life for her dedication to literature and music, among other arts. This suggests that the education of children from royal families could be more multi-faceted than most traditional university programmes permit. This nurturing of various interests would bear direct results in later life for Bhumibol's generation of royals and his offspring.

In 1927, the year of his birth, he had already received the high princely designation of *phra worawong thoe phra-ong chao* by King Prajadhipok, along with all other children of Prajadhipok's celestial brothers. As mentioned above, Prajadhipok's abdication entitled Ananda to succeed as Rama VIII.

Bhumibol was considered eligible for the throne according to the 1924 Palace Law on Succession, but he required consent and approval from the Phahon government and national assembly, which was accorded on 2 March 1935. Soon after, on 10 July 1935, Prince Bhumibol was installed as the Royal Brother after his elder brother, Prince Ananda, ascended the throne as King Ananda Mahidol.

The new king was considered an ideal choice by courtiers who had their plans for how the nation should be run; After all, he was only nine years old at the time and lived in faraway Lausanne, Switzerland. The Thai government could be unfettered to rule the country in his name. A compliant board of regency was appointed, ostensibly to represent the Boy King, but to do the government's bidding.

For almost two decades, from the mid-1930s to the mid-1950s, the Thai kings remained almost invisible in what remained a Siamese monarchy. This seemingly disadvantageous situation ironically proved to work to the monarchy's advantage.

It was not a simple example of absence making the national heart grow fonder. It was somewhat unprecedented for Thais to have titular rulers who were largely absent. Naturally, after 1932, kings were seen in pictures, and they occasionally returned to the country for brief visits, arriving in Bangkok on large ships entering the Chao Phraya River amid much pomp.

Yet for the most part, prime ministers and other government officials were given a relatively free hand to represent the nation and act independently. In theory, the monarchy was represented by regents, but their appointment needed governmental approval.

King Bhumibol changed all that, not by merely returning to reside in Thailand, but by systematically visiting remote rural regions and taking an active interest in the widest imaginable range of the life and work of his subjects, including impoverished agricultural workers. Using his musical talents to charm a nation and later, involving university students in jazz sessions, he won the hearts of his compatriots by quickly effacing the image of a privileged young man who had spent most of his life in distant lands.

By becoming identified indelibly with his nation, King Bhumibol's tireless activism ensured that the monarchy became restored after the mid-1950s. Indeed, his prestige quickly grew to the point where successive military dictators sought to legitimize their power by eliciting the king's involvement in different projects and publicizing his interest in the welfare of all Thais.

The United States backed this approach as a counter-ideology to the Communist threat that they saw spreading throughout Southeast Asia. In this way, royalists were able to reintroduce the monarchy into Thailand's political game. Bhumibol naturally became a core figure in that endeavour.[23]

The royalist spokesmen referred to King Bhumibol as the Soul of the Nation, a title drawn from a 1979 BBC documentary. Elites and the mainstream media quickly picked it up and frequently used the Thai equivalent, *kwan khong chat*, to refer to the king. To their joy, his actions were by then recognized internationally as well as domestically.

By the late 1970s, the king and his immediate family had been elevated to the epicentre of the nation, until king and nation became interchangeable. Their physical presence and activities echoed not just in the capital of Bangkok and the central lowland, but also in rural and remote border and hill areas among different ethnic groups.

King Bhumibol and Queen Sirikit, as well as his mother, Princess Srinagarindra, and the royal children visited most parts of the country and regularly stayed at provincial palaces outside Bangkok. Born Sangwan Talapat, Princess Srinagarindra was affectionately known as Somdet Ya or the Royal Grandmother, but hill tribes, whom she defended as a patron, referred to her as Mae Fah Luang or Heavenly Royal Mother.

From the early 1960s until the early 2000s, it became a constant routine for the royal family to *prae phra ratchathan*, or change royal residences, residing outside of Bangkok for brief periods. Three major residences were built in the North, South and Northeast for these visits to further solidify contacts with Thais all over the nation.

Construction began in 1962 on the Phuphing Ratchaniwet Palace in Chiang Mai, followed in 1972 by the Thaksin Ratchaniwet Palace in Narathiwat in the Deep South; and finally in 1975 by the Phuphan Ratchaniwet Palace in the northeastern province of Sakon Nakhon. Apparently, for reasons of personal preference, the northern palace was more frequented by the king, whereas the other two were more often visited by the queen. In addition, many minor provincial royal residences were built around the country, though not as regularly visited as the three major ones. They served more as physical reminders for the general populace that the monarchy was present everywhere, although Thailand remained a highly centralized nation in terms of economic and political power.

In 1988, the Princess Mother had a Swiss-style residence built atop Doi Tung, Thailand's third-highest peak at 1,200 metres above sea level. This palace benefited from cool weather in Chiang Rai Province, bordering

Burma and the area where the borders of Thailand, Laos, and Myanmar meet at the confluence of the Ruak and Mekong rivers, known as the Golden Triangle.

It was from here that she and her only daughter, Princess Galyani, diligently worked at social welfare projects until they died in 1995 and 2008, respectively.

For five decades, from the early 1960s to the early 2000s, the new provincial palaces were used by the royal family as bases for meetings provincial dwellers; here, too, they could perform a good number of inventive and effective development projects, as well as royal functions and other activities.

But Bhumibol did not restrict travel to within his kingdom. Internationally, he became the most travelled Thai king of all time, eventually surpassing the globetrotting assiduity of his grandfather King Chulalongkorn. That distinguished ancestor's thirty volumes of travel writings chronicle Chulalongkorn's royal visits to India, Malaya, Singapore, Java, Western Europe, Russia and remote corners of Siam.

Globally, the reign of King Bhumibol coincided with the second half of the twentieth century which Eric Hobsbawm termed an age of extremes.[24] During these years, East and Southeast Asia became a contested region, torn between the US sphere of influence and the Soviet Union and its partners. During the Cold War years, most Thai governments chose to cooperate with the Americans by participating in hostilities in Korea, Vietnam, Laos and Cambodia.

Until 1977, Bangkok hosted the headquarters of the Southeast Asia Treaty Organization (SEATO), founded in 1954 and situated opposite the king's residence at the Chitralada Palace. The former SEATO headquarters is now the site of the new Ministry of Foreign Affairs. SEATO was an American-led collective defence body of eight free world nations, comprising Australia, France, New Zealand, Thailand, Pakistan, Philippines, the United Kingdom, and the United States, plus South Korea and South Vietnam as dialogue partners. It was an attempt to emulate NATO, mainly used for fighting communism in Asia.

Between the 1960s and 1970s, Thailand housed six American air bases in Ta Khli, some 200 kilometres north of Bangkok, in Khorat, Udon, Ubon, Nam Phong and Nakhon Phanom. All except one, are in the Northeast close to Laos, Cambodia and Vietnam.

Like the Cam Ranh Air Force Base in central Vietnam, a naval base was established at U-Taphao near the Royal Thai Navy at Sattahip as a logistics facility, near the much-frequented Pattaya beach. At these bases, approximately 50,000 American troops were stationed, and 500 airplanes parked, including several squadrons of B-52 heavy bombers for clandestine operations in Indochina.[25]

Through SEATO and other agreements between the Thai and US governments—such as the Thanat-Rusk communiqué on mutual defence cooperation of March 1962, the Military Assistance Program (MAP), and the Joint United States Military Advisory Group, Thailand (JUSMAGTHAI)—the United States granted the kingdom over US$2 billion in military aid from 1950 to 1987, according to some estimations. The flow of money, hardware, and personnel significantly impacted Thai society and politics.

While Siam previously had been under predominantly British influence, Bhumibol's Thailand orbited around the United States. Together with the Philippines, a former US colony, Thailand became America's staunchest ally in Southeast Asia.

In this historical context, the king and the queen of Thailand visited several countries in Asia, America and Europe. Some of these state visits were explained as if the king were following in the footsteps of his grandfather, Chulalongkorn as a traveller in Asia and Europe. But a closer look at the visits by King Bhumibol revealed reflections of Thailand's close partnership with the United States during the Cold War era.[26]

Domestically, King Bhumibol's reign coincided with unprecedented rapid socio-economic changes and political turmoil in Thailand from the 1950s to the turn of the twentieth century, when the king's power and prestige reached their height. The effects of these changes have had a lasting impact on the country up until the present day. Thai society and politics have been extremely volatile throughout Bhumibol's reign.

The king had lived through more than twenty coups and counter-coups, thirteen constitutions under his name or his regents, fifty governments, and twenty-five prime ministers, from Pridi Banomyong in 1946 to Prayut Chan-o-cha in 2014.

In addition to being widely known as *khwan khong chat* (The Soul of the Nation), the king was given many other titles and appellations, with or without his consent. Some were blown out of proportion, like the Revolutionary King. Others presented him as a traditional Buddhist king, a *dhammaracha* (*dharma raja*) or righteous king. In 1987, he was officially declared a *maharat* (*maha raja*), meaning the Great—a new suffix fashioned after European monarchies.

This appellation was first given in Siam to King Chulalongkorn, who was honoured as *phra piya maharaj* (The Great Beloved) in 1907, three years before his death. The suffix the Great was bestowed upon King Bhumibol when he turned sixty and the government of Prime Minister General Prem Tinsulanonda claimed that 34 million people of a total population of 55 million replied in a nationwide poll that they wish their king to be known as *maharat*. This ranking placed Bhumibol alongside previous great monarchs from different epochs of Thailand: Sukhothai's Righteous King Ramkhamhaeng (1237–98); Ayutthaya's Warrior King Naresuan (1590–1605) and Diplomat King Narai (1633–88); Thonburi's Rescuer King Taksin (1767–82); Bangkok's Restoration King Rama I (1782–1809) and Reform King Chulalongkorn (1868–1910).

In addition to being the Great, Bhumibol officially received from Thai governments from 2001 to 2009 titles of Father of several things, such as Father of Thai Technology (2001); Royal Rainmaking (2002); Thai Innovation (2006); Thai Invention (2006); Thai Heritage and Conservation (2007); Thai Research (2008); and Thai Craftsmanship Standard (2009).[27]

Moreover, over the sixty-two years from 1950 to 2012, sixty-two Thai universities had presented the king a total of 219 PhD degrees. The fields of study in which he was so honoured ranged from architecture to agricultural and resource economics, environmental technology, aquatic science, rural development planning, soil science, and dentistry.

As for foreign universities, twenty-five honorary degrees were conferred upon Bhumibol; the first one in law was as early as 1959 from Saigon, South Vietnam, and the latest one in 2012, was in economics from Soka, Japan. Others, as with Thai institutions, mirrored his unusually broad span of intellectual concerns and talents, including engineering as well as music composition and performance.

Besides these formal honours, there was a plethora of unofficial praise and appellations respectfully bestowed upon the king. They emphasized Bhumibol's roles, such as *kasat nak phattana* (Developer King) and *kasatkaset* (Agricultural King).

Kasatkaset—or *ksatriya* and *kseshtra* in Pali and Sanskrit, respectively—means warrior king. Yet modern kings are no longer expected to descend into battlefields as the traditional warriors Naresuan, Taksin, and Rama I did before him.

As a king for modern times, Bhumibol differed from such precedent. He was deeply and sincerely concerned with the development and agriculture of his nation. Using his unique educational preparation, the king began to combine within himself *phattana* and *kaset*, or development and cultivation.

He appeared to be toiling on behalf of most Thai workers who were still mainly employed in the agricultural sector. Thus, the term *kasatkaset* was intended to reflect that the king provided protection, well-being, and prosperity for the land and the people. He was a working monarch and was so labelled by the *Far Eastern Economic Review* on 23 January 1986.

Traditionally and colloquially, Thai kings were known as *nai luang*, or He Who is Great in State Affairs. But Bhumibol, for the first time in Thai history, was also called the *pho luang*, or Great Father. The king's birthday, 5 December, became a national day or *wan chat* as well as a public holiday.

When the promoters of the Siamese Revolution of 1932 were in power, 24 June was officially declared a *wan chat* to commemorate the end of the absolute monarchy. The king's birthday was not marked as a *wan chat* on the calendar. 24 June remained a public holiday from 1938 to 1960, until Field Marshal Sarit, then prime minister, changed it to 5 December. Eventually, in 1980 the day was officially declared *wan pho haeng chat* or National Father's Day.

This adulation was justified by visible and constantly mediatized images of the king and his family caring for the humblest of his subjects in far-flung regions of the nation. This incessant focus on development and improving the lives of Thai citizens coincided with the invention of *wan mae haeng chat* or National Mother's Day, reflecting broader trends during Bhumibol's reign.

One of the longest-lasting innovations of his time on the Thai throne involves the famous and well-publicized royally initiated projects (RIP), as bolstered by members of the immediate royal family: the queen, the Princess Mother, and the royal children. The sheer application and tireless goodwill expended on strenuously visiting and carefully noting details about local conditions established a nationwide image of a royal family of activists, determined to better the lot of their compatriots.[28]

Just as French political scientists use the term *engagé* (committed) to praise private and public figures who are resolved to improve civic matters, the Thais had a constant lesson in civism from a royal family led by an indefatigable monarch. Decades of this activity were essential for creating the image that many Thais still hold of the king as protector.

NOTES
1. See *King Bhumibol Adulyadej: Thailand's Guiding Light*, 1996, first published by Post Books to mark the fiftieth anniversary of the king's accession to the throne (*kanchanaphisek* or Golden Jubilee). Three years later the book was reissued in CD-ROM form, complete with a slide show and video footage. Especially during the staunchly royalist Prem government from 1980 to 1988 and thereafter, a series of celebrations were launched to honour King Bhumibol and the Chakri Dynasty. See also Benson Tay Hock Chye, "Touching Politics, Diffusing Bombs: Royal 'Intervention' in Thai Politics" (unpublished BA Honours thesis, Department of History, National University of Singapore, Academic Year 2000/2001).

    The historian Chris Baker has summarized these events: "The second role of the king was as the focus of public ceremonial on an even larger scale than before. The bicentenary of Bangkok was celebrated in 1982, complete with a glittering royal barge procession. Seven hundred years of the Sukhothai king's legendary invention of the Thai alphabet were celebrated a year later. These were followed by the king's fifth cycle (60th birthday) in 1987; the longest reign of any Thai monarch (1988), and of any living monarch in the world (1992); the funeral of the king's mother (1995); the reign's jubilee (1996); the king's sixth cycle (72nd birthday, 1999); the queen's (2004); 60th anniversary of the reign (2006); and the king's seventh cycle (84th birthday, 2011) …"

These grand celebrations were part of the construction of the new monarchy in Bhumibol's Thailand. Prime ministers and cabinet officials were assigned to oversee the events. Seminars were organized, and voluminous commemorative volumes were published. A vast printing industry evolved around the theme of the monarchy. See Chris Baker and Pasuk Phongpaichit, *A History of Thailand* (Cambridge: Cambridge University Press, 2005), p. 241.

2. Note the use of the expression "Siamese" people or "Maha Chon Chao Sayam" here although, as discussed before, the name of Siam had already been changed to Thailand by 1939.
3. With his Cambridge education and lengthy diplomatic career, it is unsurprising that Anand borrowed the phrase about the "rights to be consulted, to encourage and to warn" from Walter Bagehot's *The English Constitution* (1867). Such a borrowing made the Thai monarch and monarchy simultaneously appear constitutional and international. Ironically, while the British have an uncodified constitution, or one that is not codified into a single document, by 1996 Thailand already had had fifteen constitutions and sixteen unelected prime ministers, including Anand himself.
4. See a recent account on eyewitness of the brutal event by Thongchai Winichakul, *Moment of Silence: The Unforgetting of the October 6, 1976, Massacre in Bangkok* (Honolulu: University of Hawai'i Press, 2020).
5. See Derek Davies, "A Right Royal Example: King Bhumibol Acts as a Catalyst for Progress", in *The King of Thailand in World Focus*, edited by Denis D. Gray (Bangkok: Foreign Correspondents Club of Thailand, 1988), pp. 110–13. See also Roger Kershaw, *Monarchy in South-East Asia: The Faces of Tradition in Transition* (London and New York: Routledge, 2001), Ch. 9, "Thailand: A King for All Seasons".
6. Besides Kukrit, two senior princes were of central importance to the restoration and promotion of the modern Thai monarchy. They were Prince Chai Nat (1885–1951) and Prince Dhani (Krom Muen Phitthayalab; 1885–1974).

Prince Chai Nat was the fifty-second of Chulalongkorn's seventy-seven children. He studied education and public health at Heidelberg University in Germany, where he met and married Elisabeth Scharnberger. The couple had two sons and one daughter. During the reign of King Rama VI, he was appointed director of public health and commander of the student doctor wing of Vajiravudh's national paramilitary Wild Tiger Corps.

Throughout the reign of King Prajadhipok, Rama VII, Prince Chai Nat recused himself from government service due to ill health. In 1939, he was accused of being involved in a plot to overthrow Premier Phibun. He was stripped of his princely rank and put under house arrest. After the Second World War, Chai Nat staged a return after his princely rank was restored. He chaired the Board of Regency after Bhumibol returned to Switzerland. In 1950 he was appointed president of the Privy Council. One year later, Chai Nat died at age sixty-six, the longest-lived male child of King Chulalongkorn. But he did not survive long enough to witness the revival and reconstruction of Bhumibol's new monarchy.

As for Prince Dhani, he was probably even more vital to the king and the new monarchy. The prince was a grandson of King Mongkut, his father being the sixty-second of Mongkut's eighty-two children. At age fourteen, he was sent to study in England. After graduating from Rugby School in Warwickshire, UK, he proceeded to study Oriental Languages, specializing in Pali and Sanskrit, at Merton College, Oxford. He graduated with second-class honors in 1908.

After his return to Siam, Prince Dhani served as education minister from 1926 until the Siamese Revolution of 1932. Like most high-ranked princes, he was dismissed from government service, but made a comeback in the postwar period. He joined the Council of Regency after the Siamese *coup d'état* of 1947. Richard Whittington, a British chargé d'affaires, described the prince as a "scholarly and distinguished gentleman [who] was educated at Oxford and has a great many English friends" in a confidential cable dated 17 March 1951.

Whittington added: "In particular, [Dhani] cannot abide the Prime Minister. He is, however, convinced of the necessity of co-operating with Field Marshal Phibun and has very healthy mistrust of the exiled former Prime Minister, Pridi Banomyong, whom he regards as a radical and an anti-monarchist." (https://www.zenjournalist.org/2012/02/13/british-cable-on-prince-dhani-1951/, accessed 19 February 2021.)

Prince Dhani was then appointed president of the Privy Council for almost twenty-five years, from 1949 to 1974. There he worked closely with the young royal couple, Bhumibol and Sirikit. The prince was also known as a scholar and served as president of the Siam Society for fifteen years, from the 1940s through the 1960s. One of his most influential research articles was "The Old Conception of the Siamese Monarchy", *Journal of the Siam Society*, 36, no. 2 (1947). It is a lofty, erudite analysis, especially compared to Kukrit's writings aiming for a more popular readership, such as Kanpokkhrong Samai Sukhothai [Sukhothai Government] and Sangkhom Ayutthaya [Society in Ayutthaya] reprinted in Kasem Sirisamphan and Neon Snidvongs, eds., *Wichaphunthan arayatham thai* [Thai Civilization Subjects] (Bangkok: Thammasat University Press, 1971).

Dhani's longevity permitted him to witness the revival and reconstruction of the Thai concepts of monarch and monarchy. For more information on Prince Dhani, see his *Attachiwaprawat* (Autobiography, 1974), reprinted to serve as his cremation volume. See also Sulak Sivaraksa, *Kromamun Bidyalabh Bridhyakorn tam thasana Sulak* [Prince Dhani as Seen by Sulak] (Bangkok: Sathirakoses-Nagapradipa Foundation, 1985).

Sulak, born 1932, is one of the best-known social critic-writers. During his early conservative royalist career, he befriended children of many high-ranked princes such as Damrong, Dhani and Wan Waithayakorn. A good number of his writings contain valuable information about the inside of the Thai aristocracy. See his strong criticism in *Sin lit Kukrit* [No more divine power of Kukrit] (Bangkok: Kledthai, reprint 2011), and *Son wai nai lueb khong kanwela* [Hidden away in the folds of time] (Bangkok: Kledthai, 2017).

7. Thai royal descendants may keep their titles, reduced from high to low according to births and parental status. It took five generations to be reduced to *samanchon* or commoners. In the late Ayutthaya period, possibly because of polygamy and limited resources, to control the number of people claiming royal status, three categories of princes and princesses were instituted: *chao fa* (offspring of a king and favoured queen). Other princely categories of *phraong chao* and *mom chao* represented gradual steps downward from the loftiest realms of royalty. After that, one was deemed a mere commoner.

But in mid-nineteenth century, major socio-economic changes came to Bangkok. With an expansion of trade, Bangkok's ruling class became more wealthy and powerful. Due to modern medicine, with smallpox vaccines and quinine introduced into Siam by American missionaries in the 1830s and 1860s, respectively, royal family members and the ruling class lived longer and grew in big number.

King Mongkut (1804–68) had an estimated minimum of eighty-two children and about thirty-two queens and concubines. One should compare this to generations before and after him. Somdet Chao Phraya Prayurawongse (Dit Bunnag; 1788–1855) was a super senior minister and head of the powerful

Bunnag family. Dit was sixteen years older than Mongkut; he fathered forty-four children with twenty-four wives. Later, King Chulalongkorn, Rama V (1853–1910) begat seventy-seven children (forty-four girls and thirty-three boys) with four chief queens and almost one hundred concubines.

Approximate numbers of wives and children of Somdet Chao Phraya Prayurawongse (Dit Bunnag); King Mongkut; and King Chulalongkorn.

Names	Wives	Children
Dit Bunnag (1788–1855)	24	44
Mongkut (1804–68)	32 (including concubines)	82 or more
Chulalongkorn (1851–1910)	116 (including consorts and concubines)	77

See David K. Wyatt, "Family Politics in Seventeenth Century and Eighteenth-century in Siam", and "Family Politics in Nineteenth Century Thailand", in *Studies in Thai History* (Chiang Mai: Silkworm Books, 1994). See also by the same author, *Thailand: A Short History* (New Haven: Yale University Press, 2003), pp. 150–51.

With growing wealth, power and numbers of royal descendants, King Mongkut, in contrast to Ayutthayan kings, augmented his large family, adding two further royal categories, *mom rajawongse* (M.R.; The Honorable, reserved for children of the sovereign's male great-grandchildren) and *mom luang* (M.L.; The Honorable, reserved for children of male *mom rajawongse*). It should be noted here that *rachasap* (royal language and vocabularies) is not required for addressing an M.R. or M.L. Ordinary language suffices, although they themselves are the same, but different, from ordinary people.

Interestingly, in 1913 King Vajiravudh (Rama VI), a grandson of Mongkut, extended royal lines still further. For the first time, the king introduced the use of *nam sakun* or family names to Siam, annexing royal descendants plus their commoner wives, but not husbands, with the suffix of *na Ayudhya* (ณ อยุธยา).

And a similar type of suffix, *na* (ณ), for example in *na Chiang Mai, na Ubol*, or *na Nagara*, was invented to apply to those outside the Chakri family, making those of *chue chao* (royal blood from Bangkok or semi-autonomous statelets) into a huge network throughout the kingdom.

There are now around thirty family names with suffix *na*. It is estimated that up to 20,000 people use the *na* suffix in family names. It should be emphasized that it is royally and officially forbidden to those not genetically related to the Chakri or premodern provincial ruling families to apply a *na* suffix to family names. Thus, the *na* is a rather exclusive form of nomenclature. It is likely that Vajiravudh, educated in Europe for ten years, from 1893 to 1902, borrowed it from the use of prepositions in English (*of*) and French (*de*) noble family names. The goal was evidently to strengthen the old Thai ruling class through cognomens.

8. Khuang Aphaiwong (1902–68), a founder of the Democrat Party, was interim prime minister three times. He was seen as a man of interregnums. The first was for one year (1 August 1944 to 31 August 1945) towards the end of the Second World War. A vacancy occurred when Field Marshal Phibun was forced to resign as prime minister on 1 August, nine days after his ally, Prime Minister Hideki Tojo, was ejected from office on 22 July 1944. Khuang eventually resigned on 31 August 1945 to make way for a new administration by Free Thai forces. The second occasion that Khuang served as prime minister was from 31 January to 24 March 1946, just after the first general election in postwar Thailand. His government lost a vote of no-confidence in parliament, and he resigned. Khuang's third opportunity was from 10 November 1947 to 8 April 1948, when the military put him into office after a coup was led by Field Marshal Phin Choonhavan. However, displeased with Khuang's government, the coup leaders forced him to resign some months later.

    Khuang was politically inactive for almost a decade. He ran again in the 26 February 1957 general election, competing again Phibun's Seri Manangkhasila Party. He won a seat in Bangkok, but his party remained in the minority. In the same year, Sarit staged his first *coup d'état* on 16 September. The next year, following another coup, political parties and elections were banned. Khuang died in 1968 at the age of sixty-five. In the shadow of Phibun and Pridi, Khuang was not successful as a premier or Democrat Party leader, but he had a rather colourful life. See his cremation volume, *Anuson ngan ... Khuang Aphaiwong*, 13 June 1968.

9. Since the 1946 version of *Anna and the King of Siam*, three more adaptations of the romantic story have been released. The most successful was the 1956, 20th Century-Fox screen musical *The King and I*, directed by Walter Lang and starring Yul Brynner and Deborah Kerr. Based on an original Broadway musical by Rodgers and Hammerstein, itself inspired by fanciful and inexact writings by Anna Leonowens (1831–1915) an Indian-born British travel writer, educator, social activist, and fabulist.

    This was followed by the 1999 animated musical *The King and I* directed by Richard Rich and distributed by Warner Bros., and in 1999, the relatively unsuccessful *Anna and the King* distributed by 20th Century Fox and directed by Andy Tennant, starring Jodi Foster and Chow Yun-fat, a popular Hong Kong actor in the role of King Mongkut.

All three movies were banned in Thailand due to allegedly ahistorical and defamatory portrayals of persons and events. Even so, *Anna and the King* was an attempt to present King Mongkut in a more acceptable way for Thai audiences. Historians of Thailand were consulted and even participated in the film-making process, but the Thai Film Censorship Board disapproved it. In February 2021, Paramount Pictures announced that, yet another film adaptation of the Rodgers and Hammerstein musical was in preparation.

In 1985, Queen Sirikit graciously attended a performance by Yul Brynner in a revival of the Rodgers and Hammerstein musical on Broadway. The show remains ever popular with frequent restaging, although it may offend some viewers who know anything about Thai history. Queen Sirikit's visit to *The King and I* was made with an entourage of thirty-four guests, including twenty ladies-in-waiting, according to UPI Archives for March 1985 (https://www.upi.com/Archives/1985/03/16/The-Queen-of-Thailand-had-a-date-with-the/1698479797200/; accessed 19 February 2021). Ms Pharani Mahanonda, a "spokeswoman for the queen", told UPI that the queen "thinks the show is fun. She and the king are open-minded, and we all know that the court would never act like that … We Thais regard it as a musical comedy, so we take it lightly."

On the other hand, Pharani explained the film being banned by suggesting, "We are afraid the majority of the Thai people wouldn't understand and be so mad at the producer they would have bad ideas about the ones who make the play or the movie." See also Denis D. Gray, ed., *The King of Thailand in World Focus* (Bangkok: Foreign Correspondents Club of Thailand, 1988), p. 149.

10. *Si Phaendin* [Four Reigns] by Kukrit Pramoj was first printed in book form in 1953 as two large volumes of over 600 pages. It was translated into English by Tulachandra (Chanchaem Bunnag), *Si Phaendin: Four Reigns* (Bangkok: Duang Kamol, 1981).

11. See my two accounts of the history of Thammasat University in Charnvit Kasetsiri, ed., *Samnaknan thammasat lae kanmueang* [That Institute Called Thammasat and Politics] (Bangkok: Dokya, 1992), and *Thammasat Kanmueang Ruang Phuenthi* [Thammasat University and the Space of Politics: 1932–2004] (Bangkok: The Social Sciences and Humanities Textbooks Foundation, 2005).

12. During the heyday of the Liberal Arts programme, 80 teachers instructed 700 first-year students each year (200 continued to pursue a Liberal Arts

degree, while other second-year students opted for the Faculties of Law, Economics, Commerce and Accountancy, Political Science, Journalism, and Social Welfare). At the time, Thammasat had no faculties of science, public health, engineering, or architecture until 1986 the university began to expand to its second regional campus in Rangsit, Pathum Thani, north of Bangkok.

13. See Charnvit Kasetsiri, ed., *Samnaknan thammasat lae kanmueang* [That Institute Called Thammasat and Politics]. I would like to thank Kanchanee La-ongsri for detailed information about the Liberal Arts Faculty in the 1960s and early 1970s when major change occurred at the university shortly before the 1973 Thai popular uprising. Kanchanee was a leading history student in 1972. Because of the faculty's policy of augmenting its teaching staff, right after graduation she was hired as an assistant lecturer at the university, where she remained until 2001. By that time, she later recalled, the faculty had increased to a staff of eighty instructors, mostly female. Interviewed June 2014.

14. Kukrit Pramoj, "Sangkhom Ayutthaya" [Society in Ayutthaya], in *Wichaphunthan arayatham Thai* [Thai civilization subject], edited by Kasem Sirisamphan and Neon Snidvongs (Bangkok: Thammasat University Press, 1971).

15. According to Prince Damrong and Thanit Yupho, *khon*—or the masked Ramayana performance—derived from a type of play called *chak nak duk damban*. In the Thai language, *chak* means to pull, while *nak* is naga or snake. But the word *duk damban* is rather puzzling. Thais use it to mean ancient or very old. But in Khmer, the phrase is comparatively clear: *chhak neak teuk tambanh*; *chhak* means stage/episode, *neak* means naga, *teuk* means water, and *tambanh* churning. I am thankful for Prem Chap of Meanchey University, Cambodia, who helped to clarify this complicated Khmer-Thai phrase.

Therefore, the whole phrase refers to the tale of churning the ocean of milk, a significant episode in Hinduism involving God Vishnu. The story was carved in stone at Angkor Wat, Angkor Thom and other Khmer temples in Cambodia, Thailand and Laos. It is likely that in the mid-fourteenth century, Ayutthaya adapted *khon* from Angkor. And this type of performance was vigorously revived in the early Bangkok period and maintained as an important symbolic repertoire by the Thai monarchy to the present days. Kings were supposed to be avatar of Vishnu. See Thanit Yupho (Fine Arts Director 1956–68) *Khon* [Masked Ramayana performance] (Bangkok: Krom Sinlapakorn, 1957).

16. Anand was a classmate of General Suchinda Kraprayoon at Amnuay Silpa School, a private boys school in Bangkok. The general happened to be a military attaché in Washington, DC, while Anand was the ambassador there.

17. See King Bhumibol's diary-article on his trip returning from Bangkok to Switzerland, "Mua khapachao chak Sayam su Switzerland" [When I left Siam for Switzerland], in *Wong Wannakam*, August 1947. The king mentioned that on 19 August 1946 (just over two months after the tragic death of King Ananda on 9 June 1946) he and the Princess Mother paid a last worship to the Emerald Buddha, the Grand Palace, and left for the Don Mueang Airport. A huge crowd of people gather in front of the temple. A voice was heard shouting "Do not abandon the people". The king wrote down: " I wish to answer that if the people do not abandon me, how could I abandon them."
18. See Supot Dantrakul, *Kho thetching kiawkap korani sawankot chabab sombun* [Facts on the Royal Death Case] (Bangkok: 3rd printing 2002); also available in e-book format: http://www.democracythai.com/pdf/who_kill_r8.pdf
19. For a useful summary of coups and countercoups in postwar Thailand up to 1957, see Thak Chaloemtiarana, *Thailand: The Politics of Despotic Paternalism* (Ithaca, New York: Cornell University Southeast Asia Program, 2nd printing 2007), Chs. 1–2. See also Thamrongsak Phetchlert-anan, *Khoang kan patiwat tatthaprahan nai kanmung thai samai mai* ["Reasons" for Coups in Modern Siam/Thailand] (Bangkok: The Social Sciences and Humanities Textbooks Foundation, 2018).
20. Phra Phinit Chon Khadi was a principal supervisor of the Ananda case until the three defendants were executed. He was responsible for compiling evidence against them to convince the plaintiff, the director of the Office of the Attorney General in Thailand. The director at the time was Phra Sarakanprasit (Phin Gunakasem) who had recently taken office in 1946. He and his acting director, Luang Atthakaiwanwathi, were forced to resign in 1948, accused of being uncooperative. The next director was Luang Atthapreecha (Cha-atth Saenkosik) who remained for fourteen years, until 1962. See *Roi pi aiyakan* [Attorney General: One Hundred Years] (1992).

    As for Phra Phinit, he had close ties to the two brothers, Seni and Kukrit Pramoj, on the one hand and to Phibun and Phao on the other. Both sides temporarily collaborated against Pridi's faction and appreciated Phra Phinit's forceful opposition to Pridi. In this context, his participation in the court case can hardly be seen as an objective fact-finding mission. In his cremation volume *Nithan tamruat* [Police Tales], published on 28 November 1970, a fabricated biography suggests that he rose from humble Chinese origins and, after benefiting from an education inside palace walls, joined and married up into the Bangkok aristocracy.
21. About the execution of the three defendants, one of Phibun's sons later wrote that his father applied for a royal amnesty, but it was refused. However, in

a detailed study, Somsak Jeamthirasakul, an exile Thammasat University historian, found these:

13 October 1954	The Supreme Court sentenced the three men to death.
25 October	Phibun's cabinet was informed of the verdict. The cabinet took note.
5 November	The three convicts formally asked for a royal pardon. Their request advanced from the Department of Corrections, an agency of the Thai Ministry of Justice, to the cabinet.
8 December	The cabinet met to discuss the request. Prime Minister Phibun, also acting as the interior minister, rejected the idea. But the matter was forwarded to the king through the Office of His Majesty's Principal Private Secretary.
16 February	The Office of His Majesty's Principal Private Secretary informed the cabinet that the request was declined.
17 February	The three men were executed by firing squad the next day. (A regulation states that as soon as a royal pardon is officially declined, punishment must ensue the following day.)

For Phibun's version, see his son Anant Phibunsongkram, *Chompon po phibunsongkram* [Field Marshal Phibun] (1976), p. 687. For Somsak Jeamteerasakul's research, see his "50 pi kanprahan chiwit 17 February 2498" [50 Years of the 17 February 1955 Execution], in *Fah Diew Kan* 3, no. 3 (April–June 2005) and his controversial *Prawattisat phueng sang* [Just invented histories] (Bangkok: Fah Diew Kan, 2011); see also Phutthipong Pong-anekul, "Kan kho aphaiyathot" [Asking for royal pardon] in *Thammachat khong kan chai amnat rat dooi kasat* [The nature of the use of state power by the king], by Phutthipong Pong-anekul (Bangkok: Shine Publishing House, 2013).

On the death of King Ananda, Rama VIII, see a revealing interview, in 1979, with King Bhumibol by David Lomax, BBC, "Soul of a Nation", in *The King of Thailand in World Focus* (Bangkok: Foreign Correspondents' Club of Thailand, 2010), pp. 162–64.

22. See Lysandre C. Seraidaris, *King Bhumibol and the Thai Royal Family in Lausanne, 2014* (also in French: *Le roi Bhumibol et la famille royale de Thaïlande à Lausanne: les souvenirs du précepteur du roi Rama IX*, and in

Thai: *phrabat somdet phrachao yuhua ratchakan thi 9 lae chaonai thai nai Lausanne*). This book was written by a son of the tutor of the two kings. His father, Cleon Seraidaris, a Swiss man of Greek ancestry born in 1906, was six years younger than the Princess Mother. At the time, Seraidaris was preparing a doctorate in law at the University of Lausanne. From the mid-1930s to the 1950s, Cleon Seraidaris was the principal royal tutor. He became close with the royal family and had no wish to write any memoir that might invade their privacy.

Eventually, his son collected letters and postcards to tell the story posthumously. One particularly telling document is the missive from King Ananda after his departure to Bangkok in 1945. His final letter, dated 11 February 1946, informs Seraidaris about new American "toys", including jeeps, mini-bikes, walkie-talkies as well as military weaponry such as long- and short-barrelled guns and rapid-firing, rifled long-barrel autoloading firearms. In one passage, the king mentions that he has experimented with firing them. Three months later, Ananda met his death.

23. See a vivid interview of King Bhumibol to a foreign reporter, early 1970s, of what he was doing was to fight against hunger not the Communists: https://www.youtube.com/watch?v=zEmz_cNZ5fY (accessed 28 August 2021).
24. Eric Hobsbawm, *The Age of Extremes: The Short Twentieth Century, 1914–1991* (London: Michael Joseph,1994).
25. As for American bases in Thailand, Thak Chaloemtiarana noted in his acclaimed study of the Sarit regime during an era of increased American involvement in Indochina, that there are "no good studies about US bases in Thailand", as if these did not exist. The Thai public was shielded from this reality. While on American campuses, attention was more on Vietnam, Laos and Cambodia. In Thailand, general interest in the topic was quite low among Thai academics.

    Nevertheless, useful books exist, such as Jeffrey Glasser, *The Secret Vietnam War: The US Air Force in Thailand, 1961–1975* (Jefferson, NC: McFarland & Co, 1995); Herman Glister, *The Air War in Southeast Asia* (Maxwell Air Force Base, AL: Air University Press, 1993); Stanley Larsen and James Collins Jr., *Allied Participation in Vietnam* (Washington, DC: Department of the Army, 1985); Robert Muscat, *Thailand and the US: Development, Security and Foreign Aid* (New York: Columbia University Press, 1990); Surachat Bumrungsuk, *United States Foreign Policy and Thai Military Rule, 1947–1977* (Bangkok: Duang Kamol, 1988); Richard Ruth, *In Buddha's Company: Thai Soldiers in the Vietnam War* (Honolulu: University of Hawai'i Press, 2011).

See also Frank C. Darling, *Thailand and the United States* (Washington, DC: Public Affairs Press, 1965), and my unpublished MA thesis, "Thailand and the United States: Partners in Southeast Asia", Occidental College, Los Angeles, California, 1967.

Last but not least, see a controversial recent bestseller by Natthapoll Chaiching, *Khunsuk sakdina lae pya insee* [Warlords, feudal, and the eagle] (Bangkok: Fah Diew Kan, 2020).

26. See Thailand, Ministry of Foreign Affairs, *Indelible Impressions of a Royal Visit-News Clippings of Their Majesties the King and Queen of Thailand's State Visit to the U.S.A. in 1960* (Bangkok: Amarin Printing, 1999).
27. For official ranks and honours presented to the king, see https://en.wikipedia.org/wiki/List_of_titles_and_honours_of_Bhumibol_Adulyadej_of_Thailand
28. Kobkua Suwannathat-Pian, *Kings, Country, and Constitutions: Thailand's Political Development 1932–2000* (London and New York: RoutledgeCurzon, 2003), see Part III "Reality: The Coming of Age of Thai Constitution Monarchy, 1932–2000".

CHAPTER FOUR

The New Monarchy: The Early Years

"They say that a kingdom is like a pyramid: the king on top and the people below. But in this country, it's upside down," His Majesty told us. "That's why I sometimes have this pain around here." He pointed to his necking shoulders and his normally scholar serious face broke into a broad smile.[1]

Denis D. Gray, 1987

Inception and Development in the 1950s

The new monarchy of Thailand began to take shape in the second half of the 1950s. By the first half of the 1990s, it was fully established, as we have seen. Black May, or Bloody May, a common name for the 17–20 May 1992 popular protest in Bangkok against the government of General Suchinda Kraprayoon and the military crackdown that followed, showed King Bhumibol at the peak of his reserved powers.

He used his *barami* to the fullest, to the point where the king's "wish became like a command".[2] This chapter will examine how this new monarchy was established in Thailand.

As Anand, the former prime minister, argued, one of the most significant identities of King Bhumibol was as a *kasat nak phatthana* or developer king. By 1996, according to Anand, his development projects (*khrongkan phra rathca damri* or royally initiated projects [RIPs]) numbered almost 2,000.

Eight years later, they had increased to over 3,000. An official statement claimed that almost 8 million people, or one in every ten Thai citizens, had benefited from them.

The history of RIPs goes back to 1951, when the young king returned from Switzerland to reside permanently in Thailand. Yet in a sense, they also had their roots in boyhood lessons inculcated by his mother, Princess Srinagarindra, who in addition to Buddhist precepts, taught her children that they had a duty to help those who were less fortunate.

The permanent impact of this early instruction was of the sources of the RIPs, their ever-expanding scope and longevity. When Bhumibol returned to Thailand in 1951 at age twenty-three, he was accompanied by his fiancée M.R. Sirikit Kittiyakorn, who would become a lifelong collaborator in RIPs, tirelessly promoting crafts and economic solutions for the nation's underprivileged. Yet for all her awareness of the need for social progress, Sirikit was a product of the aristocracy, as a grandniece of Chulalongkorn and therefore a distant cousin of her fiancé Bhumibol.

Her Majesty Queen Sirikit, the Queen Mother, as she would later be called, had attended Rajini School (Kindergarten), a private girls' school founded by Queen Saovabha Phongsri. From there she progressed to St. Francis Xavier Convent School near the palace of her father, Nakkhatra Mangala, Prince of Chanthaburi II (1897–1953). She studied English, French, and piano performance in preparation for further training at a music academy in Paris, France.

In 1947, King Bhumibol and M.R. Sirikit first met at Fontainebleau, a lush suburb of Paris. Her father was a Thai diplomat stationed in London and Paris from 1946 to 1953. Although Bhumibol quickly developed a fondness for the beautiful young M.R. Sirikit, their relationship would weather a potential tragedy that tested his stamina and resolve to commit himself to improving the lot of his fellow Thais through RIPs.

On 4 October 1948, while driving a Fiat 500, a small city car, between Lausanne and Paris, he had an accident that cost him an eye.[3] This modest vehicle, known popularly as a Topolino (or little mouse, also the Italian word for the cartoon character Mickey Mouse) did not afford protection when on the Geneva-Lausanne road, the king collided with the back of a truck that braked suddenly 10 kilometres outside of Lausanne. His injuries were severe and would delay several urgent responsibilities. They included back trauma, partial facial paralysis, and cuts on his face that cost him the sight of his right eye.

This misfortune delayed the royal cremation of his brother King Rama VIII, which had already been postponed due to unsettled conditions in 1947 after a *coup d'état*. Court astrologers had previously determined that 2 March 1949 would have been the most auspicious day for the postponed coronation, but Bhumibol was hospitalized in Lausanne, and a further extension was necessary.

Despite these serious impediments, the young man who became King Rama IX overcame physical challenges to work for well over a half-century on the RIPs that were one of the hallmarks of his reign.

His gradual recuperation was doubtless assisted by frequent visits from Sirikit, who was reportedly asked by the king's mother Princess Srinagarindra to continue her studies near the hospital so that Bhumibol could get better acquainted with her. After he finally left the hospital, Bhumibol even chose an appropriate boarding school for her in Lausanne, Riante Rive, a posh institution whose name in French means smiling riverbank.

Surely the incentive to heal from the accident and promptly pursue royal goals was enhanced by the smiles of the young woman who became his fiancée and eventually a lifelong help. A quiet engagement in Lausanne followed on 19 July 1949, and they were married on 28 April 1950, just one week before his coronation.

They were engaged in London; Bhumibol was twenty-two and Sirikit seventeen. In early 1950 the couple returned to Thailand to preside over an elaborate royal cremation for Ananda on 30 March in front of the Grand Palace. The wedding on 28 April and coronation one week later, on 5 May ensued, after which the newlyweds returned to Lausanne for still another year.

By the time of their permanent repatriation in 1951, they were ready to impact Thailand during an era marked by domestic political turmoil and the Cold War in Asia. And the royal development projects were an essential key for establishing this new monarchy.

According to the Office of the Royal Development Projects, these ventures were initially categorized under different names. They were first called *khrongkan tam phra ratcha prasong* (Royal Wish Projects, or RWP), *khrongkan luang* (Royal Projects, or RP), and *khrongkan nai phra borom racha nukhro* (Royally Patronized Projects, or RPP), according to their characteristics and when they were launched.

Over time, however, they became systematically organized and labelled by the name they have assumed for posterity, *khrongkan tam phra ratcha damri* (Royally Initiated Projects, or RIPs).

The sociologist Chanida Chitbundid has explained how the inception of RIPs coincided with the so-called semi-democratic second Phibun government, from 1948 to 1957. How the monarch and Phibun interacted will be discussed below, insofar as national distractions were plentiful that might have prevented the advance of the programme.

RIPs were contemporaneous with development projects for national security from 1958 to 1980, focused mainly on the northern and northeastern provinces. This time of Cold War, known as the American Era of modern Siam, was when the Communist Party of Thailand (CPT) was active in Thailand's north.

The CPT presence abided, despite efforts at suppression by the military regimes of Field Marshals Sarit and Thanom from the late 1950s to the early 1970s. Thailand was undergoing domestic upheaval, marked by student activism and popular uprisings.

A major opportunity for advancing the royal projects occurred in the 1980s when the impact of the Cold War and the CPT's influence were waning. All royal projects, which had previously been administered solely by the royal household as personal projects of the king himself, belatedly started to receive direct governmental support.

In 1981, General Prem Tinsulanonda, who was prime minister from 1981 to 1988, established an Office of Royal Development Projects (RDP) attached to the influential National Economic and Social Development Board (NESDB). In 1992, this office, endowed with the official status of a *krom* or department, one step below a ministry, was elevated to a bureaucratic level directly under the Office of the Prime Minister.

This advance occurred during the first government of Anand Panyarachun, from 1991 to 1992. In practical terms, it meant that RIPs would receive more attention, coordination, and, most significantly, an annual budget. Before that, in 1988, the king had personally established the Chaipattana Foundation, a non-governmental organization developing projects of national and social benefit to the Thai people, which coordinated and facilitated RIPs.

King Bhumibol was its honorary chair and HRH Princess Sirindhorn continues as current chair of the Chaipattana Foundation. Its name signifies victory (*chai*) and development (*pattana*).

On 4 December 1994, the king reportedly announced:

> Victory for this country, through the work of the Chaipattana Foundation, means peace…. for Thailand, as well as prosperity and progress. This is the victory of development as [expressed] in the name of the Chaipattana Foundation. Victory of development aims at peace, prosperity, and well-being

Chanida Chitbundid asserts that through RIP activities, the king and immediate members of the royal family were able to create *phra ratcha amnat nam*, or a royal hegemony. Citing the Italian philosopher, linguist, and politician Antonio Gramsci, Chanida argues that the monarch and monarchy had become a "national center" surrounded by a "historic bloc" and "intellectuals".

This notion presumes that charity and development necessarily result in the dominance of one social group over others. All efforts at benevolent assistance of one's fellow humans are vulnerable to such criticisms by academics who theorize about negative outcomes of charitable endeavours.

In so doing, they posit that foundations that assist people are a means of maintaining power through history, which Gramsci, speaking of European political realities that were far from Siam, described as a succession of historic blocs created by political practice, unifying groups with different interests into a social-cultural unity.

The intellectuals, according to Gramsci, may be seen as adhering to two groups, one organic, or people needed by a new class to develop an innovative social order; and the other traditional, linked to historical precedent. Extrapolating these notions of societal advance to Thailand, both the newfangled and time-honoured intellectuals would be required to collaborate to build a cultural and social unity or hegemony that is the essence of any historic bloc.

Whether or not Gramscian thought applies in any direct way to the king's RIPs, it is indisputable that in Thailand, supporters of the monarchy who collaborated in RIPs consisted of a multifarious alliance of social forces.

These included prominent monks as well as individuals recruited from urban and forest-dwelling orders. There were also doctors, nurses, teachers, academics, technicians, managers, bureaucrats from civil society, the military, and the police force, social welfare workers, journalists, writers, and artists.

By the early 1970s, this extraordinary cohesion of collective effort gave the monarchy an unsurpassed operative reach among developmental organizations. In an influential article, "Network monarchy and legitimacy crises in Thailand", the British political scientist Duncan McCargo suggested that RIPs as a form of social intervention could be best understood as part of political networks.

The principal network in the kingdom from 1973 to 2001, McCargo adds, was centred around the palace, which he terms *network monarchy* actively participating in the political process.

Implying that the diverse group of allies working for a single cause, a better quality of life for the impoverished Thais, McCargo considers this network monarchy essentially conservative, although it also assumed liberal forms during the 1990s. While conventional understandings of monarchic power worldwide benefit from fresh analysis, seeing RIPs principally, or in a major part, in the context of an effort to sustain power by the palace and its proxies, especially former prime minister Prem Tinsulanonda, negates the possibility of genuine altruistic and patriotic motives by the king, as taught by his mother Princess Srinagarindra.

Presuming, as McCargo does, that a Thai network monarchy, although it became influential, failed in aspirations to achieve conditions for domination, offers a rather Manichean view of Buddhist good works. Where Thai Buddhists speak of merit-making, political scientists may see Manichaeism, an old religion that broke down into stark contrasts of good and evil. Since the Royal Palace was obliged to work with other political institutions, mainly the elected parliament, on RIPs, this is viewed as a compromise or perhaps even partial failure. Yet the RIPs have been a noteworthy success for Thai citizens who would otherwise be struggling economically.

Without necessarily adopting a full network monarchy interpretation of the aims and effect of RIPs, we must accept that King Chulalongkorn succeeded in establishing a centralized absolute monarchy, which ended with the Siamese Revolution of 1932. His eventual successor King Bhumibol, together with what may be deemed a network monarchy, was successful in its own way in restoring, reviving, and eventually constructing a path-breaking new monarchy for Thailand.

But why were RIPs instrumental for royal restoration? To explain this point, it is necessary to place Thailand, modern Siam, and its monarchy in a broader comparative framework. In 1897 and again in 1907, King Chulalongkorn made two extended jaunts to Europe. During these trips, Chulalongkorn made every effort to meet significant European sovereigns, including Tsar Nicholas II, and Kaiser Wilhelm I. He also encountered Prince Imeritinsky, Governor of Poland; Prince Thomas of Savoy, Duke of Genoa; King Umberto I of Italy; King Oscar II of Sweden; and several other foreign leaders and dignitaries. He aimed to present Siam as a modern civilized country.

Chulalongkorn had expressed the wish to revisit Europe for the third time in 1917 but died seven years before the planned fulfilment of that project, which likely would have been stymied by the outbreak of the First World War.

During the ensuing years, both before and after the Great War, monarchies began to disappear: Portugal and Korea in 1910, China in 1912, Russia in 1917, Austria-Hungary and Germany (including a group of small Eastern European kingdoms) in 1918, and the Ottoman Turkish Empire as well as Mongolia in 1924.

In the 1930s, Spain's monarchy was suspended, and at home, there was the Thai Revolution of 24 June 1932, abolishing its absolute monarchy. Bhumibol's uncles, King Vajiravudh/Rama VI, and King Prajadhipok/Rama VII, both witnessed this monarchical decline.[4]

From 1939 to 1979, during the Second World War and the Cold War era that ensued, more monarchies disappeared: Yugoslavia in 1944, Italy in 1945, Bulgaria in 1946, Romania and almost all the princely states of India in 1947, Egypt in 1953, Vietnam in 1955, Tunisia in 1957, Iraq in 1958, Libya in 1969, Cambodia in 1970 (to be restored in 1993), Afghanistan in 1973, Ethiopia and Greece in 1974, Laos in 1975, and Iran in 1979.

As recently as 2008, Nepal abolished its monarchy. Among 193 United Nations member states today, only twenty-seven are monarchies, or a total of 13 per cent. Republics succeeding monarchies has been the international trend since the start of the twentieth century. Monarchies are fragile, and when dynasties fall, they have increasingly been followed by republics.

Nevertheless, counterexamples exist in the modern era, such as the monarchy of Spain, which since 1947 had been a regency with a vacant throne but was restored in 1975; the reinstatement in 1991 of the Emir of Kuwait following abolition in 1990 and the Gulf War; and a 1993 transition of Cambodia from a Marxist-Leninist republic to an elective monarchy. In addition, new monarchies were formed in the twentieth century, for example in Bhutan (1907), Jordan (1921), Saudi Arabia (1932) and Malaysia (1957).

King Bhumibol and his family, especially the Princess Mother, a woman of strong personality and wisdom, must have been aware of the major global trend of monarchies dissolving. Surviving monarchies, like those in the United Kingdom and Western Europe, were required to adapt themselves to new moves and behaviours, including democratic standards, while considering the needs of their subjects.

In this context, Thai RIPs simultaneously served domestic requirements and played a vital role in the combat against the spread of communism in Asia, which was in line with US regional policies.[5]

As a further frame of reference, it helps to recall that from 1945 until the early 1970s was an era of developmentalism, an economic theory which states that the best way for less developed economies to develop is through fostering a strong and varied internal market and imposing high tariffs on imported goods. This theory was conceived and promoted by the United States for their so-called Third World allies in Asia and Latin America during the Cold War.

It aimed at alleviating poverty, improving welfare, education, and social conditions. The goal was economic growth and prosperity, aided by import substitution and the expansion of industrialization, telecommunication, highways, urbanization, and middle-class lifestyles along Western lines.

The governments of Phibun, Sarit and Thanom openly took the American side in several concrete and highly visible ways. One was by sending troops to join the UN and the US in Korea in 1950. Another was by becoming a staunch US ally within the Southeast Asia Treaty Organization (SEATO), an international grouping for collective defence in Southeast Asia created by the Southeast Asia Collective Defense Treaty, or Manila Pact which went into effect in 1955. And finally, Thai troops fought openly on the US side in Vietnam.

In terms of economic policy, almost all Thai governments since then also subscribed to the US-promoted strategy of developmentalism. The first major sign of this commitment was the construction of the vast concrete arch Yanhee Dam under the Phibun government. Funded mainly by the World Bank, planning was initiated in 1951 and construction started in the mid-1950s in the mountainous area of Tak province near Chiang Mai, 480 kilometres north of Bangkok.

It blocked the Ping River flowing into the Chao Phraya, for the purposes of water storage, hydroelectric power production, flood control, fisheries, and saltwater intrusion management. A huge water reservoir was created, generating electricity for Bangkok and the central plain (22 per cent of Thailand's total usage in the 1960s). In 1957, long before the project opened in 1964, its name was changed to Bhumibol Dam.

By then, Thailand's power elite had changed. Sarit staged a second coup in 1958, seizing the prime ministership and abrogating the constitution, dissolving the national assembly. Political parties were abolished, and martial law was installed. Sarit and his successor Thanom became absolutists for a full decade, from 1958 to 1968.[6]

One of their major policies was economic development. The word *phatthana* or development became a cornerstone of their military regimes and policies. It also became a household word, broadcast almost daily on national media.

Developmentalism gave the new regime legitimacy, diverting attention from a lack of electoral democracy and constitutionalism. It enabled the junta to ward off the opposition and promote their anti-Communist agenda while winning strong support from the monarch and the United States.

In 1959, Field Marshal Sarit established the National Economic Development Board (NEDB), now known as the National Economic and Social Development Board (NESDB). Placed under the Prime Minister's Office, it is instrumental in policy planning and annual budgeting. In 1961, after much consultation with the World Bank, including American and Thai thinkers, Sarit launched his first five-year National Economic Development Plan.

Subsequently, from 1961 to 2016, there would be eleven five-year development plans. In 1963, Sarit founded the Ministry of National Development and served as its first minister. After his death in December of that year, the ministry survived for eight more years, until 1971. It was dissolved by Thanom, and development works were transferred from the government to the king.

Successive Thai governments focused on economic developments at the national level and in the urban areas, while parallel royal development activities were concerned with rural and neglected regions. In general, the two strategies were complementary, and the king became more involved by the mid-1970s.

The royal development projects adapted over time in response to changing requirements. In the early years as RWP (1951–57), they were more conventional, charity-oriented, limited, and low-key. Nevertheless, they served as essential instruments for modifying and restoring the monarch and the monarchy.

Their limitations were attributed to the unfavourable political climate during the ten years of the second Phibun government from 1948 to 1957. However, it is somewhat misleading to claim that for Bangkok royalists, the second Phibun government was as unrelentingly oppressive as his first wartime government from 1938 to 1944.[7]

Between the two eras, army leadership had changed significantly and the new Sarit-Phao-Thanom-Prapas generation had emerged.

This involved four leaders who were born in 1908, 1910, 1911 and 1912, respectively. They had been socialized in Thailand, not in the West, and were therefore less inclined to democratic and constitutional ideals, compared to the Phahon-Songsuradet-Phibun-generation.

The new army generation, all leading figures of the 1950s and 1960s, proved more cooperative with the weakened monarchy and the old Bangkok elite. As leaders of the 1932 coup, both Phahon and Phibun had been prime ministers while also controlling the post of Army Commander for a period of six years each, from 1932 to 1938 and again from 1938 to 1944. This continuity added stability to their regimes.

However, after the 1947 coup and overthrow of the Pridi-Thamrong liberal governments, Field Marshal Phin (1891–1973), and not Prime Minister Phibun, was in charge as army commander for six years from 1948 to 1954. Field Marshal Sarit succeeded Phin from 1954 for almost nine years, until his death in 1963.

The brass ring then went to Field Marshals Thanom and Prapas until immediately before the 1973 Thai popular uprising.

All postwar regimes claimed legitimacy by siding with the Bangkok elite, the Democrat Party, and the monarchy. Phibun, Phin and the army were no exception when they regained power in the twin bloodless coups of 1947 and 1948.

One of their chief justifications was a promise to resolve the tragic death of King Ananda. An investigation was launched, followed by a lengthy trial. The apparent aim was to imply that the death was a regicide rather than an accident caused by Ananda himself, which had been the explanation publicly announced by the Pridi government immediately after the tragic incident.

As mentioned, in the previous chapter, after court cases lasting several years, three defendants were executed by firing squad. In the meantime, immediately after the 1947 coup, the army appointed Khuang Aphaiwong, the conservative leader of the Democrat Party, as interim prime minister for five months, from 10 November 1947 to 8 April 1948. Then, in a bloodless silent coup that year, the military forced Khuang out of office and put Phibun back in power.

The twin coups also meant that Pridi's constitution, which had been promulgated in 1946, was abruptly abolished. The liberal constitution was replaced by a 1947 authoritative interim version approved by the military, known as *rathathammanun tum daeng* or *chabap tai tum* (red jar/hidden-under-a-water-jar constitution).

The political scientist Thanet Aphornsuwan has remarked that the 1947 coup was a

> watershed in the history of modern Thai politics ... Politically, the coup eliminated the liberals as an active political force, and at the same time, terminated the first attempt to establish constitutional democracy ... The 1947 coup also marked the beginning of a new political era in which force had become the "common currency" in Thai politics and constitutionalism declined as a source of political legitimacy.[8]

However, since the military was obliged to collaborate with the old Bangkok elite and royalists, another permanent constitution had to be drawn up. It was eventually promulgated in 1949 by Prince Regent Rangsit. This back-and-forth constitution game set a hallmark for Thai politics in the decades to come.

Thailand's recent coups of 2006 and 2014 were followed by similar rounds of constitution-writing. Once the current constitution drafting process was successful, Thailand would come to have its twentieth constitution in place. That will be a substantial number of constitutions, but still less than the Dominican Republic, which has had a total of thirty-two constitutions, the largest number of constitutions of any country, since its independence in 1844.

A large number of constitutions in any country may be said to reflect a basic lack of consensus about rules that should govern the national political life. If new governments, upon taking office, feel required to write new constitutions, changing rules to fit their agenda, this suggests continuous domestic discord and discontinuity in national norms.

Thailand's royalist 1949 constitution was less conservative than the one the military had drafted, but at the same time was also less liberal than Pridi's. To further delve into the Thai constitution game, it is worth examining three major issues which were the subject of quarrels over inclusion and exclusion for each constitution.

They involved: (1) the monarchy, (2) members of the legislative branch (elected or appointed MPs), and (3) the cabinet (prime ministers and others). The first two major constitutions of 1932 and 1946 placed limitations on the role of the monarchy, specifying that its actions must adhere to the constitution and remain above politics, along "civilized international" lines. The latter phrase implied that Western European standards set a precedent for what was civilized on an international scale.

The 1932 constitution's clause about the monarchy's remaining above politics also applied to princes and princesses of the first to third ranking, such as *chao fa, phra ong chao*, and *mom chao* or M.C. But it did not cover the fourth tier, M.R., nor the fifth, M.L., grades.

As commonly defined, the Thai term *nua kanmuang* or above politics signifies that the person concerned cannot join a political party or run for office. Otherwise, different activities that might be considered political by international standards, such as expressing solidarity by various means with a political movement, are not prescribed, at least according to the ruling class consensus.

In addition, the 1949 royalist conservative constitution increased the role and function of the advisory Privy Council. This trend continued and influenced, for example, the 1997, 2007 and 2015 constitutions to the point that the council was allowed to become involved in the royal succession, as will be discussed below.

As for National Assembly members, the 1932 constitution provided for only one house but with two types of members. Half of these members came to power from a general election and the other half was appointed. Appointments became a point of discord between King Prajadhipok and the 1932/33 People's Party government. The divisive question was who would have the privilege of making such appointments, the king or the government? The latter won the argument, leading to Prajadhipok's departure for England and his eventual abdication in 1935.

The 1946 liberal constitution provided for two houses, the House of Representatives and the Senate. Representatives were chosen in a general election and they, in turn, nominated senators. In the postwar period, the liberal and left-leaning Pridi faction won both houses. In 1947, the first Thai Senate was established with 100 members, all royally appointed.

The ensuing 1949 conservative royalist constitution led to further disagreement. The constitution prohibited civil servants, military, and police officers from being appointed to the Upper House. This meant that the legislative branch was under the control of the Democrats, rather than the military government of Phibun and Phin.

This absence of control would lead to yet another coup in 1951. As for the cabinet, both the 1946 and 1949 constitutions prohibited prime ministers and cabinet ministers from actively holding military or civil service commissions concurrently. This set the stage for another battle between conservative royalists and the military.

The Phibun-Phin government and the military needed to maintain good relations with the old elite, consisting of royalists, conservatives and Bangkok dwellers. But they also found it necessary to dispense with the 1949 constitution.

On 2 December 1951, the royal couple and their first daughter arrived from Switzerland, entering the Chao Phraya River on a grand ship from Singapore, amid much fanfare.

Just three days earlier, Thailand's Silent Coup of 29 November 1951, otherwise known as the Radio Coup, consolidated the military's hold on the country. So, the royal family had returned in style, but amidst a tense political situation.[9] The following year, the military reinstated the 1932 constitution, limiting the role of the monarchy, while increasing its powers through several amendments.

Among these was a decree effectively eliminating the Senate, by establishing a unicameral legislature composed equally of elected and government-appointed members and allowed serving military officers to supplement their commands with important ministerial portfolios.

From 1947 to 1957, a phase began that might be termed *samai ratha prahan* (*samai* = period, *ratha prakan* = coup d'état). The name contains a reference to the 1947 coup promoters (*khana rattha prahan*) as well as the political instability of the era. This period is also known as *wattachak haeng khwam chu rai* or vicious cycle, referring to coups and countercoups, generals and field marshals seizing power in turn and drafting writing new constitutions, one after another.[10]

Within this decade from 1947 to 1958, Thailand saw a total of five successful and three unsuccessful coups. Phibun returned to the prime ministership for another nine years, until the 1957 coup which forced him into exile in Japan. At that time, he was replaced by a new generation of army leaders, the Phao-Sarit-Thanom-Prapas group.

To provide more context, it is useful to know that there were three unsuccessful coups in 1948, 1949 and 1951. The 1948 coup known as *Kabot senathikan* (or chief-of-staff rebellion) was little known, being an internecine military conflict caused by a small group of liberal and conservative army leaders including Lieutenant Colonel Phayom Chulanont, father of Surayud Chulanont, who would serve as prime minister from 2006 to 2008. Most of the rebels were arrested and imprisoned for short sentences. But two other coups in 1949 and 1951 were violently and severely suppressed by the armed forces establishment.

A 1949 countercoup was an attempt to return to power by Pridi, his wartime Free Thai followers and navy collaborators.[11] This coup became known as *kabot wang luang*, or the Palace Rebellion. Most fighting occurred at the Grand Palace, then the site of the Ministry of Finance.

The ministry was Pridi's stronghold, and his followers took refuge there. The army, led by General Sarit, used heavy weaponry to subdue the insurrectionists. Pridi and his followers were outnumbered and as described in the previous chapter, he was forced into exile in China for the next two decades, followed by a dozen years in France.

The 1951 countercoup was led by a faction within the navy displeased with the dominant role of the Army. The incident became known as *kabot manhattan*, or the Manhattan Rebellion, citing the name of a vessel donated by the United States for clearing the mouth of the Chao Phraya River.

The Thai army, backed by aerial bombing by the air force, subdued the rebellion. *Sri Ayutthaya*, a large battleship, was targeted and sunk next to navy headquarters and Wat Arun, or the Temple of Dawn.

As a result, by mid-1951, the military-led government of Phibun-Phin had consolidated power, ruling without rivals or opposition from most liberals, leftists, or the navy. Exceptions were the Bangkok-centred Democrat Party and a small group of journalists, writers, and intellectuals.

Due to its collaborations with the military, the Democrats were the only political party that survived military suppression by maintaining parliamentary majorities. Liberal or left-leaning parties like the Constitution United Front led by Luang Thamrong, or Sahacheep (Trade Union) led by Luang Adul, and some Isan MP, had ceased to exist or operate.

Liberal and socialist ideas disappeared from Thailand's public political discourse for almost three decades, until after the 1973 student uprising. Meanwhile, surviving Democrats staged some minor protests and boycotted the general elections of 1952 until their party was politically and constitutionally defanged. From 1952 to 1955, political parties were banned entirely.

Meanwhile, in November 1952, the Phibun government rounded up around 200 liberal and left-wing journalists, writers and intellectuals, including Pal Banomyong, Pridi's eldest son. They included distinguished and well-known literati such as Kulap Saipradit (1905–74), better known by the pen name Siburapha, a newspaper editor and one of the foremost Thai novelists of his time.

In 1951, during the second Phibun prime ministership, Kulap established the Peace Foundation of Thailand. The following year, he protested against the Korean War. He also demanded the lifting of press censorship. When he went to distribute food and blankets to the needy in Isan, he was among more than one hundred so-called agitators who were arrested on 10 November 1952. Accused of treason and sentenced to about fourteen years in jail, he was freed in February 1957 to celebrate the advent of the twenty-fifth Buddhist century.

Siburapha served just over four years in prison, but others were even less fortunate, charged with rebellion and jailed for several years.

Their supposed crime was labelled *kabot santiphap*, or Peace Rebellion, implying they were against the military, the Americans and SEATO. They were leaning towards the Third World bloc of Red China and the Soviet Union.[12]

Although Thai authorities referred to a rebellion, a continuous series of nationwide anti-government campaigns were associated to a differing extent with the Communist Party of Thailand (CPT). By no coincidence, the arrests occurred shortly after the Asia and Pacific Rim Peace Conference, held in Beijing, China from 2 to 12 October 1952. Delegates from dozens of countries attended the conference, which included speeches by Mao Zedong.

The gathering took place against the backdrop of the Korean War and the growing Cold War between the Communist East and the Democratic West.

Viewing the arrest of suspects in Thailand as a "case of internal terrorism", the defendants' presumed association with Communists worked against them. The newspaper *Sathianraphap* (Stability) which parroted government talking points, asserted in a 10 November 1952 article about the arrests: "These villains were supported by the Communists."

In a further racist reading of the incident, *Sathianraphap* alleged that the arrestees included "more Chinese than Thai", implying that those detained at Chinese schools in Bangkok may have been involved with a Chinese Communist scheme to overthrow the Thai government.

With such strong-arm tactics, the postwar military-led government did away with most of its challenges and adversaries. Nevertheless, it also had to cope with a new political factor in the form of a revival of the monarchy following a hiatus of sixteen years.

Since Prajadipok's abdication in 1935, the country had been without the physical presence of a king, until 1951. However, with the slowly growing popularity of the young royal couple, as a public relations necessity, Prime Minister Phibun had to demonstrate that he enjoyed a cordial relationship with Bhumibol.

On the one hand, Phibun tried to maintain some of the leftover spirits of the Siamese revolution of 1932 that brought democracy to the country.

For instance, he maintained 24 June, the anniversary of the overthrowing of the absolute monarchy, as a *wan chat* (National Day), akin to Bastille Day celebrations in France every 14 July or Independence Day in the United States on the Fourth of July. June 24 became a public holiday, featuring leisure as well as abundant celebrations, plays and social activities. There were even songs expressly used for the occasion. The historian Kobkua Suwannathat-Pian noted in an essay, "Memories of My Childhood" published in *Recalling Childhood*, edited by Nicholas Tarling, how Thai children of her generation "wholeheartedly learned to sing all politico-patriotic songs such as…'24 Mithuna [June].'"[13]

During the second Phibun government, 24 June was still regarded as an auspicious day for official functions. Foundation stones were laid, new government buildings and offices opened, and bridges, as well as monuments, were inaugurated. To boost the spirit of the Siamese Revolution of 1932, a so-called *ngan chalong rattha thammanun* (Constitution Celebration Fair) had been officially organized since 1933.

This grand annual event was launched every 10 December (known as Constitution Day) and lasted for a week or two. Today, 10 December is still maintained as an official holiday. To attract popular participation nationwide, the regime used to organize beauty contests to accompany the fair. This in turn resulted in the Miss Siam/Miss Thailand competitions, ahead of which every province was encouraged to hold its own Miss *Changwat* (province) pageant, whose winners were sent to a final competition in Bangkok. The fair and the contest were suspended during the Second World War, but upon returning to power, Prime Minister Phibun revived the fair and the competitions from 1948 to 1954.

When Sarit succeeded Phibun in 1958, the constitution celebration fair was cancelled definitively, although the beauty contests were retained. Later, in 1960, Sarit also eliminated the 24 June celebrations. He officially declared King Bhumibol's birthday on 5 December as a new National Day. Thereafter, the Thai nation itself became identified with the birthday of the king rather than the Revolution of 1932.

After residing in Bangkok for almost one year, Queen Sirikit gave birth to her first and only son, Prince Vajiralongkorn, on 28 July 1952.

At the age of twenty, on 28 December 1972, he would be appointed *phra borom orotsa thirat sayam makut ratcha kuman*, a modern title for crown prince created by King Chulalongkorn in 1885 to replace the traditional designation of *wang na*, or Front Palace, the previous rather problematic office of the heir apparent which was frequently disputed.[14]

The new prince was the first male *chao fa* or first-rank prince to be born since Prajadhipok in 1893, the youngest son of King Chulalongkorn. Only fifteen days after the birth of Vajiralongkorn, the Phibun government declared 12 August, Queen Sirikit's birthday, to be another important official holiday to be celebrated annually. This was a conciliatory gesture to the monarch because, for the first time in history, the birthday of a queen was recognized as a national holiday.

Therefore, it would be misleading to assume that the prominent role accorded to the king and queen was the sole outcome of actions by a new generation of generals such as Sarit, Thanom and Prapas. Phibun, too, has his share of responsibility. By the late 1950s and early 1960s, Queen Sirikit had become a well-known public figure to the point that by 1976, her birthday was officially declared *wan mae haeng chat*, or national Mother's Day, by the Seni government. Before, Mother's Day had been celebrated on 15 April, during the traditional Thai new year water festival of Songkran.

April 15 was annually celebrated from 1950 throughout Phibun's second regime, and his wife, Thanphuying La-iad Phibunsongkram (1903–84), actively participated in events such as the National Mother Contest.

Queen Sirikit's birthday was officially recognized as Mother's Day four years before *wan pho haeng chat* or National Father's Day was introduced in 1980, and thereafter celebrated on Bhumibol's birthday. In addition, by the mid-1980s, Princess Srinagarindra (née Sangwan Talapat; 1900–95), the king's mother, was referred to as Somdet Ya (Royal Grandmother) or Mae Fa Luang (Royal Mother from the Sky or Heavenly Royal Mother). With these new appellations, a sense was created that Thai royalty comprised a single national family headed by three notabilities: the royal grandmother (Somdet Ya, Mae Fa Luang), royal father (Pho Khong Chat, Pho Luang), and royal mother (Mae Khong Chat).

At the start of the new reign in the 1950s, the royal couple's activities were confined to Bangkok and adjacent areas due to political turmoil and poor infrastructure, with one exception: in 1955, the king and queen travelled afar to the Northeast, visiting the Isan region. Before American war operations and related infrastructural developments, Thailand lacked a national airline. Thai Airways was founded only in 1960 as a joint venture with Scandinavian Airlines System, and it took years to develop into a leading airline.

The Air Force was still slowly developing. Roads and highways were scarce and in poor condition. Travel by automobile between Bangkok and the central plain could be problematic, let alone circulating in more remote provinces. In the rainy season, it was possible to be stuck on muddy roads for hours. During these years, trains were the most convenient means of transportation. Strategic Royal Railway of Siam lines linking vital border areas had been completed during the era of absolute monarchy.

The first link was between Bangkok and the Northeast (Isan). Its first section went to the Khorat Plateau in the Isan region (265 km), completed in 1900. In 1931, it was extended to Ubon (575 km) bordering Laos and Cambodia, and in the same year, to Nong Khai (624 km), across from Vientiane. In 1921, the north-south lines reached Chiang Mai in the North (751 km) and Sungai Kolok (Narathiwat 1,142 km) in the South, bordering Kelantan, a state of British Malaya.[15]

Apart from being seen at Grand Palace ceremonies and a range of Bangkok temples, the royal couple travelled by royal train between Bangkok and the Hua Hin to Klai Kang Won Palace (Far from Worry), the king's primary summer royal residence. The palace was commissioned in 1926 by King Prajadhipok, who named it by paraphrasing the French term *sans souci* (carefree), in a reference to Sanssouci, a historical building in Potsdam, near Berlin, built by Frederick the Great, King of Prussia, as his summer palace and considered among the German rivals of Versailles.

Klai Kang Won is situated 190 kilometres south of Bangkok; ironically, it was there that King Prajadhipok and his queen received news of the 24 June 1932 coup against him. After their wedding on 28 April 1950, King Bhumibol and Queen Sirikit spent much time here. After they returned to live permanently in Thailand, Hua Hin served as their first residence outside of Bangkok. Their journeys by train to and from Hua Hin became a familiar image from the early period of Bhumibol's reign.

The elegant English-made light yellow royal carriage would pull to a halting stop outside major stations along the way, for example at Nakhon Pathom, Ban Pong, Photharam, Ratchaburi and Phet Buri. At each stop, town officials, locals, and students would gather to enjoy a short audience with the king, queen, and royal children, especially the youngest two princesses, Sirindhorn and Chulabhorn, born in 1955 and 1957, respectively.

At Hua Hin, the king also began experimenting with his public projects, involving water reservoirs, roads and cooperative farming.

The Hua Hin model of royal residence was slowly extended to cover provincial towns and provinces of the Central Plain such as Lopburi, Saraburi (1952); and Ayutthaya, which had been hit by severe floods in 1953. Ban Pong district in Ratchaburi Province was added to the list in 1954 after one of the biggest fires in living memory devastated the town.

Four days after the fire, the king and queen departed from Bangkok for Ban Pong, some 70 kilometres to the southwest; Bhumibol was seen driving the car himself, without a chauffeur. Their visit was intended to be unofficial and impromptu, to avoid interrupting local officials' disaster relief work.[16] Reportedly even Special Branch Bureau police were unaware of the hasty trip but managed to catch up with the king and queen when they were lunching at Sanam Chandra Palace, Nakhon Pathom.

Driving around the affected areas himself and descending from the car to speak with local people, the king was seen as caring and empathetic, responding quickly to assist his subjects at a time of loss. By contrast, the government appeared comparatively slow-moving and ineffective due to the usual bureaucratic requirements and red tape.

By the second half of the 1950s, the young king and queen's manifold activities and visits had become the centre of national attention. The most notable one was doubtless the long and successful visit in 1955 to the Isan region, considered the poorest and least accessible part of the country and threatened by Communist incursions from across the Mekong River.

The royal couple spent nineteen days in the region from 2 to 20 November, travelling by train (680 km) and automobile (1,592 km) to fifteen of twenty provinces in the region. The trip was a noteworthy success, drawing some hundred thousand locals who welcomed the distinguished visitors. King Bhumibol was the first modern Bangkok king to journey beyond the town of Khorat or Nakhon Ratchasima, attaining Nong Khai, Nakhon Phanom, and Ubon Provinces on the banks of the Mekong.

By the end of the 1950s and the start of the 1960s, these royal train visits throughout the nation had established a practical and enduring rapport between the monarchy and the people. By the 1970s, royal train rides had been reduced and eliminated in the 1980s. But during their heyday, they were instrumental in promoting the public image of the king and queen.

Another highlight along these lines was in 1956 when the king was ordained as a Buddhist monk for fifteen days. He was depicted walking barefoot to receive morning alms and food donations, like other monks, on the streets surrounding royal Wat Bowonniwet, a temple in the Bang Lamphu neighbourhood of Bangkok.

The following year, corresponding to the year 2500 of the Buddhist Era,[17] was a watershed for Bhumibol. According to Buddhist belief, the year 2500 marks the halfway point towards completion of the current religious *kala*, the time of Lord Gautama's Buddhism. To celebrate the occasion, the Phibun government organized a series of grand Buddhist celebrations but unlike such celebrations in previous eras, without much direct input from the monarch which might have been interpreted as a political endorsement.

Meanwhile, a general election was set for February 1957. Although the government's Seri Manangkhasila Party won the election, Phibun's short-lived post-election government would be his last. The public mood in Bangkok was stirred by student demonstrations and rallies, accusing the government of rigging the elections. On 16 September 1957, tensions led to another coup staged by Field Marshal Sarit Thanarat, Phibun's minister of defence.

Field Marshal Phibun, Thailand's most durable prime minister, having served a total of fifteen years in office, was gone for good. He fled into exile in Japan, where he died in 1964 at age sixty-six.[18]

The young king's independent outreach to the rural and up-country population and the educated urban middle class might be seen in retrospect as a foreshadowing of the RIPs. For it was the visits and royal radio transmissions, documentary film showings, and music performances involving King Bhumibol that sparked the devotion of rural and up-country people. The educated urban middle class was won over by the king's regular appearances at college and university gatherings, scholarship awarding, awards, graduations and commencements. At the latter, he personally handed out individual diplomas to every single graduating college student attending the ceremonies, thereby cementing a lifelong connection with the intellectual and economic ambitions of several generations of Thai people.

This connectivity during what may be seen as a pre-RIPs era, the king and queen were the first representatives of the Chakri dynasty to be seen and heard not just in Bangkok and its adjacent provinces, but gradually throughout the nation. When the royal family was not physically present, they communicated vividly over the airwaves.

The king had long been fascinated by radio as a medium. Back in Switzerland at age ten, he reportedly constructed his own radio set with metal coils which he had won at a school raffle and spent another ten francs on black ore to build a radio wave receiver.

So, it was natural that on 15 September 1952, the Phibun government presented the adult king with a radio station. The Phibun Cabinet ordered the Public Relations Department to present the king with a 100-watt radio transmitter that he could operate from the palace. The transmitter, costing 50,000 baht, was ready to start broadcasting daily from 11:00 a.m. to 12:00 noon.

Decades later, the official handover was summarized as follows: "Amphon Palace's radio station began daily broadcasts of musical compositions by King Bhumibol ... including jazz and classical pieces. Whenever the king produced new recordings, the music was also broadcast from the station, known as Radio Aw Saw—the Thai initials of Amphon Palace—with the king as the announcer and disc jockey."[19]

In the 1950s, radio broadcasting was probably the most effective means of public relations and communication. As part of modernization, radio broadcasting had been introduced to Siam during the time of the absolute monarchy. The new political elite of the 1930s avidly used radio programmes to win popular support. During the 1940s, Premier Phibun was probably the most active broadcast personality on Radio Thailand. Yet inevitably, the king, as a gifted musician and composer, was able to charm listeners in a way that no politician could do with mere speeches, quite apart from the popular reverence felt for the monarchy across Thailand.

By enchanting audiences in multiple guises, as a performer on the saxophone, composer, announcer and disc jockey, the king furthered his brilliant record of direct communication with Thais. But before he could achieve these accomplishments, radio in the kingdom had to evolve from its initial phases.

Radio Thailand belonged to the Krom Khosanakan, or Department of Propaganda established in 1940 under the command of the Office of the Prime Minister. In 1952, to dispel the station's Second World War-era rightist associations, its name was later changed to the current Krom Prachasamphan, or Department of Public Relations when Phibun regained power. From 1951 to 1953, when the Aw Saw palace radio station was created, Radio Thailand increased its broadcasting capacity from 50 to 100 kilowatts, increasing the range wherein devotees would have access to His Majesty's broadcasts.

Aw Saw became an instrumental means for the king to be heard, as well as sharing his talents, interests, and concerns in a highly personal and individual way. As has been pointed out, at the time, the largest-selling popular daily newspaper printed around 20,000 copies, while radio could reach a vast audience of almost one-third of all Thais.[20] In 1956, the population of Thailand was 23 million, with 350,000 owning radio receivers and 10,000 television sets. The palace radio was launched with a transmission power of 100 watts, only capable of broadcasting to Bangkok and surrounding areas.

Compared to a genuine national radio, this was rather insignificant, for Radio Thailand's broadcasting capacity from 1951 to 1953 was between 10 to 50 kilowatts. But Aw Saw was slowly upgraded to 1 kilowatt, and by 1966 this had increased to 10 kilowatts, allowing Palace Radio to attain international listeners. Apart from the government-owned Radio Thailand, Aw Saw was the only station broadcast by short wave that could be enjoyed overseas.

Radio also aired the king's music. As mentioned, King Bhumibol was a skilled performer on the saxophone and the clarinet, among other wind instruments, and composed many charming melodies. All Thai people are aware of these skills, although they may lack comparative information for really evaluating King Rama IX's skills. The fact is, highly discerning musicians such as the clarinet virtuoso Benny Goodman, an early idol of King Bhumibol's, accepted to perform with him, and Goodman was notoriously judgmental about fellow musicians. Videos of King Bhumibol playing the saxophone continue to circulate on social media, showing a genuine talent for expressing emotion and a gentle swinging sensibility.

To find a place for King Bhumibol among fellow world monarchs of history with musical talents would be difficult, as he outshines most of them. In the twentieth century, King Edward VIII of the United Kingdom played jazz drums recreationally and intermittently, with none of the assiduity or accomplishment that King Bhumibol displayed with his jazz performances and compositions. Emperor Naruhito of Japan plays the viola, having switched from the violin, reportedly because he thought the latter instrument was too much of a leader in its prominence to suit his musical tastes. While King Bhumibol was an able ensemble player and assembled groups of Thai musicians who performed with him regularly, he was also capable of the solo statement in the best jazz style.

So, to find a parallel for his musical abilities among reigning monarchs, one might have to look back in history to the eighteenth century, when Frederick II of Prussia, known as Frederick the Great, played the transverse flute and wrote several works for it and other instruments. Even so, from contemporary accounts and modern recordings of Frederick's composition, they do not reflect a professional level of accomplishment.

By contrast, from 1946, the accession year, to 1994 when his sister Galyani Vadhana, Princess of Naradhiwas turned seventy-two, the king composed forty-eight songs. The first was *saeng thian* (Candlelight Blues) and the last *menu khai* (Egg Menu) because his sister was known to be fond of eggs. Except for a few songs, the king wrote the music only, leaving the lyrics to be created by men and women of his entourage. Most of the melodies were romantic and/or melancholic, except for three marches composed for the military (*Royal Guards March* (1948); *Royal Marines March* (1959); and *We-Infantry Regiment 21* (1979)).

He also wrote the school anthem or alma mater for three major national universities: *Maha Chulalongkorn*, presented to Chulalongkorn University in 1946; *Yung Thong* for Thammasat University in 1963, replacing a previous patronal song; and *Kasetsart*, for Kasetsart University in 1966. One of the king's most popular songs remains *phon pi mai* or New Year Blessing, composed in 1952. It has been a constant presence on all Thai radio and television stations every New Year for over half a century.

With the palace radio Aw Saw and his musical activities, the young king blended in well with Bangkok's entertainment circles. In 1951, Bhumibol established his band of musicians which became known as *wong dontri aw saw wan suk* or Friday Aw Saw Band. In the 1950s and 1960s, the band performed regularly, broadcasting live on Fridays between 6:00 p.m. and 7:00 p.m. It also held occasional jam sessions with popular musical legends of the time and armed forces bands.

The Friday Aw Saw Band later established links with military and police cadet school bands as well as bands from three major universities: Chulalongkorn, Thammasat and Kasetsart. The royal family became close to the young and educated urban middle class through regular performances with students from these universities. From the late 1950s until 1972, one year before the 1973 student uprising, private royal visits and casual advisory speeches on *song dontri* or music performances become social highlights on the three campuses.

The first of these visits occurred at Chulalongkorn University on 20 September 1957, four days after Sarit staged a coup, followed by Thammasat in 1963 and Kasetsart in 1966. This tradition of affectionate collaboration and mutual celebration of the arts was a unique and enduring means of rapprochement. So, it is understandable that when crowds of students marched from the Thammasat campus on the day before the 14 October 1973 student uprising, protesting the Thanom-Prapas regime, they carried flags bearing images of the king and the royal couple.[21]

More formal and close rapport with university students was achieved through graduation ceremonies and the distribution of scholarships. To the present day, receiving a degree certificate from the king or his representatives has become a highly honoured tradition and a never-forgotten personal achievement. All graduates carefully tend to their personal appearance before meeting the king or his emissaries. As part of the all-important etiquette, they must rehearse walking up to the king, and practise bowing or curtsying before him, as well as lifting one hand palm upwards to receive the diploma, a moment forever captured on photographs handed out to each graduate.

The resulting pictures will usually be framed and prominently displayed at the home of graduates. In this way, a bond was created between the monarch and the educated classes. A college education was not just a family attainment but a means of personal contact, however fleeting, with royalty. From 1950 to 1997, King Bhumibol presided over 490 graduations and personally handed out diplomas to 470,000 graduates.

This royal graduation ceremony was a newly invented tradition in Siam, first reported towards the end of the absolute monarchy. Kings Chulalongkorn and Vajiravudh never held any such public ceremonies, which only took place three times, and at a modest scale, before Bhumibol acceded to the throne. In 1930, King Prajadhipok presented medical diplomas to thirty-four graduates, and in 1946, King Ananda Mahidol presided over two graduation ceremonies just weeks before his death.

Back then, graduations were usually attended by the prime minister or education minister. Royal graduation ceremonies today represent a fundamental modification rooted in the promotion of the monarchy that began in the early 1950s. As a first step, King Bhumibol and Queen Sirikit performed the *phra ratcha than parinya* or diploma presentation at the two oldest universities, Chulalongkorn on 21 May 1950, and Thammasat eight days later. The ceremonies were simple, brief and pleasant. Over time, the graduating became vaster affairs as the number of graduates and new universities steadily increased. Yet the king continued to personally hand out diplomas, doubtless aware of the emotional significance of these brief formal encounters with young graduates for the future cohesiveness of Thailand and the educated population's rapport with the monarchy.

Using diploma conferral ceremonies as a point of contact with royals became more of a challenge as Thailand's higher educational sphere increased in importance. At first, Thailand had only five universities: Chulalongkorn, Thammasat, Medical School (renamed Mahidol, after the family name of the king's father), Kasetsart and Silapakorn. Most did not correspond to the contemporary definition of a university in terms of the breadth of subjects offered; instead, they catered to specific professional requirements.

Chulalongkorn was a training ground for civil servants, Thammasat principally a law school, Mahidol an educational institution for medical students, Kasetsart for agriculture, and Silapakorn an art school. Around the year 1950, the entire student population was about 24,000 (or a small percentage of a total population of 20,710,360). Of these, the largest student enrolment was concentrated at Thammasat; Chulalongkorn had the second-highest number of students, while the most modest programme, at Silapakorn, was attended by only a few dozen students.

By 1965, student enrolment was still underwhelming at 34,781 (of a total population of 31,822,660); but the number of universities increased from five to eight. Thammasat ceased admitting all applicants as an open institution in 1960, and in 1964, Chiang Mai was the first provincial university. A decade later, student enrolment had quadrupled to 130,875 of a total population of 42,326,312. The number of universities grew to thirteen, with the newest and largest one being Ramkhamhaeng University, the largest open university in Thailand. Ramkhamhaeng was founded in 1971, just two years before the 1973 Thai popular uprising. It was as if the sheer numbers of students newly equipped with education and heightened social awareness made demands for democratic reforms inevitable.

By 1985, after three decades of steady economic growth of over 7 per cent annually, Thailand's population stood at 52,026,901. The country had thirteen state universities and seventeen private colleges. University degrees were in high demand and education was increasingly commercialized. Student enrolment rose to 699,379, over 1 per cent of the total population, from a small fraction of that just a few years earlier.[22] The year 1985 saw 58,131 graduates receive diplomas, and there was some discussion among universities administrators that royal graduation ceremonies might be modified, as it might not be convenient, or even possible, for every student to receive a diploma directly from the hands of the king. Yet according to King Bhumibol's wish, the practice continued until 1997 at Thammasat and 1998 at Chulalongkorn, the last two ceremonies presided over by the king.

The overwhelming numbers of universities and graduates as well as the king's advanced age and health issues finally ended the much-cherished tradition. In 1997, student enrolment in state and private universities was at 861,991 or almost 2 per cent of the total population of 60,846,582. In that year, Thailand produced 90,227 graduates. At the final graduation at Thammasat with King Bhumibol's participation, 3,330 students received bachelor's degrees, while 921 were presented with master's degree diplomas. The ceremony took two days, and the final ceremony at Chulalongkorn University presided over by King Bhumibol took a day longer than that.

During the first two days, the king was accompanied by Princess Sirindhorn and handed out diplomas as usual, but on the third day, graduates merely posted before a photo of King Bhumibol. In total, there were 5,899 graduates.[23]

In addition to graduation ceremonies, strong royal rapport with the Thai urban educated classes was also reflected in scholarship grants and other awards for the intellectual endeavour. During the era of absolute monarchy, two types of scholarships were available for Siamese students who wished to further their education overseas. These were granted either by the royal family or certain ministries.

These two types of grants differed insofar as the former were available for recipients of royal blood, who were free to accept any job they wished upon returning to Siam after their studies, or indeed remaining overseas if they so desired. The latter grants, distributed by government ministries, required graduates to return to toil at certain ministries or civil service departments.

These scholarships targeted children from the extended royal family as well as the urban upper and middle classes, without overt promotion of social mobility. The grants enabled students to further their education abroad, mainly in Western Europe and, to a lesser extent, in the United States and Japan. A good number of promoters of the Siamese revolution of 1932 were one-time recipients of such scholarships, for example, Phahon (Germany) as well as Phibun and Pridi (France).

Due to political turmoil and financial issues, the king's scholarships eventually ceased, while the ministries continued to award scholarships at a sluggish pace. In the early 1950s, however, both types were revived. The King Bhumibol awards and King Ananda scholarships were particularly noteworthy and productive.

As mentioned, in 1950 King Bhumibol began to preside over graduation ceremonies at the two oldest universities. Both Chulalongkorn and Thammasat presented Bhumibol with their first honorary degrees in political science. In 1952, the king donated to each university's Faculty of Political Science seed money of 100,000 baht. That sum represented just over US$4,500 according to exchange rates then current, with the purchasing power of just under US$45,000 today.

The *kongthun Bhumibol* (Bhumibol Fund) was established, to which the two institutions contributed more money. Bank interest was used for presenting awards to the top two graduates of each university's Faculty of Political Sciences. In the mid-1960s, each awardee received the amount of 1,000 baht. There were also awards for student essays on conservative topics such as the role of the Chakri kings or national progress in the Bangkok period from 1767 to 1932.

Eventually, these funds were expanded to reward the best students in more faculties and finally, in all departments. Two more universities, Kasetsart and Srinakharinwirot, were included in this honours and cash distribution system. By 1986, 1,137 King Bhumibol awardees represented the highest academic achievement among graduates of these universities. They were personally handed diplomas by the king and received further kudos associated with the monarch.

Conveniently, the public perception of the King Bhumibol award did not recognize that the new awards were not as significant or prolonged as the king's scholarships during the time of the absolute monarchy. The Bhumibol awards were a medal, certificate and modest cash award. They did not include scholarships for further education at the master's or doctoral level. But more indirectly, the Bhumibol awards could be translated into monetary gain, because the prestige of the honour associated with the king's name facilitated its recipients' applications for higher education and professional advancement. They were regarded as having been blessed by the king. They became part of Chanida's hegemonic royal historical bloc and McCargo's network monarchy, as mentioned earlier.

Even more important was *thun anand*, or the Ananda Mahidol Foundation Scholarship. Its awardees were the national elite, hailing from the best Thai universities. After graduation with honours, they were chosen to continue studies overseas for the master's or PhD degree. This award began in 1955 and as of 2005, had been granted to 245 individuals, with 75 per cent of the scholarships for the study of medical science, engineering, pure science and agriculture. The remaining were for higher education in social sciences and humanities, including law.

As with the King Bhumibol Fund, royal seed money of 20,000 baht was granted to establish the scholarship, originally limited to medical graduates in honour of the king's father, Prince Mahidol, and his brother, King Ananda. However, the fund soon attracted major donations as a focal point for *tham bun ruam kap nai luang* or making merit with the king. Anyone could donate money to the fund, which slowly expanded until it was finally registered as a foundation. The king was its honorary chairperson and the Princess Mother as its executive director, until Princess Sirindhorn assumed those responsibilities. In 2005, the foundation's assets amounted to 600 million baht.

As these funds developed, the scholarships championed by King Ananda and his brother King Bhumibol represented a revival and modification of previous royal scholarships during the era of absolute monarchy. No longer were the recipients solely those from established aristocratic circles. A certain degree of social mobility became possible, at least for the most brilliant of students. For these honorees, intellectual accomplishment became a means of contributing to the Thai nation's future development.

Many of the grant recipients rose through the ranks of Thai public life to become prominent and influential public figures and intellectuals. Among these were the hematologist and public intellectual Prawese Wasi, the future Privy Councillor Kasem Watthanachai, and former head of the Royal Irrigation Department of Thailand Pramote Maiklad.[24]

Prawase, a socially engaged medical doctor, was born in 1932 to a middle-class Sino-Thai family based in Kanchanaburi. He was educated in his home province and finished his final two years of high school in Bangkok at Triam Udomsuksa, a training ground for future elite students. This preparation enabled him to continue studying for a medical degree at Mahidol University.

As one of the highest-ranking medical graduates, he was granted a King Ananda Scholarship for overseas study, specializing in hematology from 1957 to 1960 at the University of Colorado. He then continued his studies in human genetics at London University. Back in Thailand, Prawase became active in teaching and administration, which earned him a Ramon Magsaysay Award, sometimes referred to as Asia's version of the Nobel Prize, for public service in 1981. After the Black May protests in 1992, Prawase became a highly active public figure, receiving the popular sobriquet of *ratsadon awuso* or senior citizen. As a leading public intellectual, he was appointed as chairperson and member of many foundations and university councils, where he served simultaneously.

He was also named head of the twenty-seven-member National Reform Assembly by Prime Minister Abhisit Vejjajiva, immediately after the violence and loss of lives from the April and May 2010 Thai military crackdown. The Assembly was tasked with producing plans for positive political, economic, and social change. It was to share a reform budget of 600 million baht with the somewhat similar, but smaller, National Reform Committee.

The latter committee, also appointed by Abhisit, had nineteen members and was headed by Anand Panyarachun. Its task was to formulate reform strategies and action plans. Both bodies proved futile, as political developments and social upheaval from 2010 until the 2014 Thai *coup d'état* prevented any serious study, let alone implementation of recommendations.

Similar to Prawase, Kasem Watthanachai was a medical doctor by training. He was born in 1941 to a middle-class family in Phichit Province and completed his first medical degree at Chiang Mai University. Subsequently, Kasem was awarded a King Ananda scholarship to study internal medicine and cardiovascular disease at the University of Chicago from 1969 to 1975. He became a long-time instructor at his alma mater in Chiang Mai and served as rector from 1989 to 1992. Kasem was known for promoting rural doctors and medicine for hill tribes in the North, an activity that brought him close to the royal family and their activities among inhabitants of rural areas.

In 2001, Kasem joined the Thai Rak Thai Party of the Thai businessman and politician Thaksin Shinawatra, won a seat in the Parliament, and became Thaksin's Minister of Education. However, less than four months later, he resigned from the cabinet and was immediately appointed member of the Privy Council, headed by ex-Premier General Prem Tinsulanonda.

Like Prawase, Kasem held various important educational positions and was chairperson, as well as member, of foundations and university councils.

Pramote Maiklad was known for his role as director of the Royal Irrigation Department and an active RIP hydrology adviser. Pramote was born in 1940 to a fruit orchard-owning family on the outskirts of Bangkok. After he graduated from Kasetsart University, he received a King Ananda scholarship to study irrigation engineering at the University of California, Davis, from 1964 to 1966.

He worked at the Royal Irrigation Department, where he became director in 1997 as well as deputy permanent secretary of the Ministry of Agriculture and Cooperatives in 1999. Mr Pramote was seen as promoting policies and projects akin to those presented by RIPs on irrigation issues. This basic agreement was especially noteworthy over the controversial issue of building the Pa Sak Cholasit Dam. Located in the upper part of Lopburi and Saraburi Provinces, the dam, one of the biggest ever built in Thailand, was completed in 1999 on the king's seventy-second birthday.

Its main function was to prevent floods in the central plain and Bangkok, a plan that failed in 2011 during some of the worst floods in recent memory. Mr Pramote ran for a Bangkok senatorial seat in the 2000 election and received a plurality of votes. During the 2013–14 political crisis leading up to the 2014 Thai *coup d'état*, Pramote was politically outspoken. He joined Suthep Thuagsuban's anti-democratic People's Democratic Reform Committee (PDRC) which prepared the ground for the 2014 coup, toppling Thailand's first female Premier, Yingluck Shinawatra.

These prominent graduates were just a few among those who reached positions of influence in Thailand's modern development, made possible by royal support of their education. The legacy of intellectual growth and training represented by the instructional philanthropy of the monarchy had been, at one time, one of the brightest contributions to national growth and the maturing of public consciousness.

NOTES

1. Denis D. Gray, "Thailand's Working Royals", in *The King of Thailand in World Focus* (Bangkok: Foreign Correspondents' Club of Thailand, 2010), p. 120.
2. Ibid., in the 2010 expanded version of the Foreign Correspondents' Club of Thailand (FCCT) volume (1988) edited by Denis D. Gray, *The King of Thailand in World Focus*, is an article by Alex Spilliu, a British correspondent for the *Daily Telegraph*, dated 23 September 2006, four days after the coup led by General Sonthi Boonyaratglin. The revealing title is "The Thai King's wish is his people's command." It includes this interesting observation:

   > Our own royals [in the United Kingdom] can only dream of such reflex loyalty. And in modern Britain of course, even standing up for the national anthem would be met with utter derision by teenagers and their parents. But Thai subjects seems to enjoy any opportunity to demonstratiie their allegiance to King Bhumibol. If there are any republicans, they do a good job of disguising themselves. Which is why the fact that the king seems to support the coup in Thailand is crucial to its success—King Bhumibol's wish is his people's command. (p. 116)

I am thankful to Sinae Hyun, professor in the History Department at University of Wisconsin-Whitewater, who pointed out that "This is one of the best sources to see how the Western journalist projected their expectations towards the role of the king." (Private communication dated 26 July 2014).

3. Associated Press, "Siam's King Hurt in Auto Crash", FCCT, 2010, p. 24.
4. Benedict Anderson, *Useful or Useless Relics: Today's Strange Monarchies* (Working Paper Series No. 32, Afrasian Centre for Peace and Development Studies, Ryukoku University, 2007). I am thankful to Benedict Anderson of Cornell University for pointing out this global perspective and thereby *Kob Nai Kala* or extracting the frog from the coconut shell.
5. See Daniel Fineman, *A Special Relationship: The United States and Military Government in Thailand, 1947–1958* (Honolulu: University of Hawai'i Press, 1997); Thomas David Lobe, "U.S. Police Assistance for the Third World" (PhD dissertation: Political Science, University of Michigan, 1975); Donald E. Nuechterlein, "Thailand: Another Vietnam?", *Military Review* 47 (June 1967): 59–63; David Morell and Chai-anan Samudavanija, *Political Conflict in Thailand: Reform, Reaction, Revolution* (Cambridge: Oelgeschlager, Gunn & Hain, 1981); Prakan Klinfung, *Tam Roi Phrayukhonlabat: Kansadet Phraratchadamnoen Chonabot Kap Kantotan Communit* [In His Majesty's Footsteps: Royal Visits to the Provincial Areas and Anticommunism], *Fa Diew Kan* 6, no. 4 (October–December 2008): 176–212; Vasit Dejkunjorn, *In His Majesty's Footsteps: A Personal Memoir* (Bangkok: Heaven Lake Press, 2006; original in Thai); and finally, with much appreciation to Sinae Hyun and her "Indigenizing the Cold War: Postcolonial Nation-Building and Spread of Royalist Nationalism by the Border Patrol Police of Thailand, 1945–1980", (PhD dissertation, University of Wisconsin-Madison, 2014); see especially sub-chapter 3.3, "Rise of the Indigenous Cold War Patrons".
6. See Thak Chaloemtiarana, *Thailand: The Politics of Despotic Paternalism*, Chs 3–5.
7. Charnvit Kasetsiri, "The First Phibun Regime and Its Involvement in WWII", *Journal of the Siam Society* 62, no. 2 (July 1974): 25–88. See also Benjamin A. Batson, "The Fall of the Phibun Government: 1944", *Journal of the Siam Society* 62, no. 2 (July 1974): 89–120.
8. See Thanet Aphornsuwan, "The United States and the Coming of the Coup of 1947 in Siam", *Journal of the Siam Society* 75 (1987): 187–208 and his revised version in Thai, "Khon Cha Thueng Ratthaprahan 2490 nai sayam", *Sinlapawatthanatham* 35, no. 10 (August 2014): 88–113. It was generally accepted that the authoritative new 1947 constitution was drawn up and

hidden under a red water jar or traditional Thai ceramic container to hold water during the summer season, by a coup member named Colonel Kat Katsongkhram (Luang Kat Songkhramchai or Thian Kengradomying).

Colonel Kat (1893–1967) had a colourful political life. He was among the Siamese revolution of 1932 promoters and was wounded in the fight suppressing the 1933 royalist rebellion. He was promoted in the military during the Second World War and joined Pridi's Free Thai movement. After the war, he was associated with left-leaning bureaucrat politicians and was a member of Adul's Trade Union Party (Sahacheep). After the death of King Ananda, he switched sides again and became vocal against Pridi, accusing him of regicide in the tragic death of King Ananda, an allegation to which King Bhumibol did not lend credence.

Kat was deputy head under Phin in staging the Siamese *coup d'état* of 1947. His so-called red jar constitution was actually drawn up by the two royalists Seni and Kukrit Pramoj. In 1948, he staged another coup, forcing the Democrat leader Khung Aphaiwongs from office. Finally, in 1950, he ran into trouble with Phibun and Phao, who arrested him on charges of plotting against the government and sent him into exile in Hong Kong. He lived there for seven years, only to return when Phibun left after the 1957 coup. His final army rank was Lieutenant General, and he died in 1967 at age seventy-four. See his cremation volume *Nangsue Nai Ngan Phra Ratcha Than Ploeng Sop Phol Tho Kat Katsongkhram*, 20 April 1967; see Yuad Lertrit's obituary in the cremation volume of *Khemmachat Bunyaratphan*, 25 February 1995. See also Theerat Pulthuam's cremation volume, *Prawat Khana Phukokan Plianplaeng Kan Pokkhrong 24 Mithunayon 2475* [Biographies of the 24 June 1932 promoters], at Wat Sraket, Bangkok, March 1996.

9. In his memoir *Attachiwaprawat* (Autobiography, 1974), with second edition serving as his cremation volume, Prince Dhani, the then regent, declared that the military sent its representatives to him on the night of the 29 November 1951 coup, asking him to sign the abrogation of the 1949 constitution. The military explained that with this constitution, the government would lack power to defeat the Communists. Dhani refused and asked them to wait for the king to arrive in three days' time, on 2 December. In the event, the military claimed that the Regent had agreed with them and proceeded to declare suspension of the 1949 constitution in his name. They brought back the 1932 charter with some modifications in 1952 to fit their needs and facilitate their grasp on power. See Dhani, p. 146. Also, Paul M. Handley, *The King Never Smiles: A Biography of Thailand's Bhumibol Adulyadej* (London: Yale University Press, 2006), Ch 6.

10. See the Introduction of Suchit Bunbongkarn, *The Military in Thailand Politics 1981–1986* (Singapore: Institute of Southeast Asian Studies, 1987).

11. See *Nangsue Nai Ngan Phra Ratchathan Ploeng Sop Pholrua Tri Luang Sangwon Yutthakit 2516* [Cremation Volume for Rear Admiral Sangwon Yutthakit], 1973, and *Prawat Khana Phukokan Plianplaeng Kan Pokkhrong 24 Mithunayon 2475* [Biographies of the 24 June 1932 promoters].
12. See Supot Dantrakul, *Khabot 10 Pho.Yo. 2495: Tamnan Khabuankan Ku Chat* [10 November 1952 Rebels: Legend of the National Rescue Movement], 1986; see also Wiwat Khatithamnit, *Khabot Santiphab* [Peace Rebellion] (Bangkok: Khobfai, 1996). This study originated as a Master of Arts thesis at Chulalongkorn University (1989); Sirilak Chantornwong, Takahashi Katsuyuki, Somsak J., and Cholthira Satayawatthana, eds., *Kung Sattawat Khabuankan Santiphab Khamching Keokap Khabot Santiphap: Samnuk Thang Prawattisat Khong Khon Samrun* [Half a Century of the Peace Movement, "Truth" About Peace Rebellion: The Historical Consciousness of Three Generations] (Bangkok: Meak Khao, 2002).
13. Kobkua Suwannathat-Pian, "Memories of My Childhood", in *Recalling Childhood*, edited by Nicholas Tarling (London: Hamilton Books, 2017), p. 173.
14. See David K. Wyatt, *The Politics of Reform in Thailand: Education in the Reign of King Chulalongkorn* (London: Yale University Press, 1969), Ch. 2. See also Charnvit Kasetsiri, "The Front Palace: The Office of the Heir Apparent?", in *The Emergence of Modern States Thailand and Japan*, edited by Carl K. Trocki (Bangkok: Institute of Asian Studies, Chulalongkorn University, 1976).
15. Summary of Road Construction by the Department of Highways:

Year	Distance (km)	Percentage (%)
1959	8,285.347	
1960	8446.707	1.94%
1970	10,401.481	3.14%
1980	28,150.621	170.64%
1990	45,445.042	61.43%
2000	60,788.897	33.76%
2010	67,315.270	10.39%
...	...	...
2013	68,252.688	1.39% (from 2010 to 2013)
1960 and 2013	68,252.688 − 8,446.707 = 59,805.981 km	= 708.03%

Source: Department of Highways (21 July 2014) and *Statistical Yearbook*, Thailand, Number 24/1960, Ministry of National Development State Highway Department.

For railways in Thailand, see R. Ramaer, *Railways of Thailand* (Bangkok: White Lotus, 2009), and Ichiro Kakizaki, *Rails of the Kingdom: The History of Thai Railways* (Bangkok: White Lotus Ltd., 2012). On these three grand tours, the Royal couple had to travel by automobile, train, and airplane. Travelling by auto was still an exception, considering the limited number of highways at the time.

16. The 1954 Ban Pong Fire highlights how King Bhumibol's new monarchy developed in its early stages. The fire broke out on 9 September 1954 and destroyed 800 houses, almost the entire town. Three deaths were recorded, 6,000 people were affected and 60 million baht in damages added up. Three days later, on 12 September, Prime Minister Phibun and his wife visited Ban Pong. Phibun donated 200,000 baht from his own fortune to help the stricken.

    The next day, 13 September, the king and the queen departed from the Royal palace on a private visit to Ban Pong. The king reportedly drove the car himself. When they arrived, a huge crowd gathered to welcome them. The Royal couple drove around to see the damage and the king eventually donated 100,000 baht. On 15 September, Phibun and his wife returned to Ban Pong. This time, he asked his cabinet to approve funding of 2 million baht to assist Ban Pong.

    The whole event was abundantly covered by newspapers, including Kukrit's *Siam Rath*. There were some puzzled remarks from journalists about the role of the king, but the overall impression was highly positive. Whereas the government was seen as doing its duty by offering financial aid to the victims of the fire, the king's unexpected appearance, and the personal nature of the young couple's personally rushing to offer any assistance that they could, deeply impressed local observers and the nation as well. Unlike Phibun's efforts as part of an entire government's bureaucratic reaction to an emergency, albeit with the personal touch of donating money from his pocket, the Royal couple's appearance was seen as an impulsive, good-natured act of benevolence and caring, underlining national solidarity and love of the monarch for his people. See the cremation volume: *Mae Klab Chak Ban Pong Thueng Paknam* [Mother: Back from Ban Pong to Paknam], 2010, Appendix 6.

17. The Buddhist Era in Thailand differs by one year from other Southeast Asian countries. For example, 1957 CE in Thailand is BE 2500, but in Burma and Cambodia, it is written BE 2501.

18. See Kobkua Suwannathat-Pian, *Thailand's Durable Premier: Phibun through Three Decades, 1932–1957*, 1995, see Ch 4.

19. *Nai Luang Kab Prachachon* [The King and the People], printed by Palace Radio Aw Saw on the occasion of the king's seventy-second birthday in 1999.

See p. 38 of the Radio programme. This vast volume of over 1,000 pages is highly informative, with photos and charts fully documenting how Palace Radio Aw Saw became influential among urban dwellers of the 1960s and 1970s, before television took over in the late 1970s.

20. Chanida Chitbundid, *Khrongkan an nueng ma chak phraratchadamri: kan sathapana phraratcha amnat nam nai phrabat somdet phrachao yu hua* [Royal Initiative Projects: Foundation of Royal Hegemony of His Majesty the King] (Bangkok: The Social Sciences and Humanities Textbooks Foundation, 2007). p. 98.

21. See Charnvit Kasetsiri, ed., *Chak 14 Thueng 6 Tula* [From 14 to 6 October], 1998.

22. *Thailand, Statistical Yearbook*, No. 34, 1985–86, p. 535, No. 35, 1987–1988, pp. 136–37.

23. By 2006, the year of the coup which toppled Premier Thaksin Shinawatra, Thailand had 110 universities, state- and privately run, with a total student enrolment of 1,592,600 or 2.53 per cent of a total population of 62,828,700. Thai graduates from 110 universities received diplomas from the hands of the Crown Prince (the future King Vajiralongkorn) and princesses who by this time attend on behalf of King Bhumibol, Rama IX.

    The Crown Prince presided over the ceremonies at Thammasat, the Open University of Sukhothai, and at forty-one Rajabhat universities (upgraded from teacher training colleges and spread across the country) numbering 43 in all.

    Princess Sirindhorn presided at Chulalongkorn University, Srinakharin, Burapha, Naresuan, Mahasarkham, Thaksin, Chiang Mai, Khon Khaen, Mahidol, Ramkhamhaeng, Silapakorn, Nakhon Phanom, King Mongkut's University of Technology, Ubonratchathani, Narathiwat Rajanagarindra Collage of Music, Mae Fah Luang, Suranari, the National Institute of Development and Administration (NIDA), nine Raja Mangala Universities (upgraded from vocational and technical colleges), Phatthanasilp, and Phayao, for a total of thirty-two.

    The youngest princess, Chulaborn, presided over Kasetsart, Maejo, Songkhla Nagarindra, Walailak, and seventeen campuses of the Institute of Physical Education, for 21 in all. For Chulalongkorn University, see Chulasamphan, 41:25, 20 July 2541.

24. See *Kung sattawat munnithi Ananda Mahidol* [Half a Century of the Ananda Mahidol Foundation] (Bangkok: Chomrom, 2005).

CHAPTER FIVE

The Princess Mother and the New Monarchy

My good people (khon di)? It must be one who does not lie, does not flatter, does not envy, does not deceive, and does not have mad ambition, but does his best. In the realm of morality ...

The Princess Mother

Somdet Phra Srinagarindra Boromarajajonani (Sangwan; 1900–95)

In the history of Thailand or old Siam, no mother of any king played a more important role in national affairs than Somdet Phra Srinagarindra Boromarajajonani. She was the mother of two monarchs, King Ananda (1925–46) and King Bhumibol (1927–2016). A self-reliant, highly independent woman, she is among the most flamboyant characters of twentieth-century Thailand. Her strong willpower and resolve arguably played a role in a historic battle against the spectre of Communism in the Kingdom.

Best known as Somdet Ya, the Royal Grandmother, or Princess Mother, her original name as a commoner was Sangwan. By the middle of the 1960s, at the height of the Cold War in Asia, the Princess Mother had become a leading national figure.

In 1964, she returned from Switzerland to live permanently in Thailand. She was sixty-four years old, and her nation had become a staunch ally of the United States of America. In that same year, Prime Minister Field Marshal Thanom Kittikachorn strongly supported the US Congressional resolution on the Gulf of Tonkin incident.[1]

The Gulf of Tonkin incident was an international confrontation that led to the United States engaging more directly in the Vietnam War. It involved a confrontation on 2 August 1964 and a claimed or presumed confrontation two days later between ships of North Vietnam and the United States in the waters of the Gulf of Tonkin. In this incident which occurred in a medium-sized gulf at the northwestern portion of the South China Sea, located off the coasts of Tonkin (northern Vietnam) and South China, the original American report blamed North Vietnam for both incidents.

Although later informed reports discounted the veracity of the second incident, it was used at the time by the US State Department and other government personnel to justify an escalation by the United States to a state of war against North Vietnam.

On Sunday, 2 August 1964, the destroyer USS *Maddox* claimed to have been attacked by North Vietnamese Navy torpedo boats. In response to the two reported incidents, the US Congress passed the Gulf of Tonkin Resolution, granting President Lyndon B. Johnson authority to assist any Southeast Asian country whose government was considered to be jeopardized by "communist aggression".

The resolution would provide legal justification for President Lyndon B. Johnson to deploy US conventional forces and begin open warfare against North Vietnam. As the war in Vietnam burgeoned menacingly, the Maoist Cultural Revolution was also growing in China. And the Communist Party of Thailand (CPT) was redirecting its struggle to rural areas in the North and the Northeast.

Before the Princess Mother, other strong women had made their mark in Thai-Siamese history, for example, King Chulalongkorn's Queen Saovabha (1864–1919), who was highly esteemed. A principal consort of Chulalongkorn, she was also the mother of two monarchs: King Vajiravudh (1910–25) and King Prajadhipok (1925–35).

Queen Saovabha was accorded a supreme title as Queen Mother Sri Patcharindra and became active to develop modern efforts at social work like the Thai Red Cross Society, which was established in 1893 and quickly became one of the major humanitarian organizations in Thailand. Queen

Saovabha likewise founded schools for girls, which were referred to as Saovabha Schools and Rajini or Queen's Schools, starting in 1904.

In 1910, she was honoured with a new title as the princess mother, Somdet Phra Phanpi Luang or the great thousand years, probably borrowing from Imperial China. Thus, Queen Saovabha became the first queen regent in Thai history, serving as regent when King Chulalongkorn travelled to Europe.

The second queen regent in Thai history would be Queen Sirikit, so named in 1956. And since 2020 her grand title was Phra borom ratcha chonni phanpi luang [Great mother the grand thousand years], likely inspired probably borrowed from the titles for empress dowagers or *huang tai hou* of China. Examples included Empress Dowager Cixi (1835–1908) or Empress Dowager Longyu, who would abdicate on behalf of Emperor Puyi, the renowned Last Emperor of China, in 1912.

However, unlike Bhumibol's Princess Mother, Saovabha's activities did not extend across the nation. Instead, her work was mostly limited to Bangkok and a few other urban areas.

Somdet Phra Srinagarindra Boromarajajonani was born ten years before the death of King Chulalongkorn, on 21 October 1900. She was ninety-five years old when she died, one year before King Bhumibol's Golden Jubilee in 1996 (*kanchana phisek*), and two years before the 1997 economic crash in Southeast Asia, known in Thailand as the Tom Yam Kung crisis.

Her remarkable story may be divided into three parts: 1900 to 1935, starting with her humble birth up to the point where she became the Princess Mother when her son Ananda was crowned king. The second part starts in 1935 and ends in 1964, including the tragic years of the Second World War, the death of King Ananda in 1946, and the early years of the reign of her son Bhumibol who acceded to the throne as Rama IX.

During these two eras, the Princess Mother lived in Europe and America for almost half of the sixty-four years. She returned to live permanently in Thailand in 1964, a time when the Cold War was intensifying on the eastern border. The final portion of her life, from 1964 to 1995, featured her activism in the fields of social welfare, health services, rural development and national security.

This was when she became popularly known as Somdet Ya, or Royal Grandmother, and Mae Fah Luang, or Heavenly Royal Mother. Whereas the King and Queen of the Ninth Reign were seen as father and mother of the people and the Thai nation, the Princess Mother had become the grandmother of them all.[2]

She was born Sangwan Talapat to a middle-class Sino-Thai family. Her father, Chu Chukramol, was a goldsmith working in the Thonburi area of Bangkok west of the Chao Phraya River. Her parents had four children, of which the first two died at a young age. The Princess Mother lost her father and mother when she was three and nine years old, respectively.

Her family must have had good connections with members of the royal family because, in 1908, she entered a traditional patron-client relationship, *thawai tua* (given oneself to), with Princess Valaya (1884–1938). The princess was the forty-third child of King Chulalongkorn; she was also an older sister of Prince Mahidol (1892–1929) who later became the Princess Mother's husband and father of King Rama VIII and King Rama IX.

Thereafter, Sangwan received a solid Western-style education at two recently established Bangkok centres of education for girls, Suksanari School and Satriwithaya School, established in 1900 and 1910, respectively.

In 1913, she was admitted to nursing and midwife training courses at the Faculty of Medicine, Siriraj Hospital. This new and modern hospital and medical science centre of Siam had been founded by King Chulalongkorn in 1888. It was named after the king's son, Prince Siriraj, who had died at the age of eighteen months from dysentery one year before the hospital opened.

The immediate motivation for the new healthcare centre was provided by the fifth major international outbreak of cholera in the nineteenth century, from 1881 to 1896, termed the fifth cholera pandemic. It spread throughout Asia and Africa, and reached parts of France, Germany, Russia and South America, claiming 90,000 lives in Japan alone between 1887 and 1889.

Due to King Chulalongkorn's adoption of preventive and proactive health policies, subsequent outbreaks of cholera that affected Siam in 1891, 1900, and from 1907 to 1909 were gradually less severe in effect.

With Siriraj Hospital, which would develop into a leading national hospital and medical school, the policy was no longer to wait for outbreaks of disease before making curative attempts. Anticipating future health issues became the forward-looking approach.

The development of Siriraj Hospital was accelerated by the presence of an American Protestant missionary, Dr George Bradley McFarland (1866–1942). Born in Bangkok to a missionary couple, McFarland graduated with medical and dental degrees from American universities before returning to Siam for the remainder of his life.

Dr McFarland produced many translations into the Thai language of essential medical texts, in addition to revising a pioneering Siamese-English dictionary first published by his father.

For several decades thereafter, the Siamese government, through the tireless efforts of HRH Prince Mahidol, the father of modern medicine and public health of Thailand, felt a strong need to modernize Siriraj Hospital as well as the medical school and its medical curriculum.

Thus, the Rockefeller Foundation was called upon to help revise and improve medical teaching in 1923. The foundation sent Professor Errett Cyril Albritton, an American research physiologist and medical administrator, to the medical school to improve instruction methods in physiology.

Professor Albritton revised the content of the physiology course to include not just physiology, but also pharmacology and biochemistry. He also established a physiology laboratory, thereby adding a laboratory course to the medical training curriculum.

Apart from Siriraj Hospital's link to Prince Mahidol, who worked as a medical trainee there briefly, the Princess Mother and her only daughter, Princess Galyani, were hospitalized and died there in 1995 and 2008, respectively. Siriraj was also the residence of King Bhumibol from September 2009 to August 2013. He entered the hospital for treatment of a respiratory condition. In October 2014, King Bhumibol would receive gall bladder surgery at Siriraj and died there on 13 October 2016.

Before Siriraj Hospital had developed into a major institution, education for the elite was seen as a matter of overseas training.

In 1917, Sangwan Talapat was sent to further her studies in the United States, as part of a group comprising another female student and eighteen young men. This was one of the largest groups of Thai students ever sent to the United States for higher education, as the previous preference had been to choose Europe as an educational destination for privileged young people.

However, that same year, Siam had declared war against Austria-Hungary and Germany on 22 July, three months after America's war declaration on 6 April. The Great War in Europe was seen by King Vajiravudh as an opportunity to create and promote Siamese nationalism. He aligned Siam with the Allied Powers and expelled German and Austrian officials from the Railway Department and Siam Commercial Bank. He also put the properties of the Central Powers under a Siamese government protectorate. Participation in the war allowed Siam to later negotiate with the Western powers as a junior partner.

So, amid these international developments, Sangwan spent one year in Berkeley, California, learning English and becoming acquainted with American lifestyles before travelling to the East Coast to attend nursing school. There she met Prince Mahidol, who earned a certificate in public health from Harvard in 1921 and later returned to Boston to study at the Harvard Medical School, where he earned his MD cum laude in 1928.

Later celebrated as Thailand's "Father of Public Health and Modern Medicine, throughout his studies, Prince Mahidol preferred to be known to his classmates as Mr Songkhla and did not reveal that he had royal status. His official name was Mahidol Adulyadej, Prince of Songkhla. He would later be accorded the title Mahitala Dhibesra Adulyadej Vikrom, the Prince Father.

During his time at Harvard, the prince negotiated an agreement with the Rockefeller Foundation to provide funding for education in medicine, nursing and public health in Siam. His educational belief, as he once stated, was that "true success is not in the learning, but in its application to the benefit of mankind."

Sangwan became engaged to Prince Mahidol and the couple returned to Siam in 1920 to attend the funeral of Queen Saovabha. While there, they married under the royal blessing of his half-brother King Vajiravudh at Sapathum Palace.

Between 1920 and 1928 the couple travelled frequently between Siam, Europe, and the United States. After Prince Mahidol received his Certificate in Public Health in 1921, he went to Edinburgh on vacation, but his duties in representing the Siamese government in negotiations with the Rockefeller Foundation for donations and technical assistance to improve his country's medical and public health education led him to London.

There his first child, Princess Galyani Vadhana, was born in 1923. He returned to Siam that year to assume the job of Director-General of the University Department in the Ministry of Education. Apart from administrative duties, he also taught preclinical medical students at the Royal Medical College.

In 1925 Prince Mahidol went to Heidelberg, Germany for medical treatment for a kidney ailment. Ananda, the couple's first son, was born there in 1925. The family returned to Harvard University, where the prince studied medicine, and it was here that Bhumibol, their second son, was born in 1927 in Cambridge, Massachusetts.

When he returned to Siam in December 1928, Prince Mahidol promptly established scholarships for students of medicine, nursing, and public health. He intended to return to Siriraj Hospital to serve his internship. However, it was felt that his royal rank made this unsuitable.

Instead, Prince Mahidol chose to be an intern at a more egalitarian-minded hospital, the McCormick Hospital Chiang Mai, which had been founded in 1889 by Presbyterian missionaries.

For three weeks, he worked there tirelessly for patients who affectionately referred to him as *Mho Chao Fa* or Doctor Prince. Unfortunately, his kidney ailment flared up again, and after visiting Bangkok to attend the funeral of an uncle, Prince Mahidol was unable to return to Chiang Mai. His health continued to fail, and he died on 24 September 1929, aged thirty-seven.

After the death of her husband, Sangwan and her three children continued to live in Bangkok for three more years until shortly after the Siamese revolution of 1932, when the absolute monarchy was abolished. Like many senior members of the royal family, Sangwan decided to move to Europe. She chose Switzerland, a favourite vacation site of her late husband's.

By contrast, other princesses, princes and aristocrats preferred to relocate to monarchies such as the United Kingdom or European colonies in Penang, Singapore, Saigon, Phnom Penh and Bandung. In April 1933, Mom Sangwan and her children duly departed for Switzerland.

After King Prajadhipok abdicated in 1935, he was replaced by Ananda Mahidol, who became Rama VIII at age nine. The King and his Queen Consort, Rambai Barni, were childless, so other successors had to be sought.

The 1924 Palace Law of Succession promulgated by King Vajiravudh (Rama VI) had placed Sangwan's two sons prominently in the line of succession. Incidentally, it was also Vajiravudh, who had studied and travelled abroad extensively, who initiated the custom of retroactively attributing numbers to previous kings as Rama I, Rama II, and so on. His motive was to make things easier for foreigners who were sure to have difficulties remembering exotic Siamese names.

As a mother to a family which had also had extensive experience outside of their homeland, Sangwan saw her life dramatically altered after Ananda's accession. Then aged thirty-five, instead of Mom Sangwan,[3] she would eventually become known as Somdet Phra Srinagarindra Boromarajajonani or Princess Mother of a King.

Over the next twenty-nine years, from 1935 to 1964, the Princess Mother spent most of her time in Switzerland, during an era of uncertainty. The royal family, consisting of a mother and three children, lived in Lausanne throughout the Second World War.

Back in Thailand, the Phibun government had allied itself with Imperial Japan and on 25 January 1942, declared war on Great Britain and the United States. Three years later, as soon as the war ended, Pridi Banomyong issued a Declaration of Peace on 16 August 1945. Formerly Finance Minister in Phibun's government, Pridi was at the same time Regent on behalf of King Ananda and leader of the underground anti-Japanese Free Thai Movement, in a dizzying range of responsibilities.

Pridi claimed that Phibun's declaration of war was null and void, and Thailand immediately returned territories that had been seized from British

Burma and Malaya. The new Thai government, strongly backed by the United States, was ready to negotiate a peace settlement with British and French forces.

Four months later, on 5 December 1945, the Princess Mother and her two sons were flown back to Bangkok by the British Air Force. Her elder son, King Ananda, had just turned twenty. His duty was to preside over Siam's problematic transition to peace.

In Bangkok, the king received British troops and Lord Louis Mountbatten (1900–79), Supreme Allied Commander South East Asia (SACSEA). The British unfurled an impressive military parade in front of the Grand Palace, presided over by the young king and the British Lord.

Mountbatten would later possibly overstate in his diary for 1946 the stress this represented on the new king, whom he described as a "frightened, short-sighted boy, his sloping shoulders and thin chest be hung with gorgeous diamond-studded decorations, altogether a pathetic and lonely figure". At a public event, Mountbatten added, King Ananda's "nervousness increased to such an alarming extent, that I came very close to support him in case he passed out".

Whatever Mountbatten's impression may have been for six months the king, always accompanied by his mother and brother, valiantly maintained a busy schedule. Ananda attended numerous Buddhists and royal ceremonies, receiving members of the cabinet and armed forces. He opened parliament twice and appointed new prime ministers: Khuang Aphaiwong on 31 January 1946 and Pridi Banomyong on 24 March 1946.

He also promulgated a new constitution on 9 May 1946, ceremonially attended two trials of the Courts of Justice, and presented diplomas to small groups of graduates at Chulalongkorn and Thammasat Universities.

Probably his most impactful initiative was to visit Sampheng, a historic neighbourhood and market in Bangkok's Chinatown. He aimed to boost the morale of the local Chinese population, who had suffered persecution under Phibun's xenophobic Thai nationalistic programmes, as well as from the wartime Japanese Occupation.

Therefore, the Chinese residents of Sampheng in Samphanthawong District were much relieved at the news of the Allied victory. This also represented a victory for the Kuomintang (KMT, or Nationalist Chinese Party), as a result of which China was granted sovereignty of Taiwan after the Japanese were defeated in 1945. The KMT received the Japanese surrender, and the island became part of the Nationalist China of Chiang Kai-shek, at least for the time being.

Meanwhile, in late September 1945, a three-day riot broke out, known as the Yaowarat Incident (Yaowarat is the Thai term for Chinatown). The incident began as a clash between Chinese demonstrators preparing to celebrate the anniversary of the establishment of the Republic of China, and Thai police, who demanded that demonstrators display the Thai national flag along with the national flag of the Republic of China.

Violence broke out, and the Thai military and police killed seven Chinese demonstrators. Shops and houses were looted for a week before local Chinese representatives and Thai authorities were able to bring the situation under control.[4] Eight months after the incident, on 3 June 1946, King Ananda and his brother Bhumibol visited and met Chinese residents.

This noteworthy encounter occurred a mere six days before the tragic and still-unsolved death of Ananda on 9 June. Two months later, on 19 August, the new king and his mother departed again for Switzerland. Bhumibol would not return until 1950, while the Princess Mother stayed away even longer.

As for the third part of her life and work, the Princess Mother returned to live permanently in Thailand in 1964. Until her death in 1995, she participated in charitable work alongside the king, queen, royal children, and the military, especially the Border Patrol Police (BPP), a Thai paramilitary police under the jurisdiction of the Royal Thai Police, responsible for border security and counterinsurgency.

The efforts of the royal family in the 1960s and the 1970s to bolster goodwill for the monarchy among rural communities complimented the anti-Communist mission of the Thai military and Americans in mainland Southeast Asia.

To fully understand the importance of the Princess Mother's goodwill activism and charitable efforts, it is necessary to look at the context of the national struggle over what appeared to successive regimes to be a threat from the burgeoning Thai Communist Party, as well as Communism elsewhere in Southeast Asia.

Confronting National Peril?

In 1964, barely less than one year that Princess Mother returned to Thailand,[5] the Gulf of Tonkin Incident erupted, an international confrontation that led to the United States engaging more directly in the Vietnam War.

On 2 August, the destroyer USS *Maddox*, while performing a signals intelligence patrol, was claimed to have been approached by three North Vietnamese Navy torpedo boats of the 135th Torpedo Squadron. The North Vietnamese boats attacked with torpedoes and machine gun fire.

The USS *Maddox* launched a sea battle, which left one US aircraft and three North Vietnamese torpedo boats damaged, with four North Vietnamese sailors killed and six wounded. There were no US casualties.

A second Gulf of Tonkin incident was alleged by the National Security Agency to have occurred on 4 August 1964, but this later proved to be a myth.

Nevertheless, the two incidents led to a US Congressional resolution that enabled intensification of American involvement in Vietnam. President Lyndon Baines Johnson was granted the authority to conduct military operations in Southeast Asia without the benefit of a declaration of war.

The resolution gave Johnson approval "to take all necessary steps, including the use of armed force, to assist any member or protocol state of the Southeast Asia Collective Defense Treaty requesting assistance in defense of its freedom".

The Thai government of Field Marshal Thanom, succeeding Sarit in 1963, fully supported American actions, leading to enhanced US military presence in Thailand, as well as the construction of naval and military bases. Soon, Thai soldiers were sent into combat alongside Americans in Vietnam in 1966, along with troops from South Korea, Australia and New Zealand.

Meanwhile, Thailand was still ruled by martial law. No political parties were allowed, and no elections were held. The Communist Party of Thailand (CPT) had aligned itself with Maoism and changed its focus from urban to rural areas. It slowly reinvented itself in the countryside, especially in the North and the Northeast, and partly in the South.

Compared to other Southeast Asian countries, leftist ideologies and organizations occurred rather belatedly in Thailand. The Communist Party of Indonesia (PKI) was founded in 1914, the Indochinese Communist Party and the Communist Party of Malaya were formed in 1930.[6] Meanwhile, Thailand successfully pushed back against communism, and immediately after the Siamese revolution of 1932, an anti-Communist law was passed.

Pridi Banomyong, a French-educated member of the People's Party, was accused of being a Communist. Although he was officially cleared of the charge, it would remain a burden for him. Therefore, communist activities remained mostly underground from the 1920s to the end of the 1930s and were mostly confined to people of Chinese or Vietnamese origins.

Only in 1941, with the Second World War raging, was the CPT established. At the end of the conflict, the anti-Communist legislation was suspended as the postwar government yielded to demands by the Soviet Union, one of five permanent members of the United Nations Security Council.

From 1946 to 1952, the small CPT was legally recognized and could operate openly in urban areas, especially Bangkok. In 1946, Prasert Sapsunthorn (1913–94) born in Kanchanadit District, Surat Thani Province, became the first and the only Communist representative elected to the National Assembly.

But with the return of a military dictatorship, a new anti-Communist law was issued in 1952 and the CPT was forced underground. In the late 1950s and early 1960s, hundreds of its leaders and sympathizers were arrested and jailed at Bang Kwang Central Prison in Nonthaburi Province. Even today, Bang Kwang remains the site of the men's death row and execution chamber of Thailand.

Many leading Communists were summarily executed by Sarit. Among them were politician and democracy activist Khrong Chandawong and his associate Thongphan Sutthimat, who were publicly executed by firing squad in Sawang Daen Din district, Sakon Nakhon Province on 31 May 1961.

Khrong's last words would be cited in later contexts: "May dictatorship be wrecked. May democracy flourish."

Another well-known case was that of Ruam Wongphan, a Chinese-trained Thai Communist and member of the CPT Central Politburo from Suphan Buri Province. He was executed in Bangkok on 24 April 1962.

Meanwhile, in 1962, The Voice of the People of Thailand (VOPT), a CPT Thai-language radio station, was established in Yunnan, southern China. The party launched the Thai Patriotic Front in early 1965 and proclaimed that an "era of armed struggle had begun".

The first gunshot of the reported struggle was fired on 7 August 1965, supposedly in Renu Nakhon District of Nakhon Phanom Province in the Northeast, on the banks of the Mekong across from Thakhek in Laos. The CPT called this *wan siang puen taek*, or the day of the first shot.

While in its early stages, CPT leadership mainly consisted of urban Sino-Thais, by the late 1950s the party was joined by rural local leaders from the North, Northeast, and South.

By the 1960s, it had even attracted hill tribes like the Hmong. By this time, it was estimated that the CPT had roughly 1,200 armed fighters under its command.[7] Despite these meagre numbers, the Thai and American militaries used harsh measures to suppress leftist activism and ideas.

While the CPT stepped up activities in the North and Northeast, the king, queen and Princess Mother became actively engaged regionally. During the twenty-one years between the CPT's Third and Fourth Party Congresses in 1961 and 1982, respectively, four features of the party became prominent: First, it sided with Communist China and Maoism rather than with the Soviet Union, obtaining its support and backing from Yunnan and Laos.

As mentioned, a short-wave radio station had been established in Kunming. By the early 1970s, the programme had received more attention, especially among educated young people in urban areas. Although the CPT was strongly opposed to American and Thai intervention in Vietnam and Laos, it did not align itself with Vietnamese Communists. As early as 1966, relations with the Communist Party of Vietnam (CPV) became frayed, after the CPT blamed the CPV for failing to take a clear pro-China stance.

Secondly, the CPT took up armed struggle with guerrilla warfare strategies, or *pa lom muang* (jungle surrounding the cities). The CPT probably borrowed this phrase from the Chinese Communist phrase *nóng cūn bāo wéi chéng shì* or the countryside enclosing the cities.[8]

From this term, a popular expression among idealistic students during the 1970s was derived: *khao pa* or going to the jungle.

In 1965, the Thai Patriotic Front was established and in 1969 the Supreme Command of the People's Liberation Army was founded. From its stronghold in the Northeast, it spread over the mountainous areas of the North bordering Laos and close to Yunnan. It also established a presence in the South.

Thirdly, by then the CPT leadership was increasingly recruited from among Sino-Thai party members rather than ethnic Chinese, though many of the former still retained a sense of cultural Chineseness.

A partial list of these activists would include the poet, short-story writer, and literary critic Atsani Phonlajan, who published under the pen name *Nai Phi* or Master of the Spirits such incisive works as *Intharayut*, a critique of Thai literature and myth. Then there was Udom Sisuwan, who produced a chronicle, *Banjong Banjerdsilp*.

Among several other left-leaning authors of polemic texts, novels, and translations was Pleung Wannasri, a respected poet who signed his verse *Nai Sang*. Both Atsani and Pleung's pen names translate as Specter, and both were prominent Thammasat University students in the 1950s.

Thong Jamsri, who edited the first underground newspaper *Mahachon* or *The Public*, first printed in March 1942, died in 2019 at age ninety-eight.

And although he did not survive long enough to become a political leader, Jit Phumisak (1930–66) a philologist, historian, poet and songwriter, wrote the influential *Chom na khong sakdina thai nai patchuban* [The Real Face of Thai Feudalism Today], 1957.[9]

Jit, sometimes described as the Che Guevara of Thailand for his charisma, was killed by local residents near the village Nong Kung in Waritchaphum District, although published reports have alleged that Jit was executed by government officials near the Phu Phan Mountains shortly after being released from a jail sentence.

In the mid-1970s Jit's powerful writings were rediscovered by progressive students, as well as those by Atsani and Pleung.

Those who survived were active CPT members from the 1960s to its decline at the end of the 1970s.[10]

While the first Party Secretary-General was Chinese, the second was a Sino-Thai from Khorat. His name was Song Nopphakhun (known as Comrade Ba or Prasong Wongwiwat. Song had a Khorat Thai mother and a Teochew father of Chinese origin who ran a rice mill in Buriram.

He was sent to a Chinese school in Bangkok and in 1934 joined the Communist Party of Siam, a precursor of the CPT. As a young man during the Second World War, Song fought underground against the Japanese Occupant. He wrote for Thai and Chinese political newspapers and claimed to be in contact with Pridi's Free Thai Movement.

Song was a persuasive propagandist, drawing well-educated mainstream Thais to the CPT. To make the CPT more ethnic Thai, Song stepped aside from a leadership role, alleging health problems, and a third secretary-general, Charoen Wanngam, was chosen.

Of all the mainstream Thais who joined the CPT, one of the most noteworthy and complex cases was Lieutenant Colonel Phayom Chulanont, known as Comrade Khamtan. Born to an aristocratic family in Phet Buri Province, Phayom graduated in 1931 from a military academy and married a daughter of Phraya Si Sitthisongkhram (born Din Tharap), deputy commander of the royalist troops during the failed Boworadet Rebellion of 1933, led by Prince Boworadet (1877–1947).

Phayom's son General Surayud Chulanont would be a future prime minister from 2006 to 2008, after the 2006 Thai *coup d'état* against the elected caretaker government of Prime Minister Thaksin Shinawatra.

During the Second World War, Phayom was on active duty on the Thai borders in the east, north and south. In 1947, he was elected to the National Assembly, the same year he joined the coup-makers Phibun and Phin in their move against the Pridi-Thamrong government.

The following year, he collaborated in the failed Siamese *coup d'état* of 1948, which forced him to go underground. Phayom probably became an exile in Beijing, where he joined the CPT.

In 1958, he returned to Thailand to run in the general election, unsuccessfully. During the ensuing regime of Field Marshal Sarit, Phayom decided to go to the jungle, where he rose in the ranks of the CPT People's Liberation Army. His area of operation was the mountainous Nan province bordering Saiyabuli Province in northwest Laos, near Luang Namtha, a province of Laos in the country's north. In 1980, Phayom was hospitalized and died in Peking at the age of seventy-one.[11]

That such an establishment figure decided to take to the forests and follow his unexpected trajectory indicates the unsettled nature of the era, which made the stability and patriotism exemplified in Royal Household activities all the more essential to the Thai people. If Phayom could fulfil such an unusual destiny, it might seem possible for any number of well-born and otherwise accomplished Thais to do so.

How important to have a counterexample that showed the monarchy as a viable and key element of Thai national development, to oppose what was seen by the military as an insidious Communist threat.

An official count of casualties in the war between the CPT and the Thai government from the 1960s to the 1980s listed 10,504 fatalities and 17,771 injured. The CPT suffered 4,588 deaths and 1,830 wounded, while the government lost 5,916 soldiers, with an additional 15,941 wounded.

The numbers were published by General Saiyud Kerdphol, Supreme Commander of the Royal Thai Armed Forces from 1981 to 1983. His statistics excluded civilian victims.[12]

More reason to understand the Princess Mother's valiant participation in the Thai state's fight against the spread of communism in the provinces. Her energetic social work and dedication were legendary, exemplified by a story about her ascending to the top of Doi Inthanon Mountain in Chiang Mai in 1964.

At 2,565 metres, Doi Inthanon is Thailand's highest peak. The area surrounding it was once rich in teak wood, as royal property claimed by rulers of Chiang Mai and by extension, by the Chakri kings. Its name is in tribute to the last semi-independent Chiang Mai king, Inthawichayanon (born Prince Inthanon), who reigned as Seventh Ruler of Chiang Mai and Ruler of Lanna from 1870 until his death in 1897.[13]

In the 1960s and 1970s, Chiang Mai developed from a traditional small town to a bustling northern capital. Its location was ideal in terms of cultural, climatic and strategic matters. The city is close to the Golden Triangle between Myanmar, Laos, and Xishuangbanna, an autonomous prefecture for Dai people in the extreme south of Yunnan Province, China, bordering both Myanmar and Laos.

In addition to the 33rd Military Circle Kawila Camp located in Chiang Mai City Municipality, the region also hosts the 7th Infantry Division, an Alpine Infantry division of the Royal Thai Army, currently part of the Third Army Area.

The 7th Infantry Division supervises the northern provinces of Chiang Mai, Chiang Rai, Lamphun, Lampang, Phayao and Mae Hong Son. As mentioned, Bhubing Palace (Phuphing), King Bhumibol's royal winter residence, the first such built outside Bangkok, was constructed here in 1961.

The palace is located 1,300 metres above sea level in a hilly area surrounded by forests, in proximity to villages of ethnic Karen, Hmong, Lahu, Yao, and Lawa people. Three years later, Chiang Mai University, the first major Thai university to be founded outside of Bangkok, opened its doors. As an institution of higher learning, it became especially renowned for medical and anthropological studies.

In addition to Bangkok and Hua Hin, Chiang Mai and Bhubing Palace became a focal point for the royal family to launch social and welfare development projects. Chiang Mai achieved international prominence due to its cultural attractions, as well as the fact that King Bhumibol entertained foreign heads of state at Bhubing Palace.

In 1962, the King and Queen of Denmark were the first royal guests to stay at the palace, followed by many world leaders and their families: Juliana of the Netherlands and her consort in 1963; Baudouin of Belgium and his wife, Queen Fabiola, in 1964; President Ferdinand Marcos of the Philippines and his wife Imelda Marcos in 1968; and Elizabeth II, Queen of the United Kingdom and Prince Philip, Duke of Edinburgh in 1972.

Until the late 1990s, King Bhumibol continued to visit Bhubing Palace annually, mainly during the cool months from January to March, before confining himself to Bangkok and Hua Hin.

On 26 April 1964, when the Princess Mother reached the top of Doi Inthanon, the mountain still represented rough terrain.[14] No paved road led to the top and walking and climbing were the sole means of ascent. However, the event was well organized, and the Princess Mother was accompanied by a party of BPP.

At the foot of the mountain, Hmong and Karen people awaited to accompany and assist her climb. At the time, Thai and American authorities feared that ethnic minorities in the mountains might be receptive to communism.

To demonstrate official benevolence and draw them into the orbit of the state, the Princess Mother handed blankets and first aid medicine to these representatives of the hill tribes. She stayed overnight on the mountain. Upon her descent, the king and queen arrived with their entourage to greet her at the foot of Doi Inthanon. The king reportedly played his saxophone to celebrate the happy occasion.

In official palace history, and to the wider public, the event was seen as a turning point for the Princess Mother; it marked a break from her earlier urban-centred, traditional roles in social welfare and health care. Instead, she began to embody a more proactive approach to development and reform that proved a powerful response to the potential enticement of communism.

Her new activities aimed at rural development in the hill areas and eventually turned her into a leading patron of three major efforts: medical volunteer work, the BPP, and primary schooling for children of the northern ethnic minorities.

Upon her first visit, it was reported that she witnessed the hardship and material scarcity suffered by the minority groups, particularly the apparent neglect on the part of the central government.

This clearly differentiated the royal household from whichever government might be in power at the moment and reminded the Thai people that monarchical constancy was a precious attribute for improving the lot of those living in the kingdom.

The following year, the Princess Mother climbed the mountain again. This time she brought two medical doctors along with her and began to offer treatment to the hill tribes. In 1969, she established a mobile medical volunteer unit known as the Princess Mother's Medical Volunteers (PMMV or in Thai language, *po oo so wo*).

Just as lastingly, the image of a diminutive woman in her sixties dauntlessly scaling a mountain to show solidarity with a remote population touched the hearts of her compatriots. An athletic achievement, her ascent, echoing the tradition of Buddhist pilgrimages for an added aura of sanctity, was even more a demonstration of grit and determination that set an example for an entire nation.

In this context, it is important to note that this was an era of volunteer work. Founded in 1961, the Peace Corps, an independent agency and volunteer programme run by the US government, was intended to provide international social and economic development assistance. The Peace Corps was a specific response to the Cold War. President John F. Kennedy pointed out that the Soviet Union "had hundreds of men and women, scientists, physicists, teachers, engineers, doctors, and nurses ... prepared to spend their lives abroad in the service of world Communism". The United States lacked any such programme, and Kennedy sought to involve Americans actively in the cause of global democracy, peace, development and freedom.

Peace Corps volunteers have served in Thailand since the programme first sent them out in 1962. They worked on a wide range of projects, teaching American English, physical education and hygiene in Thailand's urban areas. A number would later become experts in Southeast Asian or Thai studies.

In 1966, two years before the PMMV was established, the military regime of Thanom launched its version of the Peace Corps, sending fresh graduates to rural areas around the country. The *asa samak*, or young volunteers, spent time in *khai asa*, or volunteer camps, "helping villagers to help themselves". The work could be dangerous at times.

Dedicated, bright young teachers such as Komol Kheemthong, a Chulalongkorn graduate, and Ratana Sakunthai were shot and killed by Communist insurgents in the South. It was difficult to judge if the achievements of the volunteers justified the risks they took, insofar as the immediate impact of their efforts was unquantifiable.

Nevertheless, the young educated corps members interacted with rural people, conveying the notion that as Komol put it, being a teacher meant helping to create thoughts rather than merely transferring knowledge.

One direct effect of contact with teaching volunteers is that some rural populations became increasingly dissatisfied with the military regime and authoritarian government. This evolution would eventually make possible the 1973 Thai popular uprising.

To avoid duplicating the work of Thai and American volunteers, the PMMV operated primarily along the border of northern Siam which was not already covered by the corps.

To qualify for receiving assistance, areas had to be located in remote and rough terrains with no paved access. Naturally, this put the PMMV in close contact with the BPP as it quickly grew and expanded its coverage of more areas in the Northeast and South.

In 1974, it acquired the status of a foundation, as did most royal projects, receiving 1 million baht as an initial donation from the Princess Mother. Its main office was located at Sra Pathum Palace in downtown Bangkok, where its personnel dressed in uniforms and otherwise comported themselves much like government officials.

The PMMV's high profile attracted considerable funding and assistance from government and private sectors, including foreign aid. Its activities quickly expanded to other border areas in the South. By 1970, it covered thirty-one provinces or 43 per cent of the total area of the country.

By 1995, at the time of the Princess Mother's death, her medical volunteer teams were present in forty-eight provinces, or over 66 per cent of the nation. Her only daughter, Princess Galyani, took up her work until she died in 2008. Since then, the organization has been led by Princess Chulabhorn, King Bhumibol's youngest daughter, with a reduced profile and public standing.

Although a modest growth record continued, with a reported 50,000 PMMV volunteers active in fifty-four provinces by 2011, the organization's heyday was doubtless during the life of the Princess Mother.

The PMMV was especially interesting organizationally and operationally. Groups of volunteer teams made regular visits to border areas, usually on weekends and on an entirely unremunerated basis. By the 1970s, the Princess Mother routinely accompanied the volunteers.

Each team consisted of doctors, nurses, and dentists, mostly drawn from local government hospitals. Each provincial governor would head the overall effort, assisted by the armed forces and BPP. The military and the police would supply logistics such as helicopters, planes and automobiles. Provinces covered by PMMV activities were designated as *changwat po oo so wo* (PMMV provinces). This set-up was strikingly similar to *changwat thahan bok*, or military provinces.[15]

Again, in retrospect, it is difficult to precisely evaluate the success rate of the PMMV. One attempt was made by Arwut Srisukri, a medical professor and a former rector of Chiang Mai University:

> In terms of medical care, I don't think much advance was made. But psychologically, there was considerable advance. [The hill tribes] receive the message that they are not abandoned ... This inspires them to be honest with us and join our national community. And that gives them a morale boost. I think this project has even further value. Ordinary people like ourselves lacked the sophistication to create it. Had the great *somdet* [Princess Mother] not initiated it, we could never have achieved it, even with substantial funding. It was only possible with the great *somdet* as patron...[16]

Since one of its main objectives was to operate only along borders, the PMMV worked symbiotically with the BPP, which oversaw the 4,800 kilometres of land borders in Thailand. Established in 1953 as a paramilitary force, it was heavily supported by the Central Intelligence Agency (CIA) and closely connected to the Remote Area Security Development (RASD) of the United States Operations Mission to Thailand.[17]

The BPP waxed and waned, with its heyday being in the mid-1950s. Shortly thereafter, it was downgraded to the point of being dissolved immediately after Sarit's coup in 1957. However, it made an energetic comeback by the mid-1960s.

Its founder and patron was Police General Phao Sriyanond (1910–60). Phao became one of a powerful triumvirate, alongside Prime Minister

Phibun and Defence Minister Sarit. Phao was director-general of Thailand's national police from 1951 to 1957, and Minister of the Interior until Sarit's coup forced him into exile in Switzerland. There he died in 1960, three years before his rival Sarit.

Phao's Police Department and the BPP were generously backed with American dollars and heavy weaponry when the Cold War heightened, and Thailand became a major front line in mainland Southeast Asia.

The police had their tank unit, and the BPP was supported by regular annual paratroop training for what was known as the BPP Aerial Reinforcement Unit (PARU). Since 1954, the BPP PARU had annually recruited 50 to 100 student trainees.

They were educated in combat skills at King Naresuan Camp, neighbouring Rama VI military camp and near Klai Kangwon Palace. In practice, the BPP was fairly autonomous but retained close links with the military. It also enjoyed a special relationship with the royal family, including the king, queen, and Princess Mother.

The last-mentioned became their patron after Police General Phao left the scene. The BPP combined the functions of a national police force and an army ostensibly fighting external enemies. Whence their slogan: "What neither soldiers nor regular police can do, the BPP can."

Regularly, the BPP gathered information from local authorities, village headmen, and average citizens. Since 1966, it also collaborated closely with the clandestine Communist Suppression Operation Command (CSOC). CSOC had been established in 1965 to combat Communists, left-wing politicians, and students.

After the 1973 Thai popular uprising, CSOC was rejuvenated and retitled Internal Security Operation Command (ISOC). But its function remained more or less the same. Apart from suppressing Communists, the BPP was entrusted with eradicating and preventing the trade in opium and other drugs as well as illegal logging and migration.

Officially, the BPP was confined to border areas, but by the late 1960s, its operations had expanded to urban locations, including Bangkok. Most notable were the BPP offshoots, the Volunteer Defense Corps, or VDC (*Or Sor*, meaning volunteer), and Village Scouts (VS, or *luk sua chaoban*).

The VDC, rural-based and active in the late 1950s and the 1960s, was closely associated with the Ministries of Defense and the Interior. The VS was more urban and Bangkok-oriented, becoming politically instrumental and directly linked with the royal family by the 1970s.

The highest-profile action by the VS was during the 6 October 1976 massacre, where it slaughtered students and other young protestors on the Tha Prachan campus of Thammasat University. Administratively, the VS was attached to the BPP. In practice, however, their status and strength stemmed from royal patronage and their self-proclaimed patriotic mission to defend the national triad of Nation, Religion, and King.[18]

The Princess Mother's aforementioned contacts with the BPP originated during her visits to the Bhubing Palace in Chiang Mai and her expeditions to Doi Inthanon.

As early as in 1962, during her first brief stay at Bhubing, she encountered Praphan Yuktanond, at the time a young police captain. Praphan commanded a BPP unit guarding the rear entrance of the palace. When Praphan first introduced himself to the Princess Mother as a border police officer, she remarked "I thought you were a soldier."

He and Salang Bunnag, another police captain, were assigned as her personal bodyguards. Salang Bunnag later rose through the ranks to become a police general and Deputy Director of the Police Department. He was considered an adviser behind the scenes for the forces involved in the 6 October 1976 Thammasat massacre of students, among later instances when according to media reports, he meted out "rough justice".[19] Salang made headlines again in February 2018, when as an ailing octogenarian, he threw himself off a seventh-floor interior balcony at Central Chaeng Wattana, a mall in northern metro Bangkok, leaving behind a suicide note justifying his action.

The support from Princess Mother for the BPP was timely, as the organization had recently been downgraded by Sarit and attached to the less prestigious provincial police force. Royal patronage helped restore its bureaucratic status.

In return, the Princess Mother received assistance and service from the BPP for her activities in the mountainous areas along the border. In

1967, a foundation for the welfare of BPP officers and their families was established with a 1.5 million baht donation by the Princess Mother. Until the end of the 1980s she, her PMMV, and the BPP worked hand in hand.

Annual visits by the Princess Mother along the border were made in police helicopters or jeeps. Omnipresent images distributed by Thai media showed her distributing medicine and other basic necessities, garbed in a volunteer team uniform and beret. Walking alongside her in the photos were invariably BPP officers.

BPP members began to affectionately refer to her as Somdet Ya and Mae Fa Luang, terms ostensibly coined by hill tribe people who had become familiar with the sound of her helicopter approaching, whence the term Princess from the Sky.

Although these appellations might have been initially considered over-familiar or quaint as applied to the king's mother, they soon caught on with the general population and indeed the BPP.

While BPP sources have commonly claimed that the hill people, naively lacking knowledge of proper court language and etiquette, began to refer to the king and the queen as *pho luang* and *mae luang*, the origin of these terms may have another source.

Rather than inventions of the hill tribes, these appellations may have been spoken by BPP officers straining to speak Northern Thai, the language of the Northern Thai people of Lanna. From these efforts by the paramilitary group, ethnic groups echoed the phrases, since in the Northern Thai language *pho luang* means father as well as village headman.

Traditionally, Thais had never considered kings and queens to be their fathers or mothers. In the thirteenth century, Ramkhamhaeng, the third king of Sukhothai was reportedly called *pho khun* (Father Ruler). Yet this innovation which created the concept of paternal rule, in which a monarch governs his people as a father would oversee his children, was a transitory phenomenon.

Since the late 1980s, an acrimonious scholarly debate has erupted over whether the Ramkhamhaeng Inscription, a stone stele bearing inscriptions traditionally regarded as the earliest example of Thai script, is authentic. Discovered in 1833, it was deciphered and dated to 1292. It offers a description of the Sukhothai Kingdom during the time of King Ramkhamhaeng,

Although art historians such as Piriya Krairiksh have cast doubt on the bona fides of the stele, the controversy itself underlined how little is known today about Ramkhamhaeng's era, apart from what is communicated in the inscription.

The Sukhothai period was doubtless a golden age for the development of Thai arts, yet the reigns of its leaders were brief and, in some ways, evanescent. In any event, despite any concerns, the Ramkhamhaeng Inscription was honoured by inclusion in UNESCO's Memory of the World Programme in 2003.

And the concept of a paternal monarch also proved to be resistant to the vagaries of time. A poem written in 1879 by King Chulalongkorn, then in his twenties, echoed the notion. It formed part of his 1879 *Nitthra Chakrit*, a Thai adaptation of "The Sleeper and the Waker" from the eleventh volume of *The Arabian Nights* as translated by the Victorian adventurer Richard F. Burton.

The key line from Chulalongkorn's poem was "*tuy rat rak bat mae ying dui piturong*", or the people love him (the king) more than their own fathers.[20]

King Chulalongkorn's poem praised the *barami*, or moral authority, of a ruler from the Harun al-Rashid caliphate in Baghdad. It was used in court circles to praise Chulalongkorn himself. It is unknown, however, if the idea became popular with the general population. In any case, the poem was cited to elevate Chulalongkorn to a status superior to that of a merely paternal role for the Thai people. And at no time were his four principal queens referred to as mothers of the people.

Not until the 1980s did a paternal cult arise around King Chulalongkorn, by then referred to as *latthi sadet pho ro. 5*, or the cult of the Royal Father, the Fifth Reign. King Chulalongkorn was therefore worshipped like a father, but not until long after his death in 1910.

To the rising urban middle class, the paternal King Chulalongkorn became a symbol of good luck, prosperity, and happiness, as explored in

Irene Stengs's *Worshipping the Great Modernizer: King Chulalongkorn, Patron-Saint of the Thai Middle Class.*[21]

Photos, statues, medals, and charms with the effigy of King Chulalongkorn were in great demand, sold all over the country. From the late 1980s until the 1997 Asian financial crisis, Bangkokians flocked in droves to the equestrian statue of King Chulalongkorn at the Royal Plaza almost every Tuesday evening, the weekday upon which the king was born.

During Chulalongkorn's second Grand Tour of Europe in 1907, he had visited the Palace of Versailles in France and reportedly remarked that he was impressed by the Equestrian Statue of King Louis XIV, designed and partially executed by the Italian artist Gian Lorenzo Bernini. The King considered that if an equestrian statue of himself were installed at a public thoroughfare, a majestic impression would be made, like those in European capitals.

Chulalongkorn had also made a comparable remark about the equestrian statue of King Victor Emmanuel II in Milan, Italy, designed by the nineteenth-century Italian sculptor Ercole Rosa. Indeed, Chulalongkorn had demonstrated interest in Italian sculpture and metallurgy since his first Grand Tour of Europe in 1897.

Crown Prince Vajiravudh, then regent of Siam, organized a project accordingly, and in 1907, Chulalongkorn visited the renowned Susse Frères bronze foundry in Paris to pose for an equestrian statue. It was initially modelled after the Monument to Alfonso XII designed by José Grases Riera and located in Buen Retiro Park in Madrid, Spain.

However, since Alfonso XII was exceedingly tall, the proportions of the resulting image of King Chulalongkorn had to be adjusted accordingly.

The statue reached Bangkok in November 1908, coinciding with the Rajamangalabhisek Royal Ceremony commemorating the fortieth anniversary of Chulalongkorn's accession to the throne.

It was installed before Ananta Samakhom Throne Hall or place of immense gathering, a royal reception hall within Dusit Palace in Bangkok, commissioned by King Chulalongkorn in 1908. Candles and incense sticks as well as pink roses and European brandy or wine—favourite amenities of the modern monarch—were offered by worshippers of the king, who had died shortly before, in 1910.[22]

So, the idea of King Bhumibol, Queen Sirikit and Princess Mother Sangwan as the nation's father, mother and grandmother, respectively, essentially originated in the early 1960s. Its use supposedly originated among the hill people, for whom it was deemed acceptable, as they were considered uncultured and uneducated. Nothing unseemly was seen in their referring to Bangkok royalty in terms of affectionate kinship.

Yet soon, the terms were co-opted by BPP officers. At first, this usage raised strong objections from the Bangkok-educated elite. As late as September 1982, debates over such niceties were printed in Kukrit Pramoj's daily *Siam Rath* between the academic Chulathat Phayakharanond and general readers.

Chulathat maintained that it was inappropriate for commoners to relate to the Princess Mother as if she were their own grandmother. Some readers faulted this viewpoint for failing to appreciate that the king, queen, and Princess Mother had come down to meet the people. By sharing the people's happiness and sorrow, the royal family behaved in a parental role, and therefore it was suitable to refer to them as Somdet Pho, Somdet Mae, and Somdet Ya or Mae Fah Luang.

According to this logic, there should be no objection to the terms. Finally, the debate reached the Princess Mother, who reportedly opined: "Yes, I have become their grandma."[23] In any case, this newly adopted usage had its limits. No other member of the royal family has ever been referred to in kinship terms, so there has been no Somdet Pa, or Royal Auntie, for example.

Instead, other honorific allusions are made, so that Princess Maha Chakri is commonly referred to her as Phra Thep or Princess Angel.

Throughout these innovations, the BPP was vital for promoting the Princess Mother as the national grandmother, underlining the close cooperation between her and the officers. One of their most extensive projects was establishing temporary primary schools for children of the hill tribes and borderland peoples.

By the late 1950s, it was estimated that around 300,000 people belonged to these minorities in Thailand. Among them were the Hmong, Yao, Musur, Karen and Lisu. Thai authorities intriguingly also included the Ho, or Yunnan Chinese, in their definition of hill tribes. These were KMT soldiers and their families who had been defeated by the Communist Chinese in 1949 and were obliged to flee to Burma, Laos and Thailand.

In terms of promoting schools, a precedent had been set as early as 1962 by Queen Sirikit, who donated 13,500 baht to the BPP to build a small wooden primary school for children of local ethnic groups in Fang District, Chiang Mai.

The BPP grandly named the school *Chao Mae Luang Uppatham* (Under the patronage of the Great Royal Mother).[24] In the following year, the king donated 30,000 baht for another primary school in Hang Dong District, Chiang Mai, again to be called *Chao Pho Luang Uppatham* (Under the patronage of the Great Royal Father).

Royally patronized schools sprang up in different remote areas of the North. They were further symbolic evidence of the king and queen's new roles as mother and father of people on the borders of Thailand. The Princess Mother followed suit by likewise funding schools in the border areas.

In 1921, the Compulsory Primary Education Act became law, requiring compulsory four years of schooling in modern Siam. After the Siamese revolution of 1932, the focus on education heightened, due to the new constitutional requirement for a literate population capable of participating in democratic elections. Government efforts attempted to bolster primary education, with private schools in Bangkok and some provincial centres depended on for most of the teaching, especially at the high school level. Despite widespread efforts, accomplishments were few.

In most rural and mountainous areas, primary schools did not exist until the late 1950s. One complicating factor was the ambiguous legal status of the hill people; Thai government policy was unclear about their citizenship status. Therefore, the education of children of hill people was not seen as a primary concern of the Ministry of Education.

In 1956, the BPP, still under the direction of Police General Phao Sriyanond, was the first organization to establish temporary primary schools for hill children, one of which was situated in Don Hma Wan village near Chiang Khong, a small town in Chiang Rai Province. It was named *rongrian tamruat trawen chaidaen bamrung 1* or BPP Maintained-Patronized School No. I.

The educational resources were rudimentary, with simple wooden buildings in which BPP officers served as teachers. This was a classic case of lowland people versus highlanders, in which the former tried to impose their language on the latter. After the BPP found that they could neither communicate with nor control the hill tribes, they considered that the best long-term solution would be to open schools for their children.

According to BPP Deputy Commander Lieutenant General Chan Ungsuchot, four main reasons were behind BPP's involvement in education: (1) older hill people could be reached through their children; (2) the young were easier to teach; (3) the young were more receptive to compromise; and finally, (4) a substitute was needed for neglect by the Ministry of Education.[25] By 1958, the BPP had founded about 70 schools for around 4,000 students, mostly in the North.

As mentioned, a few years later, the BPP schools attracted the attention of the royal family. Starting in 1964, the Princess Mother became a major patron of the schools. From 1964 to 1981 she would establish 185 BPP schools, 29 funded by her personally. She attended opening ceremonies for most of these schools and donated Thai national flags, Buddha images, and framed pictures of the king and queen, helping to educate rural children about the three pillars of Thailand: *chat-sasana-phra maha kasat*, or Nation, Religion, and King.

Along with these items, the Princess Mother distributed elementary school textbooks, notebooks, and pencils. The textbook titles were intriguing: *udomkan niyom Thai* (The Ideology of Thaiism), *ku chat* (Rescue the Nation), *chan pen Thai* (I am Thai), *rao yu yang thai* (We Live the Thai Way), *krongkan laeng nam tam phraraatchdamri* (Royal Water Resource Initiative), and *mae lao hai phang* (Princess Mother Tells Stories).

Other giveaways included jigsaw maps of the Thai state. The maps were divided with a province drawn on each piece, so children learned about the region they lived in and the form of the Thai nation when the puzzle was assembled.

By 1980, Princess Maha Chakri Sirindhorn had become the patron for the schools. In 2011, there were 169 schools, with 52 in the North, 39 in the Northeast, 41 in the Central Plain, and 37 in the South.[26]

As with the PMMV, it is difficult to precisely measure the success or failure of BPP schools. Most children who attended did not go beyond primary education. Only in very few cases were schools elevated to secondary status and delegated to the Ministry of Education. Perhaps the most useful outcome was that after a few years of study at BPP schools, the new generation in the northern borderlands could communicate in the Thai language and felt that much more of a sense of belonging to the nation.

According to Deputy Royal Secretary-General Khwankeo Vajarodaya (1928–2017), the Princess Mother's main concern was that the students become aware that "they are Thai, they have settlements in Thailand, though, in some places, they speak Khmer, Lao or Pattani Malay."[27]

In the mid-1980s, the Princess Mother turned her attention to her final projects in Chiang Rai. These consisted of three related schemes: first, an orchard known as the *Rai Mae Fah Luang*, second, an admonitory historical museum called The Hall of Opium, and finally, Doi Tung Development Project (DTDP) palace. The Rai Mae Fah Luang Orchard, which opened in 1984, was located within the city. Its quiet attractions included a variety of traditional northern wood buildings, cultural artefacts, gardens, plants and flowers. It was used as an occupational training camp for hill people as well as tourism.

The Hall of Opium Museum was a graver venture, aiming to educate visitors about opium wars and warlords, drug smugglers and the nefarious effects of the drug. Also described was how the Golden Triangle, the area where the borders of Thailand, Laos, and Myanmar meet at the confluence of the Ruak and Mekong Rivers was recuperated from its former status as an internationally infamous drug trading zone. Among the exhibits in the Opium in Siam section was a reconstruction of a Chinese tea house in Yaowarat where customers formerly smoked opium.

The DTDP palace, completed in 1988, had been conceived in 1980 when the Princess Mother celebrated her eightieth birthday. It was a more ambitious project entirely. The aim was to transform a large, deforested opium-growing area of just over 48,000 acres around Doi Tung, a mountain in the Thai highlands of Mae Fa Luang District, into farmland and a tourist attraction.

The area was partly reforested and replanted with cold climate fruit trees and flowers. The agricultural yield would be processed for sale onsite or in shops at major airports and cities. The projects resembled a more modest one at Doi Ang Khang, a mountain in Fang District, Chiang Mai Province, where the first research agricultural station was established by King Bhumibol in 1969.[28]

Reportedly the Princess Mother had visited the area in 1980 and liked it because, according to members of her Bangkok entourage, Doi Tung was akin to the Swiss Alps, without any snow. The Princess Mother reportedly remarked, "Build a house for me here, and I will take care of reforestation."

This request led to her new development project and a residence for herself, a mountain villa built in a style blending Swiss and Lan Na architecture. It was situated near Ban Ego Pa Kluay or the village of Akha banana forest.

The villa sits atop a peak of Doi Tung, opposite the ancient Wat Phra That Doi Suthep, a sacred pilgrimage site housing a relic that according to lore dating back to the Sukhothai Kingdom, was identified as Gautama Buddha's shoulder bone.

Doi Tung is the third-highest peak of Thailand, 1,200 metres above sea level, located in the Golden Triangle area on the Burmese border. In the early 1980s, Doi Tung was still a major opium-growing area, comprising a population of 10,000 hill people, most of them Akha, Musur, Shan and Yunnan Chinese.

According to information from General Pang Malakul na Ayudhya, an aristocratic senior army officer in charge of military operations in the area during the 1980s and 1990s, the Yunnan Chinese consisted of two groups who had crossed the border and stayed in Thailand.

The first was comprised of KMT soldiers and their families. After being defeated by the Communists in 1949, they took refuge in Burma and Laos until they were driven further into Chiang Rai, where the Sarit government allowed them to stay.

By 1984, over 8,000 of them lived in thirteen villages scattered on Doi Mae Salong, slightly to the south of Doi Tung. The KMT became allies of the Thai army and fought against the CPT. The KMT who did not return to Yunnan or move to Taiwan were provided with land and Thai citizenship in exchange for their collaboration.

Apart from the KMT, there were two other categories of civilians from Yunnan. First, a group that the Thai called the Ho, consisting of Muslims and non-Muslims. Some claimed to be related to Zheng He, the celebrated court eunuch and fleet admiral of the Ming Dynasty who according to historical accounts was 7 feet tall, with a waist 5 feet in circumference, and a voice "as loud as a bell".[29]

Officially, Thailand had banned opium smoking and growing since 1958. But the valuable crop continued to be cultivated for four more decades throughout the 1980s. The Princess Mother's development project was welcomed by many people at a time when the *barami* and prestige of the royal family were extremely high.

Social and economic development, especially in rural areas, had become more associated with the royal family than with the Thai government. The Ministry of National Development had already been dissolved in 1971, its responsibilities divided among several ministries and government agencies.

Consequently, the Doi Tung Project was much needed and appreciated. It attracted widespread attention and cooperation in Thailand and overseas. The Sasakawa Peace Foundation, a Japanese private entity founded in 1986 to enhance international cooperation, donated 1.6 million baht annually for a decade.

The army and ISOC, led by General Chavalit Yongchaiyudh, assisted the Princess Mother's endeavour. The government of General Prem Tinsulanonda, in power from 1981 to 1988, pooled resources, technical know-how, and staff from six ministries and thirty-three governmental departments to implement the project promptly. By 1988, it was functioning, and the villa was completed in 1989.

Several ethnic groups who had decided to remain onsite became hired labourers, working on freshly cultivated land or in the reforestation programme. Their incomes reportedly rose threefold. Remote areas formerly used to grow opium became the site of housing projects. As highland people moved out, lowland people moved in.

The projects resulted in intense land speculation and bustling tourism. Because of the Doi Tung Project, Mae Sai, a small town nearby that served as a gateway to Burma's Shan State and Keng Tung, boomed.

This was an area where Khun Sa, a Shan drug lord born in Burma, once operated. The town, known as a transit site for opium and drug smuggling as well as human trafficking, became a border centre for business and tourism. Soon, it boasted branches of all the major commercial banks of Siam.

Mae Sai became a symbol of the so-called economic miracle in Southeast Asian countries like Thailand, Malaysia, Indonesia and Singapore. They were turning into so-called tigers and newly industrialized countries (NICs) alongside Hong Kong, Korea and Taiwan.

This all occurred before the Princess Mother died in 1995, the king celebrated his Golden Jubilee in 1996, and the 1997 Asian financial crisis. Meanwhile, the Cold War had drawn to a close, the CPT was disintegrating, and some thousand students who had joined the Communists after the 6 October 1976 massacre returned from the jungle, in response to a government offer of amnesty.

Among them were two leaders: Seksan Prasertkul, who returned in 1980, and Thirayuth Boonmee, who emerged from a clandestine life the following year. Seksan proceeded to earn a PhD degree at the Department of Government, Cornell University in New York, writing a dissertation on "The Transformation of the Thai State and Economic Change (1855–1945)". Thirayuth's return to academia included relocating to the Netherlands to study philosophy, science and anthropology. Ultimately, he earned a PhD in sociology and anthropology at Radboud University Nijmegen.

As these societal reconciliations occurred, Thais experienced what was felt like a profoundly personal loss when on 2 June 1995, the Princess Mother was hospitalized at Bangkok's Siriraj Hospital where she had trained as a nurse some eight decades earlier. She died on 18 July 1995, at age ninety-five.

One of the most elaborate royal funeral ceremonies ever seen in Thailand was held for her. It equalled the obsequies that might be expected upon the loss of a much-revered queen, with official mourning and merit-making for 100 days.

Cremation followed in a pavilion constructed to evoke Mount Meru, the sacred five-peaked mountain of Buddhist cosmology considered to be the centre of all the physical, metaphysical and spiritual universes. The rite was held on royal grounds before the Grand Palace.

In 1999, the Chuan Leekpai government honoured the Princess Mother by nominating her as one of UNESCO's world's great personalities of the century for the year 2000. However, the centenary of Pridi Banomyong, a leader of the Siamese revolution of 1932, was also commemorated in 2000, and there was popular support for his nomination as well.

Prime Minister Chuan encountered some difficulties. As mentioned, after the death of King Ananda in 1946 and the Siamese *coup d'état* of 1947, Pridi went into exile in China and France, where he died in 1983. At one point, Pridi had been accused of being involved in the regicide of King Ananda, and even though King Bhumibol did not lend credence to these rumours, the stigma was enduring.

It took much time and effort for Pridi's admirers, sympathizers, and students, mostly from Thammasat University, to rehabilitate his name posthumously. Therefore, a major effort was made to nominate him for the UNESCO honour. Finally, the Chuan government compromised, and both Thai candidates, Pridi and the Princess Mother, were registered among the world's great personalities of the century by UNESCO simultaneously.

NOTES

1. *Bangkok Post*, 7 August 1964.
2. This brief biography of the Princess Mother derives from three authoritative sources. The first is the Princess Mother's daughter, Princess Galyani Vadhana,

Mae Lao Hai Fang [What Mother Told] (Bangkok: Electricity Generating Authority of Thailand, 1980). The book was reprinted repeatedly and was sold and distributed gratis by the Ministry of Education and BPP. Around 100,000 copies were printed. The book traces the Princess Mother's ancestors back only two generations, as part of an incomplete genealogy. It recounts that the Princess Mother's father was a goldsmith from Nonthaburi by the name of Chu. Chu's father was Chum, but Chu's mother was neither known nor remembered.

The Princess Mother's mother was named Kham, and she was born into a family of six brothers and five sisters. According to anecdotal tradition, her maternal side might have migrated from Vientiane because their family enjoyed eating sticky rice! In many ways the Chinese background, if there was any, was covered up like most middle- and upper-class Thai since the turn of the nineteenth century.

See also *Song Sadet Somdet Ya* [Sending off the Princess Grandma], compiled by H.R.H. Galyani Vadhana, 10 March 1997, published 100 days after the royal cremation of the Princess Mother. This volume interestingly details a Chinese ceremony, or *Phithi Kongtek*, arranged repeatedly for the Princess Mother. *Kong Tek* is Teochew or *gong de* in Mandarin, meaning merit, virtue, charitable pious deeds. It is a Chinese mourning ritual. At one ceremony, the Princess Galyani Vadhana and Princess Sirindhorn were seen garbed in *Kong Tek* mourning clothes of sack and raw cotton. They were to perform a *Kong Tek* rite of crossing the bridge between the human world and heaven. Paper effigies of a Mercedes Benz automobile, a plane, and the Princess Mother's Doi Tung villa were ritually burned on this occasion.

The third source was Sumalee-Sukanya Bamrungsuk and Suppharat Lertphanitkul, eds., *Phraratcha Prawat Lae Phraratcha Koraniyakit Nai Somdet Phra Sri Nagarindra Boromjajajonani* [The Biography and The Royal Duties of Princess Srinagarindra] (Bangkok: Thai Studies Project, Chulalongkorn University, 1984). The editors were college classmates of Princess Sirindhorn and their volume was printed before the Princess Mother's death.

For an official cremation volume, see: Literature and History Division, Krom Sinlapakorn (Department of Fine Arts), Sivalee Phuphet, ed., *Phraratcha Prawat Lae Phraratcha Koraniyakit Nai Somdet Phra Sri Nagarindra Boromjajajonani* [Life and Work of the Princess Mother] (Bangkok: Department of Fine Arts, 1996). Fifty thousand copies were printed for distribution on the cremation day at Sanam Luang, Bangkok, 11 March 1996, almost nine months after her death.

3. The word Mom is a title for female commoners who become wives of princes of Mom Chao, Phra Ong Chao, and Chao Fa ranks.
4. See G. William Skinner, *Chinese Society in Thailand: An Analytical History* (Ithaca: Cornell University Press, 1957), pp. 279–80.
5. The Princess Mother returned to Thailand on 9 November 1963, *Bangkok Post*, 10 November 1963.
6. See Benedict Anderson, "Radicalism after Communism in Thailand and Indonesia", *New Left Review* I, no. 202 (November–December 1983): 3–14.
7. See Tho Phianwitthaya (tr. Chris Baker), "The History of Our Party and Some of Its Lessons", republished online as "An Internal History of the Communist Party of Thailand", file:///C:/Users/VRF/Downloads/Baker_InternalHistoryofCPT_JCA(2003).pdf (accessed 11 March 2021). See also M. Ladd Thomas, "Communist Insurgency in Thailand: Factors Contributing to Its Decline", *Asian Affairs* 13, no. 1 (Spring 1986): 17–26. Also see Chai-anan Samudavanija et al., *From Armed Suppression to Political Offensive* (Bangkok: Institute of Security and International Studies, Chulalongkorn University, 1990).

    Or, see this important writing of the CPT's own history translated by Chris Baker (2003) "An Internal History of the Communist Party of Thailand", *Journal of Contemporary Asia* 33, no. 4 (2003): 510–41, http://dx.doi.org/10.1080/00472330380000311 (accessed 18 August 2021).
8. My thanks to Mr Sa-nguan Khumrungroj, a knowledgeable freelance journalist, for information concerning Thai Chinese cultural connections.
9. Craig J. Reynolds, *Thai Radical Discourse: The Real Face of Thai Feudalism Today* (Ithaca: Cornell University Press, Southeast Asia Program, 1987).
10. See Chs 3 and 9 of Kasian Tejapira, *Commodifying Marxism: The Formation of Modern Thai Radical Culture 1927–1958* (Kyoto: Center for Southeast Asian Studies, Kyoto University, 2003).
11. Lieutenant Colonel Phayom Chulanont was likely one of the most semi-officially celebrated Communists. This was partly because his son Surayud became a prime minister and partly because he brought several Communists to interact with the Thai government in a less hostile manner. In 1978 and 1979, regional Communist insurgencies erupted. Vietnamese troops brought the Cambodian politicians Heng Samrin and Hun Sen to Phnom Penh and drove the Khmer Rouge and their allies to the Thai border. Consequently, the Chinese became involved to retaliate against the Vietnamese. Civil war in Cambodia continued for a decade.

    The CPT aligned itself with the Chinese and no longer received support from Laos or Vietnam. Meanwhile, Thai prime ministerships, including those of General Kriangsak Chamanan from 1977 to 1980 and General Prem Tinsulanonda from 1980 to 1988, tried to broker a compromise with the CPT. This became known as the 66/23 reconciliation policy, after the administrative number that had been assigned to Prime Minister Prem's order.

Approximately 3,000 students who had gone into the jungle, including leaders such as Seksan Prasertkul and Theerayuth Boonmee, gradually began to return to Thai society with guaranteed immunity from prosecution for anti-government political activity. Rural Communists returned to their provinces and some were given land for residence and cultivation in Phetchabun, Uttaradit, Phisanulok and Nan.

Surayud, at the time Commander of the Fourth Infantry Battalion, closely aligned himself with General Prem and received permission to see his ailing father for the first and the last time in twenty years.

The father made the request that his jungle comrades be looked after; many of them were ethnic Hmongs in Phetchabun and Nan. These jungle returnees became known as Phu Ruam Patthana Chat Thai Phorotho, or Joint Developers of the Thai Nation. As part of the incentive to surrender, they were offered arable land and Thai citizenship, otherwise difficult to obtain.

As late as the 2010s, royal-affiliated Communists from Nan protested against Yingluck Shinawatra's government, in power from 2011 to 2014. See a popular account of the life and work of Phayom Chulanont by Thanphong Rasananond, *Lung Kham Tan Chiwit Udomkan Khwamwang* [Comrade Uncle Kham Tan, Life, Ideology, Hope] (Bangkok: Matichon, 2007).

12. Saiyud Kerdphol, *The Struggle for Thailand: Counter-insurgency, 1965–1985* (Bangkok: Security Research Center, 1986); see also Chai-anan Samudavanija et al., *From Armed Suppression to Political Offensive*, quoting casualty statistics from research by General Surayud Chulanont, p. 65. See also note 7 above.

13. In 1886, this Chiang Mai king sent his thirteen-year-old daughter, Dara Rasami (1873–1933), to Bangkok. For Siam's national integration in which Chiang Mai had to be under Bangkok's control, the little princess became a consort of King Chulalongkorn. In 1892, they had one child, a daughter who lived for only two years. Dara Rasami is now best remembered for retaining her Chiang Mai cultural identity. While living in Bangkok, she maintained her traditional hair style, long enough to touch the floor. She always wore *Lanna pha nung*, also known as *pha sin* or *pha thung*, a long fabric wound around the waist to resemble a long skirt, similar to *longyi*, a sheet of cloth widely worn in Burma and Laos.

She eschewed cutting her hair short or wearing *sompot chong kben*, a unisex, lower body wraparound cloth worn in Cambodia, Laos, and Thailand as the preferred garb for upper- and middle-class women for daily wear.

Rather than imitating major queens, concubines and Bangkok court ladies, Dara Rasami and her Chiang Mai entourage were conspicuously different in the Grand Palace. They were looked down upon and sometimes verbally accused of being Laotian, rather than Thai. For two decades from 1886 to 1908, the princess was not permitted to revisit her Northern home; nor was she allowed to attend her father's cremation in 1897.

Only in 1908, two years before King Chulalongkorn's death, was she granted permission to visit Chiang Mai. At this point, she was also accorded a royal title. Instead of being merely a Chao Chom Manda (mother of a king's child), she became a Phra Ratcha Chaya (king's wife). Upon arrival at Chiang Mai, she arranged for elaborate stupas to be constructed at Wat Suan Dok, a Royal Temple of the Third Class. The stupas were to house the ashes of her Chiang Mai royal family.

Her father's ashes were sent to the summit of the highest peak in Siam. There a Lanna-style stupa was raised to house the ashes of the last Chiang Mai king. Interestingly, two even grander stupas were built in contemporary Bangkok style atop Doi Inthanon in recent decades, a bit further down from the prior one. They are called Napamaytanidol and Napapon Phoom-siri. Part of these two names are taken from the names of King Bhumibol and Queen Sirikit. They were built for the sixtieth birthdays of the king and queen, in 1987 and 1992 respectively.

Princess Dara Rasami continued to live in Bangkok until the death of her husband. In 1914, King Vajiravudh, Rama VI, granted her permission to return home to Chiang Mai. There she became active in promoting Lanna traditional culture for about twenty years. On 30 June 1933, one year after the Siamese revolution of 1932, the princess died of a lung ailment at age sixty.

14. Public Relations and Distribution Section, Samnak Phraratchawang (Bureau of the Royal Household), *Sadet Phichit Yod Doi Inthanon 26 Maysayon 2507* [Conquering the Peak of Doi Inthanon 26 April 1964] (Bangkok: Bowonsan, 1988).
15. In operation and chain of command, the Thai Army is divided into four military areas: Bangkok, Nakhon Ratchasima, Phitsanulok and Nakhon Sithammarat. Each region consists of a number of *monthon thahan bok* or military mandala/circles. There are fourteen *monthons* or mandalas. Within these *monthons* are thirty-six *changwat thahan bok* or army provinces in total. Curiously, there is no *changwat thahan rua* or *changwat thahan akat* for the navy or air force.

16. Sumalee-Sukanya Bamrungsuk and Suppharat Lertphanitkul, eds., *Phraratcha Prawat Lae Phraratcha Koraniyakit Nai Somdet Phra Sri Nagarindra Boromjajajonani*, p. 243.
17. See Raymond I. Coffey et al., *Thailand: Public Safety/Border Patrol Police, Remote Area Security Development: An Approach to Counterinsurgency by the Border Patrol Police* (Bangkok: US Operation Mission/Thailand, Agency for International Development, 1971).
18. Katherine A. Bowie, *Rituals of National Loyalty: An Anthropology of the State and the Village Scout Movement in Thailand* (New York: Columbia University Press, 1997). See also Kawirat Khunaphat, *Luksua Chaoban*: "*Bangsing Bangyang Chak 6 Tula 2519*" [Village Scouts: Some of the Things from 6 October 1976], *Warasan Thammasat* 3, no. 15 (January–March 1986): 151–65.
19. Benedict Anderson, "Withdrawal Symptoms: Social and Cultural Aspects of the October 6 Coup", *Bulletin of Concerned Asian Scholars* 9, no. 3 (July–September 1977): 13–30. See also in the same issue: Puey Ungphakorn, "Violence and the Military Coup", pp. 4–12.
20. This poem was composed by King Chulalongkorn when he was twenty-six and still not in full control of the Siamese government and administration. It was part of his 1879 *Nitthra Chakrit*, a Thai rendering of "The Sleeper and the Waker" from *The Arabian Nights*, possibly inspired by the translation into English of Richard Francis Burton.
21. Irene Stengs, *Worshipping the Great Moderniser: King Chulalongkorn, Patron Saint of the Thai Middle Class* (Singapore: NUS Press & University of Washington Press, 2009).
22. Nidhi Eeoseewong, *Latthi Phithi Sadet Pho Ro. 5* [Ceremonial Cult of the Fifth Reign Father-King] (Bangkok: Matichon, 1993). This well-thought-out analysis by Nidhi was widely criticized by the Bangkok elite, who asserted that it was inappropriate to use the term Sadet Pho Ro. 5 to refer to King Chulalongkorn. But the book sold well and was regularly reprinted. It probably reflected the temperament of the rising Bangkok middle class. The cult extended from performing at Chulalongkorn's Equestrian Monument on only Tuesday nights weekly to a second performance on Thursdays as well. Candles, incense sticks, pink roses, wine, and brandy, as supposed favourites of the king, were prominent offerings. In 1997 the cult died down and worshippers began to vanish when the economic crash came.
23. *Song Sadet Somdet Ya* [Send off the Royal Grand Ma], compiled by H.R.H. Galyani Vadhana, 10 March 1997 on the occasion of 100 days after the Princess Mother's death on 18 July 1995.

24. According to its website (10 June 2014), the school is now under the Office of the Basic Education Commission, Ministry of Education, no longer officially affiliated with the BPP. It has 16 teachers for an enrolment of 405 students (62 in kindergarten, 226 in primary school, and 117 in secondary school.) See http://data.bopp-obec.info/emis/schooldata-view.php?School_ID=1050130194&Area_CODE=5003 (accessed 11 March 2021).
25. Chan Ungsuchot (1914–2001), *Khwam Pen Ma Khong Kan Chat Tang Rongrian Tamruat Trawen Chaidaen* [History of Border Patrol Police Schools] (Bangkok, 1958), p. 14. See also a writing along the same line, *Rongrian Chao Khao Lae Prachachon Klai Komnakom* [Hill Tribe Schools and People Far from Main Communications] (1982); see various articles in the 500-page commemorative book on *40 pi rongrian to.cho.do* [40 anniversary of Border Patrol Police 1956–1996] (Bangkok: O.S. Printing House, 1996). Much thanks to Khun Chaiyasit A. of Thammasat University Library for locating these two books.
26. See its website: http://www.bpp.go.th/bppmain_school/news/0030.175-0033-08102553.pdf (accessed 11 March 2021).
27. See note 24 above. Note the use of the words Yawi for Melayu or Malaya. Bangkok Thai officers and Bangkok elites usually avoid using the word Melayu/Malaya, for it might be interpreted as implying that local people in the far South (Pattani, Yala, Narathiwat, and part of Songkhla), are Malay, rather than Thai, creating problems of nation, ethnicity, and nationality.

It is similar to the word Isan (*phasa* or language, *ahan* or food, *watthanatham* or culture) that replaced the word Lao. Formerly ethnicity, languages and cultures on both sides of the Mekong River, now part of Laos and Thailand, were generally called Lao or Laotian. For example, the administrative area centred in Ubon was called the *monthon*, or mandala, of Lao Kao. But after the French took over the area on the left bank of the Mekong and included it into French Indochina, old appellations became problematic for the Thai nation. To stress that the area and people on the right bank were not part of French Indochina, all words labelled with Lao had to be abandoned and renamed.

Therefore, the administrative area of Monthon Lao Chiang centred at Chiang Mai became Monthon Phayap, with the word Lao dropped. Monthon Lao Klang (Khorat) became Monthon Nakhon Ratchasima; Monthon Lao Phuan became Monthon Udorn; and Monthon Lao Kao became Isan (or Northeast). The word Isan became widely used for whatever was formerly called Lao in northeast Siam. See the informative MA thesis on this subject by David Streckfuss, "Creating the 'Thai': The Emergence of Nationalism in Non-Colonial Siam, 1880–1920" (University of Wisconsin, Madison, 1987).

28. It should be noted once again that in 1969, Bhumibol's first rural development project (Khrongkan Luang) was established at Doi Ang Khang, Fang District, Chiang Mai. Its primary goal was to eradicate the opium trade and turn the native Hmong population into cash crop cultivators. By the 1970s, the royal projects had expanded into a network of thirty-eight small ones.

    The most important overseer of the project from the beginning was Prince Bhisadej Rajani, a son of Prince Dhani, born in 1920. As of March 2021, he is one of the longest-living royal personages in the Thai history at age ninety-nine. He was a close "friend" of the king, seven years his junior. Prince Bhisadej graduated from Debsirin School in Bangkok and continued his education at Dulwich College in England where he played rugby, tennis and squash. During the Second World War, he joined the London chapter of the Free Thai Movement and enlisted in the British Army at the same time as Puey Ungphakorn, future governor of the Bank of Thailand from 1958 to 1971 and rector of Thammasat University from 1974 to 1976. Prince Bhisadej was sent for military training along the Himalayan Mountains, near Darjeeling Hill Station.

    After the war, Prince Bhisadej returned to Siam and worked with the BPP for a few years. The prince led a hard-working, dedicated and simple life. He was also a writer. His older sister was Princess Vibhavadi Rangsit, a lady-in-waiting to Queen Sirikit who was also a well-known author of children's novels signed with the pen name V. na Pramuanmarg. The Princess, in late 1950s and early 1960s, accompanied the royal couple on their state visits to twenty-one countries around the world.

    In 1977, at age fifty-seven, she died after an army helicopter in which she was travelling to visit some royal development projects in a Communist-dominated area of Surat Province, was attacked by machine gun fire. A highway between Bangkok and the previous Don Mueang International Airport was renamed as Vibhavadi Rangsit in her honour. For the Princess, see her cremation volumes: *Anuson Ngan Phraratchathan Plerng Sop Vibhavadi Rangsit* [In memory for the royal cremation of Vibhavadi Rangsit], 1977 and *Vibhavadi Rangsit Ramluk* [In Memory of Vibhavadi Rangsit] (Bangkok: Vabhavadi Foundation, 1977). For the prince, see his autobiography, *Chiwit chan* [My Life] (Bangkok, 2002), and his account of working for the king in *Phrabat Somdet Phrachao Yuhau Lae Khrongkan Luang* [The King and the Royal Projects] (Bangkok: Royal Projects, 1988).

29. In 2009, General Pang Malakul na Ayudhya, at age seventy, began to write his online memoirs (http://www.pangmalakul.com/; accessed 11 March 2021) about his life and work, especially in the northern part of Thailand and Laos, his dealings with the CPT, and more importantly, his service to the Princess

Mother and her rural development projects. In 1980, General Paeng led a grand celebration in Chiang Rai, Wai Sa Mae Fah Luang (Paying Homage to the Heavenly Grandmother). General Pang was a key protagonist of the military television Channel 5, which he directed from 1995 to 1999. During these years, he also chaired the Television Pool of Thailand (TPT), a powerful media body controlled by the army which can unite all stations to broadcast a single programme simultaneously throughout the whole country, if required. TPT has usually been under the control of a trusted army general.

General Pang was also a younger brother of Piya Malakul na Ayudhya, a mass media tycoon. Mr Piya, along with General Surayud Chulanont (then a member of the Privy Council), Ackaratorn Chularat (President of the Administrative Court), Charan Pakdithanakul (Secretary General of the Supreme Court), Charnchai Likhitjitha (President of the Supreme Court), and Pramote Nakornthap (a freelance academic), were accused by Thaksin Shinawatra of plotting to overthrow him. The accused supposedly spread the so-called Finland Charter rumour, about a plot to overthrow the monarchy, a factor that contributed to the 2006 Thai *coup d'état*. See Duncan McCargo and Ukrist Pathamanand, *The Thaksinization of Thailand* (Copenhagen: NIAS Press, 2005); and Pavin Chachavalpongpun, ed., *Good Coup Gone Bad: Thailand's Political Developments since Thaksin's Downfall* (Singapore: Institute of Southeast Asian Studies, 2014), Section I.

CHAPTER SIX

Twilight of Two Reigns in Siam and Thailand

The term barami *refers to the accumulation of goodness.*
Royal barami *derives from a belief in rebirth.*
All humans are considered to be reborn.

Those reborn at a higher status than others are great kings. Therefore, it is believed that great kings possess more barami than anyone else.

This hearkens back to the Traiphum Phra Ruang, a religious and philosophical text describing diverse worlds of Buddhist cosmology, and the way in which karma consigns living beings to one world or another, through a belief in ancestry or making merit from past lives.

We believe that all human beings made merit during past lives. But in Buddhism, this belief is not mandatory. It may be accepted or not. But most Buddhists believe in merit-making during past lives. Those who have done so more than others will achieve a loftier level as great kings, situated above other humans.

However, Buddhism simultaneously advocates that regardless of the merit of their past lives, if great kings fail to act according to the Ten Royal Virtues, their merit vanishes, and they are subject to dethronement or deposition. This is essential to understand.

Sulak Sivaraksa, August 2021[1]

One Coup for the Brother, Another for the Sister

Historical perspectives from the past can clarify events occurring in the present. Although certainly familiar with the phenomenon of *coups d'état*, many historians and political scientists in Thailand viewed the 22 May

2014 coup staged by General Prayut Chan-o-cha, then Chief of the Army, against Prime Minister Yingluck Shinawatra, who had been elected to office, as unprecedented.[2]

It arguably differed from the 2006 coup by Army Chief General Sonthi Boonyaratglin against her brother Thaksin Shinawatra, a billionaire businessman who started as a police lieutenant colonel before becoming a politician and being elected to office.

After the Second World War in Thailand, coups against elected governments, usually headed by military or civilian bureaucrats who had turned politicians, had become traditional. These events, it might be pointed out, always involved male politicians, unlike the developments of May 2014.

Before 22 May, Prayut seemed to enjoy a good working relationship with Thailand's first-ever female Prime Minister. In another first, for just under a year, starting in June 2013, during one of several cabinet reshuffles, Yingluck also concurrently took on the responsibility of serving as Thailand's first female defence minister in her cabinet, while still holding the prime ministership.

At the time, she claimed that she took on the role of defence minister to improve cooperation between her office and the military, although some observers believed that this manoeuvre was intended to permit her to influence military reshuffles that would occur the same year. Still, others thought that by serving as defence minister, Yingluck might offer added protection to her government and ward off any military coup, like the one that ousted her brother from power in 2006, after which he was found guilty of corruption in 2008 and chose a life of long-term self-imposed exile in Dubai.[3]

To an external observer, Yingluck might have been seen as coping adequately with such challenges as the catastrophic 2011 Thailand floods that hit the nation only a few months after she took office in August of that year. For thirty months or so, Yingluck's administration appeared to weather a variety of street protests and efforts to shut down Bangkok by the People's Democratic Reform Committee (PDRC), which advocated changing Thailand into a complete democracy with the king as head of state.[4]

This umbrella political pressure group was more specifically aimed at removing the influence of former Prime Minister Thaksin from Thai politics and achieving political reforms by an unelected royalist council.

The group was formed in November 2013 by Suthep Thaugsuban, a Thai politician and former Member of Parliament for Surat Thani Province, who resigned from his post as Democrat Party secretary-general and MP and appointed himself as PDRC secretary-general.

Although much of the movement's message revolved around the ill deeds of politicians, the PDRC mostly consisted of members of the Democrat Party, the People's Alliance for Democracy (a coalition of opposition to Thaksin), student activist groups, state worker unions and pro-military groups. The PDRC was notably supported by wealthy Bangkok dwellers and inhabitants from the south of Thailand.

By accusing Yingluck's government of lacking legitimacy, Suthep announced the PDRC's plan to seize sovereign power from the government and put through national reform.

Yet despite these initiatives which were clearly aimed against the abiding political power of her brother as much as Yingluck, some politicos predicted that she might indeed follow Thaksin's accomplishment of being the first prime minister of Thailand to complete a full four-year term in office.

Yet that was not to be. Instead, analysts of the Thai political scene wondered why still another coup had occurred, followed by the drafting of still another new constitution, the nation's twentieth.

Speculations abounded, over whether the military directorship and establishment were acting on their own or following instructions from some higher power. Did the military position itself into power in order to be controlled at a time of great transmutation, the Royal succession from the Ninth Reign to the Tenth? Or did they read the twenty-first-century global situation of Thailand through an antiquated and no longer relevant Cold War optic, mimicking the military absolutist spectre of Field Marshal Sarit Thanarat from 1958 to 1963 and others of his era?

King Chulalongkorn, Rama V of Siam, and King Bhumibol, Rama IX of Thailand

Rather than offering any grand theory for analysing the Thai military's historical rapport with the Royal Palace, it may be more illuminating for understanding Thailand's chaotic opening of the twenty-first century to look farther back in time.

To better perceive the closing years of the Ninth Reign, of His Majesty King Bhumibol, as well as his connection to the military, a long-term approach helps. By examining a comparative study on the twilight of two exceptional reigns, those of King Chulalongkorn, Rama V (1868–1910) of Siam, and King Bhumibol, Rama IX (1946–2016) of Thailand.[5]

As might be expected, the two reigns offered similarities as well as differences. They represent the longest such reigns in Thai history; and King Bhumibol's record of service to his people of 70 years and 126 days, is exceeded only by King Louis XIV of France, known as the Sun King, who reigned 72 years and 110 days.

Yet France's Sun King was only four years old at the time of his coronation, so King Bhumibol retains the record as the longest-reigning monarch to have served only as an adult.

Beyond such issues of impressive endurance and longevity, King Chulalongkorn was probably the first, and almost the last, absolute monarch of Siam. To understand the end of his reign, it is essential to look at how he arrived there.

He was crowned in 1868 at age fifteen. He ruled for forty-two years before dying in 1910 at the age of fifty-seven. His long reign can be divided by decades. During the 1870s, the junior king studied and experimented with statecraft, developing modernizing reforms for his kingdom. The 1880s marked the early stages of building absolutism and centralization. The 1890s represented the height of success for his reign, with internal reform and external accommodation with colonial powers; Siam remained the only independent, uncolonized country in Southeast Asia. Finally, the 1900s were the twilight years.

Chulalongkorn's lengthy reign coincided with the height of British and French colonialism in Asia. In 1868, at age fifteen, he was traditionally chosen by an assembly of royals and nobles to succeed his father, King Mongkut. He was nominated along with his elder cousin Prince Wichaichan (1838–85), the eldest son of Vice-King Pinklao and nephew of King Mongkut.

Prince Wichaichan held the title of *uparaja* of Siam, colloquially known as the Front Palace, after the place of residence of the titleholder. Apart from Front Palace, other translations of *uparaja* included viceroy, vice-king, and Lord/Prince of the Front Palace, all traditional titles for heir presumptive.

For five years until 1873, Chulalongkorn prepared to assume his duties by observing court business and travelling to observe colonies in British Malaya and the Dutch East Indies in 1871 and to Malaya, Burma (Myanmar), and India in 1871–72.

By making these trips, Chulalongkorn became the first Siamese monarch to travel outside the kingdom. It may be noteworthy that Chulalongkorn prioritized observing colonial conditions in British and Dutch colonies, rather than French ones for example. Yet in his remarkably determined globe-trotting, King Chulalongkorn would eventually visit Paris in 1897 and 1907.

Whereas his father, the brilliant and innovative King Mongkut, corresponded with foreign leaders and invited international experts to help advance Siam's intellectual and technological capacities, Chulalongkorn assumed an innovative public relations drive through international diplomacy.

With governmental press relations, the image of Siam as a civilized nation not requiring colonization was advanced, each time that the diminutive and dapper monarch arrived energetically in a foreign land.

With prescience comparable to that of his father, Chulalongkorn was media-savvy to an extraordinary degree, and became the first Siamese to be filmed, during a royal state visit to Berne, Switzerland on 25 May 1897. Less than a year before, he had first become intrigued with the cinematic art, then in its infant stages, when during a visit to the British colony of Singapore, he was shown a short film on cockfighting which required peering into a kinetoscope, a newfangled invention by Thomas

Edison. In doing so, Chulalongkorn became the first Siamese person to see a moving picture.⁶

The surviving short silent movie in which Chulalongkorn made his screen debut, entitled *Berne: Arrival of the King of Siam* or *The King of Siam in Berne*, was filmed by the Swiss Victorian cinematic pioneer François-Henri Lavanchy-Clarke. It shows the royal procession in the streets of the Swiss capital.⁷

A second such newsreel-like image of the king was soon produced, during Chulalongkorn's visit to Stockholm, Sweden on 13 July 1897. This film, directed by Swedish royal photographer Ernest Florman, was entitled *King of Siam Landing at Logårdstrappan* or *The Arrival of the King of Siam in Stockholm*. Logårdstrappan is a stone staircase used since the early nineteenth century as a parade entrance for important visits by sea to Stockholm Castle. Remarkably, this image of Chulalongkorn was the first film ever made in Sweden. The Siamese King hops jauntily out of a boat to visit a fair and is formally embraced on the dock by the Swedish King Oscar II, who towers over him.⁸

The impact of these brief images cannot be underestimated. The film of King Chulalongkorn arriving in Sweden created a sensation back home, and just one month after the Berne visit of May 1897, the first public screening was held in Siam at Mom Chao Alangkarn's Theatre, the Kingdom's first version of cinema, opened for business near the Sam Yot city gate on Charoen Krung Road.

The king's half-brother Prince Sappasartsupakij, now considered the father of Thai cinema, purchased a combined movie camera and projection while accompanying his brother on a European tour in 1897, and later proceeded to film Chulalongkorn performing official duties and capturing other palace events.

In part because of such efficient and memorable propaganda through then new technology, Siam avoided the fate of all its neighbours and was not colonized by British and French imperialist forces.

During one 1871 voyage alone, lasting from 9 March to 15 April, the eighteen-year-old king was accompanied by an entourage of 208 on official visits to Singapore, Batavia and Semarang.⁹

Again, in late 1871 and early 1872, for ninety-two days, the king and an entourage of forty took an extended jaunt to Singapore, Melaka, Penang and Burma, stopping in Moulmein and Rangoon, as well as an extended stay in India. Part of the trip was by the Imperial Indian Mail, a train from Bombay to Calcutta during the British Raj.[10] As in the case of the previous trip, the official stated purpose was for the new young King of Siam to study. In 1873, Chulalongkorn celebrated his twentieth birthday. After his second coronation began the long process of extensive reforms for Siam, including abolishing slavery, improving judicial and financial institutions and instituting appointed legislative councils.

As discussed above in Chapter 1, the administrative reforms patterned on Western models, especially the Dutch East Indies, British Malaya, and British Raj, developed a bureaucratic state, or in the Dutch term *beamtenstaaten*, for colonial administration, or in the case of independent Siam, self-administration.

These innovations carefully were tailored to follow established models comprised rationalizing and centralizing the royal government, eliminating traditional semi-autonomous tributary statelets, and promoting economic development, somewhat along colonial lines.

First Two Decades of Chulalongkorn's Reign: 1870s–1880s

Chulalongkorn's goals were progressive, especially in the early stages of reform. His first proclamation, in 1873, addressed the abolition of prostration and crawling.[11] The practice of social subjugation, in which the Siamese were accustomed to prostrating themselves at the feet of those of higher social status, was seen as retrograde and unproductive, part of the past rather than the future. Bowing to dignitaries instead became the recommended form of expressing respect and deference.

The king noted in comments published in the *Royal Gazette*: "The practice of prostration in Siam is severely oppressive ... Subordinates have been forced to prostrate in order to elevate the dignity of their superiors. I do not see how the practice of prostration will render any benefit to Siam."

Typically, the proclamation revealed a comparative international perspective, with the king keenly aware of what worked and what did not in other nations. So, he observed that in other East Asian kingdoms, including China, Yuan (Vietnam), Japan and West Asia (India) the practice of commanding subordinates to prostrate themselves before superiors and nobles, had been abolished in the name of rebuilding more equal relationships between different social groups in society to reduce "class oppression". As a key conclusion, the king added that since abolishing prostration, the aforementioned nations became "more prosperous". He saw the practice of prostration in Siam as reaffirming the "existence of oppression which is unjust", in addition to holding back the kingdom economically. Finally, he warned that other reforms would be on the way, but to eliminate all retrograde social practices simultaneously would not be practical, so a "gradual and timely" approach would be taken, by the end of which "Siam will re-emerge as a much more prosperous kingdom."

Likewise, King Chulalongkorn slowly and systematically abolished slavery or *that* system, as well as the corvée or *phrai*, i.e., use of forced labour exacted in place of taxes. In doing so, he was following the precedent of his father King Mongkut, who began the gradual reform of the complex and specifically Siamese forms of personal bondage and servitude.

While not comparable to Western forms of slavery, these systems did inevitably lead to human oppression and above all, hindered Siam's economy by making previous workforces beholden to individual owners. Looking to a future Siam in a commercialized, international economy, the king saw that workers, especially in underpopulated areas, had to be made readily available, rather than tied down by permanent obligations.

Previously, commoners or *phrai* were required by corvée obligations to serve as unpaid labour to their *nai* or officials in the nobility, from two to six months annually. Eventually, commoners were permitted to escape these obligations by payment of a fee.

Slaves in Siam comprised war captives and those in debt bondage. Instead of seeking territory, as European forces did in wars, traditionally Southeast Asian kingdoms sought to capture workers.

Already due to King Mongkut's initiatives, the arcane varieties of debt slavery began to be abolished, with avenues of escape provided. Yet people continued to be treated as a form of property. Some of those experiencing both fates even preferred slavery over corvée labour, due to various intricacies in each condition.

As ever, King Chulalongkorn had in mind the international image of Siam, and what formal freeing the slaves, which occurred in 1905, would mean to the world political image of Siam.

By the late nineteenth century, Europe's imperial powers used supposed backwardness in matters of civilization as an excuse to invade and dominate colonies. This was one purported reason given by France for launching the Franco-Siamese War of 1893. So, the ongoing existence of slavery in Siam was significant in Western eyes.

After his decree of 1874, it later became notably easier to envisage officially terminating the practice of slavery in 1905. King Chulalongkorn realized that the practical effect of any such final abolition would be limited, as other forms of economic bondage persisted, but the need to demonstrate to Western powers that Siam was a modern power worthy and capable of self-government was primordial.

The 1905 decree did not specify this motivation, instead stating that slavery was being abolished for "the progress and happiness of the nation". If economic and political pressures helped end the corvée and slavery systems, King Chulalongkorn's centralization of taxation and financial control ran into trouble.

In 1873, supported by young princes, mostly his brothers and half-brothers, and nobles who formed a group that called itself Young Siam, the King established three new offices to bolster his reform programmes: a twelve-member Council of State, a Central Revenue Office (*Ho Ratsadakonphiphat*), and a forty-nine-member Privy Council. Most important was a progressive reorganization of the antiquated Great Royal Treasury Department or *Phra Khlang Maha Sombat*.

The old *Phra Khlang* had developed into an organization for collecting revenue on major coastal towns in the Gulf of Siam, while at the same time supervising foreign affairs (*Krom Tha*). In the initial period of reform, tax collecting was to be directly and tightly supervised by the King's close senior relative Prince Maha Mala, a half-brother of King Mongkut, and the *Krom Tha* became a separate entity, paving the way to the modern Ministry of Foreign Affairs.

These new measures of tax collection raised heckle among traditional-minded conservative factions at court and led to a political crisis early in 1875. The opponents were older princely relatives and nobles. The Front Palace Crisis or Wang Na Incident occurred from 28 December 1874 to 24 February 1875. In the power struggle, against the reformist King Chulalongkorn was the conservative Prince Wichaichan, the vice-king.

These reforms looked to Prince Wichaichan and the nobility as diminishing their power and influence. In December 1874, Wichaichan received an anonymous letter that threatened his life. In response, he mobilized troops and ordered them to the Front Palace, in a worrying show of power that outnumbered the king's royal guard. The king in turn assembled his royal troops.[12]

When, apparently accidentally, a fire broke out inside the Grand Palace, Wichaichan's Front Palace troops fulfilled their duty to protect the monarch by rushing to assist, but this was seen as a potential move to arrest the king, so the royal troops barred their entry.

Despite this confrontation, the fire was extinguished, although rumour had it that the Front Palace might have been at its origin. Since Prince Wichaichan was not personally at the head of Front Palace troops offering aid, as he should have been, King Chulalongkorn ordered his troops to surround the Front Palace.

Fearing for his own life, Wichaichan fled in the early hours of 2 January 1875 to the British Consulate. The crisis was finally resolved by Sir Andrew Clarke, Governor of the Straits Settlements, who elected to back the king, rather than his cousin. Afterwards, the Front Palace's powers were removed, and after Wichaichan's death in 1885, the title ceased to be used.

Once again, it may be that King Chulalongkorn's early international outreach in 1871 and 1872 during much-publicized visits to British Malaya, Singapore, Burma and India likely worked in his favour. British mediation ensured that the forward-looking king eager to incorporate

Western know-how in his political policies were preferred to Prince Wichaichan's Old Siam forces; although the latter's revenue and armed force were thenceforth confined and limited, King Chulalongkorn realized that his centralizing reform had to be a gradual process to avoid any such collisions in future.

The first sign of success in centralization and absolutism occurred a decade later when senior members of the Old Siam began to die and otherwise fade from the scene. In early 1887, Chulalongkorn appointed his eldest son, nine-year-old Prince Vajirunnahis (1878–94) as heir apparent.

In doing so, Chulalongkorn did not follow the old Siamese tradition of consulting an assembly of royals and nobles and even bypassed the 300-year-old Office of the Heir Presumptive or Wang Na. Prince Wichaichan had died in 1885, following the 1882 demise of Chuang Bunnag, Somdet Chaophraya Si Suriwongse, senior head of an influential family of nobles, who had served as regent during the early years of the reign of King Chulalongkorn.

For the benefit of his son, the king created an office of Crown Prince or Siamese Crowned Royal Son (*Sayam makut ratcha kumar*). Traditional European primogeniture styles of royal succession were thereby introduced to Siam for the first time and would endure, sometimes problematically, until today. Issues of the protocol in royal successions since this innovation of the Fifth Reign would be seen, notably between the Sixth and Seventh reigns, as well as the Ninth and Tenth.

Subsequent Decades of Chulalongkorn's Reign: 1890s–1900s

Internally, Chulalongkorn succeeded in centralizing on four fronts: primarily, financial (*klang*); military (*kalahom*), provincial administration (*mahatthai*); and educational (*suksathikan*). Traditional departmental names such as *klang, kalahom* and *mahatthai* were retained but were not merely modified in the shift from the former departments (*krom*) to the new ministries (*krasuang*) as decreed by the king in his 1892 reform statement.[13]

In 1890, fifteen years after the Front Palace crisis and over halfway through his reign which would end in 1910, the problematic financial administration was finally reorganized as the Ministry of Finance (*krasuang phra khlang maha sombat*; literally the Ministry of the Great Royal Treasury). The new Ministry consisted of thirteen departments charged with overseeing all financial affairs: tax and duty collecting, accounting, budgets, coining and printing money, and operating the crown property. The king named close, highly trusted officials to run the operation, including a number of his close relatives.[14]

On the military front, the King bypassed the old defence ministry (*krom kalahom*) and, in 1887, established a new War Department (*krom yutthanathikan*). In the eventful year 1890, it would be elevated to Ministry of War (*krasuang yutthanathikan*), before being renamed yet again two years later as the Ministry of Defense (*krasuang kalahom*).

During the Ayutthaya Kingdom, the *krom kalahom* did not supervise military forces. There was no standing army in old Siam, except royal guards and a small number of conscripts under the six traditional departments (*krom*) of *kalahom, mahatthai*, capital/*wiang*, palace/*wang*, and rice fields/*na*.[15] By the early Bangkok Period, *krom kalahom* had acquired a more territorial function, overseeing the area to the south of Bangkok; it was in charge of corvée labour conscription, tax collecting, and judicial functions, among other responsibilities.

Chulalongkorn's military reform created a modern standing army, up-to-date military training, education, and conscription. Military recruitment or conscription (*ken thahan*) finally replaced corvée labour in 1905, and modern weapons were purchased from Western armaments suppliers.[16] As one historian put it:

> The development of a modern military was slow. The "pilot model" was the elite Royal Pages Bodyguards created by King Chulalongkorn in 1870/71. In 1874 the various guards' units were consolidated into the Royal Infantry of the Line, which, like Royal Pages Bodyguards, followed British patterns of military organization. Later, in 1880, the process of modernization shifted to the First Foot guards, who protected the capital. This revitalization force, organized on the continental rather than the British model, recruited paid volunteers, thus providing the means for creating a standing army. The Royal Military Academy, founded in

1885, began to educate a Thai officer corps ... The National Defense Plan of 1904 prepared the way for universal conscription ... By 1910 Thailand [still Siam then] had achieved a standing army of 20,000 men that was headed by Thai officers trained in either the Royal Military Academy or Europe.[17]

Neo-mandala: Internal Colonialism

So, by the middle of his reign, Chulalongkorn had a modern army that, on the one hand, was not strong enough to protect Siam during the Paknam Incident, a military engagement fought during the Franco-Siamese War in July 1893. While sailing off Paknam on Siam's Chao Phraya River, three French ships entered the Siamese territory. Warning shots were fired from a Siamese fort and gunboats were deployed, but France won the ensuing skirmish and blockaded Bangkok, which ended the war. As a result, Siam agreed to cede Laos to France, an act that led to the significant expansion of French Indochina.[18]

Even so, King Chulalongkorn's army was capable of suppressing the so-called Holy Man's Rebellion in 1901 and 1902. In the former year, supporters of the *Phu Mi Bun* religious movement began an armed rebellion against French Indochina and Siam, to install their leader, the sorcerer Ong Keo, whose name meant Precious Jewel, as ruler of the world. By 1902, the uprising had been eliminated in Siam, although it continued in French Indochina until 1936.

According to one story, Ong Keo was executed for being unacceptably arrogant by a French Commissioner of Salavan Province in southern Laos in 1910; the French civil servant summoned the religious leader to a meeting, hiding a gun in his hat, which was used to kill him.[19]

Along with financial and military control, Chulalongkorn was able to transform Siam and its formerly semi-autonomous princedoms like Lanna/Chiang Mai, Isan and Muslim Pattani into a unified kingdom. This meant abandoning claims and sovereignty over areas adjacent to the British in Burma and Malaya (Kedah, Kelantan, Terengganu and Perlis) and the French in Laos (Luang Prabang, Vientianne and Champasak) as well as Siem

Reap, Battambang in Cambodia. However, internally, and innovatively, a neo-mandala system had been created to replace older structures.

The centralized provincial administration was referred to as *mandala desa abhibala*, supervised by the Ministry of Interior with Prince Damrong, founder of the modern Thai educational system as well as the modern provincial administration, in charge. Half-brother of King Chulalongkorn, Prince Damrong was a self-taught historian, and one of the most influential Thai intellectuals of his time. Of this neo-mandala system, the historian David K. Wyatt has written:

> In what he termed the *thesaphiban* [*desa+abhi-bala*] system, introduced at Nakhon Rachasima (Khorat) ... Prince Damrong grouped a number of provinces into a single administrative unit (*monthon* [mandala] "circle") under the control of a resident commissioner in a manner similar to the royal commissionerships earlier established in Chiang Mai, the northeast, and Phuket. Given the power to override the semi-hereditary provincial governors, the commissioners began almost immediately to take control of local revenues and expenditures, overhaul the courts, introduce new police units, and curb corruption and injustice. Some older officials were retired, and others were incorporated into the new system. All were encouraged to send their sons to schools in Bangkok, that they might carry on their families' noble profession (but in other provinces).[20]

This neo-mandala system to centralize administration was a protracted process, taking some two decades to complete. It was slowly introduced in the early 1870s in the North, then the Northeast, and finally in the South. Under the ancient mandala system, these so-called outer provinces (*hua muang*) were semi-autonomous. They had their own hereditary ruling families and separate cultural identities in spoken and written languages.

They had their own legal codes, customs and religions, with different Buddhist practices in the North and Northeast, and Islamic observance in the Deep South. In the North, centred in Chiang Mai, most of the population were Tai Yon, known to central Thailand as Lao people; their own ruling family dated back to the late eighteenth century, the era of Kings Taksin and Rama I.

Their cultural identity included an individual brand of Buddhism, garb and language, especially the writing system, which was more similar to the Shan and the Burmese than the central Siamese-Thai. But the British, advancing into Burma, had already accepted Bangkok's suzerainty over the area by signing the first Anglo-Siamese Chiang Mai Treaty in 1873 with Bangkok. This was followed by the second Chiang Mai Treaty in 1883; both secured Siam's cooperation with British India and Burma in dealings with the teak business, extraterritorial consulate court, and criminal extraditions.[21] King Chulalongkorn was able to station agents as commissioners or *kha luang yai* to wrest administrative control from Chiang Mai and other northern ruling families from Lampang, Lamphun, Chiang Rai and Nan. The most celebrated commissioner was Prince Phichit Prichakon (1855–1909), half-brother to the king.

In 1884 while stationed in Chiang Mai, the Prince imposed Bangkok rule over the northern capital and arranged a political marriage between Chulalongkorn and a Chiang Mai princess, Dara Rasami (1873–1933). This was done to ensure that the northern region would not become part of British India or Burma. An engagement was made with the eleven-year-old princess and two years later, she was sent to live in the Bangkok Grand Palace as one of Chulalongkorn's concubines.

Dara Rasami had only one daughter with the king, in 1889, who died at age four. The king chose another Chiang Mai princess as an additional concubine, Thip Keson, who bore him a son, Prince Dilok (1884–1912). The prince was among the first Siamese to graduate from the University of Tübingen, Germany, where in 1908 he received a doctoral degree in economics.[22]

Bangkok also claimed suzerainty over vast areas in the Northeast, including the Lao regions of Luang Prabang, Muang Phuan, Vientianne and Champasak, as well as several centres east and west of the Mekong River. On one side is present-day Laos, with the Khorat Plateau on the other, comprising Nakhon Ratchasima, Loei, Nongkhai, Nakhon Phanom, Ubon and Buriram-Surin, including Siem Reap and Battambang.

Yet as we shall see, King Chulalongkorn's centralized reform project was more complicated in the Northeast, the area today known as Isan, than in the North, and less successful. In exchange, Siam had to relinquish control over what is now Laos and Cambodia. By contrast, after the French colonized Vietnam, they also claimed Laos and Cambodia as former vassals of that nation, bundling them all into what became known as French Indochina in 1887.

France had obtained control over northern Vietnam following its victory over China in the Sino-French War of 1884–85. French Indochina was formed in October 1887 from Annam, Tonkin, Cochinchina, which together form modern Vietnam, and the Kingdom of Cambodia; Laos was added after the Franco-Siamese War in 1893.

In short, politico-historical developments in King Chulalongkorn's reign resulted from an internal need for centralization as well as Siamese accommodation of France's colonial expansion. Three influential factors were prominent: the Haw Wars, fought against Chinese quasi-military forces invading parts of Tonkin and Siam from 1865–1890; northern Lao principalities as tributary states of both Vietnam and Siam; and finally, French influx into Indochina. These phenomena added up to create and influence Chulalongkorn's policies towards the Northeast and Laos.

Remnants of the aftermath of the Taiping Rebellion, the civil war waged in China from 1850 to 1864 between the established Qing dynasty and the theocratic Taiping Heavenly Kingdom led by Hong Xiuquan, a heterodox Christian convert, spilled over into the northern part of mainland Southeast Asia. The invaders were confused with Chinese Muslims from Yunnan called Haw, resulting in the misnomer of Haw Wars.

During the latter half of the nineteenth century, bands of Chinese warriors known as flag gangs ravaged large areas of northern Laos. Outlaws and freebooters, the flag gangs were fleeing the suppression of the Taiping Rebellion in China. Tonkin, now northern Vietnam, was invaded first when units of the Black Flags and rival Yellow Flags crossed the China-Vietnam frontier in 1865 and established bases in the upper reaches of the Red River Valley.

By the 1870s, other bands, brandishing Red Flag and Striped Flag banners, moved south to occupy almost all of northern Laos.

Forces sent by King Chulalongkorn, Rama V failed to suppress the various groups, the last of which eventually disbanded in 1890. Neither the Vietnamese nor Thai overlords could help their Laotian tributaries, who instead sought French protection. Yet in 1875, 1883, and again in 1884–85, Chulalongkorn sent modern armies to ward off the Haws.

Of these expeditions, the last mentioned one is the best documented, as it included James Fitzroy McCarthy (1853–1919), an Irish surveyor and cartographer who played a prominent role in the delimitation of Siam's borders in the late nineteenth century, helping transform the country into a modern nation-state. McCarthy would serve as the first Director-General of the Royal Thai Survey Department, established in 1885.

Several other Europeans participated in the 1884–85 expedition to suppress the Haw rebels, which was marked by poor planning, causing exceptional sufferings for the troops involved.

While McCarthy was impressed by the beauty and natural wealth of the regions he visited, he sympathized with the difficult lives of local residents, who were often victimized by roving bands of robbers, while also being in debt to regional governors. Regional Buddhist temples were regularly plundered by marauders.

Into this problematic situation arrived some notable commanders of Siamese forces, including the King's younger half-brother Prince Krom Mun Prajak (1856–1925) and his associate Chamuen Waiwaranat (1851–1931; accorded the title of *Chao Phraya Surasakmontri-Choem Sang-Xuto*).

According to James McCarthy, transport issues as well as the difference in character among Siamese commanders made their mission difficult from the start. One commander, who had been raised around the Royal Court, was displeased to be associated with a fellow military officer with a more rustic, provincial background.

To some extent, the Siamese commanders with royal connections underestimated the Haw rebels and were mistakenly under the impression that the mere arrival of Siamese troops on the scene would be enough to cause them to scatter. As it happened, the Haw turned out to be a tenacious foe, with well-fortified stockades. As in the North, the incursion of the

Taiping splinter groups, and the involvement of the French were useful reasons for Chulalongkorn to station Bangkok commissioners in the area.

The final outcome in 1890–91 was new administrative units known as *huamuang/monthon/mandala* Lao Klang, Lao Phuan and Lao Kao. In 1892, after the Paknam Incident, the areas to the east of the Mekong were annexed to French Indochina. They were followed by Champasak in 1904 and Siem Reap-Battambang in 1907. What remained with Siam is now known as Northeast Thailand, with three centres under new mandala names: Nakhon Ratsima (replacing Lao Klang), Udon (replacing Lao Phuan, with its administrative centre moved from Nong Khai to Udon), and Isan (replacing Lao Kao, with its centre moved from Champasak to Ubon).

The reason for discarding the term Lao was to avoid political confusion, insofar as the other portion of Laos became part of French Indochina. What remained in Chulalongkorn's Siam could no longer use the Lao appellation. King Chulalongkorn reportedly explained these place name revisions by commenting, around the year 1900, that ancient Siamese administrative polity was an empire (*rachathiracha*) consisting of different peoples and languages. To retain the old administrative form would be detrimental to the nation, the king asserted. His Siam had become a kingdom or *phrarat anakhet*.[23]

Gone were the days of vassal kings given a high degree of autonomy, provided that they made an annual tribute of gold and silver, traditionally modelled into trees, as symbolic gifts given in tribute to overlords. The *bunga emas dan perak* (golden and silver flowers), sometimes termed *bunga mas* (golden flowers), was a tribute triennially to the King of Ayutthaya (Siam) from vassal states in the Malay Peninsula, especially Terengganu, Kelantan, Kedah, Pattani, Nong Chik, Yala, Rangae, Kubang Pasu (a district in northern Kedah) and Setul. The tribute consisted of two small trees made of gold and silver, plus costly gifts of weapons, goods and slaves.

Such tributes, also including corvée labour, had led to such outbreaks as the Lao–Siamese War of 1826–28 over a half-century earlier. So, the king concluded, the people and their area in the northeast and north of Siam should no longer be referred to as Lao (or Kaek Malayu). Instead, they should be termed Thai of the North, Northeast, and South.

Echoing Chulalongkorn's associations with two Chiang Mai princesses, at least two Bangkok Prince Commissioners married into local ruling noble families. Prince Krom Luang Sanphasit (1857–1922), a half-brother of the king was stationed in Ubon; he married Mom Chiang Kham and Mom Boon Yuen, both from ruling Ubon families. Prince Krom Luang Prajak (1856–1924), another half-brother of the king, was stationed in Nong Khai and Udon; he married no fewer than seven local Nakhonthab noblewomen, named Suwan, Phring, Chaem, Chan, Nuam, Toem and Keo.[24]

In the South, historically the control by Ayutthaya and Bangkok was through a semi-autonomous statelet at Nakhon Si Thammarat. Noi na Nagara (1776–1838), or Chao Phraya Nakhon Si Thammarat, was governor of Nakhon Si Thammarat or Ligor and a son of King Taksin. His modern descendants bear the surname na Nagara, Komarakul na Nagara, and Chaturangakula. Chao Phraya Nakhon Noi was known in contemporary British sources as the Raja of Ligor.

Further south were Malay states such as Pattani, Kedah, Kelantan and Terengganu, all with their own ruling families, but different religious and ethnic groups. The Malays were loosely governed from Nakhon Si Thammarat and were required to pay gold and silver flower tributes to the Bangkok kings. By the mid-nineteenth century, these coastal areas had become more economically important to Bangkok.

Tin mining and rubber plantations provided new economic resources. Meanwhile, the British were advancing across the Andaman Sea. Penang's history begins in 1786 when Captain Francis Light (1790–94) made a pact with the Sultan of Kedah. He acquired Penang on behalf of the East India Company from the Sultan and in return, the company promised to give Kedah protection from powerful neighbours. And in 1819, Stamford Raffles, Temenggong Abdu'r Rahman and Sultan Hussein Shah of Johor signed a treaty that gave the British East India Company (EIC) the right to set up a trading post in Singapore.

By 1885, British annexation was complete, from the coast of Tenasserim to Mandalay and beyond. With the opening of the Suez Canal in 1869, the western coast was booming from Moulmein through Ranong, Phuket, Penang and Singapore. Tin and rubber became vital parts of economic life for the South, along with an influx of overseas Chinese, especially Hakka Han people. Some old towns were revived, as new ones sprang up: Songkhla and Hat Yai, Phuket, Phang Nga, Trang, Takau Pa, and Ranong. Old urban centres at Nakhon Si Thammarat and Pattani would be overshadowed by Songkhla and Hat Yai as well as Phuket and Ranong. Traditional ruling families, including the Bunnag, were replaced by new arrivals, especially the wealthy and willful na Songkhla, na Ranong and Jotikasthira clans. They were originally impoverished groups in China who made fortunes in business after arrival in Siam. The na Songkhla clan, for example, traces its origin back to Chin Yiang Sae Hao, the clan founder, who migrated from Fujian province to Siam in 1750 and established political influence in Songkhla Province. Since the beginning of Bangkok, these families have been a highly significant part of Thai economic and political life.[25]

Chin Yiang Sae Hao (1716–84) was a Hokkien. At age thirty-four he sailed from Amoy to settle in Songkhla. His business acumen soon became visible in the edible bird's nest trade, centred around Bird's Nest Island (*Koh Rang Nok*) in Songkhla Lake.

In the Pak Phayun district of Phatthalung Province, islands serve as home to flocks of swiftlets whose nests are made of solidified saliva, the main ingredient in making bird's nest soup, a delicacy especially prized in Chinese culture due to their rarity, high nutritional value in protein, and flavour. So renowned were edible bird's nests collected from Phatthalung that King Chulalongkorn once visited Koh Rang Nok, the island of bird's nests, and had his royal initials inscribed on a cliffside.

Chin Yiang Sae Hao's expertise in other agricultural products also caught the attention of Bangkok kings from Taksin to Chulalongkorn. From 1775 to 1901, seven members of his family, including himself, were appointed governors of Songkhla. This titular eminence was the source of their Thai family name.

The height of their power coincided with the second half of the nineteenth century, during the governorship of Bunsang (1847–65) and Chao Phraya Wichian Khiri, Men (1865–84). The na Songkhla clan essentially represented an extension of Bangkok control on revenue collection as well as provincial administration of the eastern coast of southern Siam, including the Malay areas.

The western coast was controlled by the na Ranong family, who took their Thai surname from the province, where they resided, Ranong. Khaw Soo Cheang (1797–1882), the founder of the family, was also a Hokkien. He arrived in Siam in 1922 and eventually established a tin mining and shipping empire. He was appointed governor of Ranong Province in 1854 and given the princely title of Phraya na Ranong by the royal family. He became the primogenitor of the Khaw na Ranong family, one of the most prominent Thai Chinese families in Thailand.[26]

With all these carefully interwoven allies, King Chulalongkorn was poised to attain even greater achievements, as his new Siam became a secured buffer state between the British in Burma and Malaya and the French in Indochina.

Yet he would die in 1910 at age fifty-seven, a considerably younger age than his father King Mongkut, whose own untimely demise at age sixty-three was due to malaria caught during an astronomical expedition to Wa Ko village in Prachuap Khirikhan Province, south of Hua Hin, where Mongkut had correctly predicted a solar eclipse.

His son, King Chulalongkorn, who was present for the expedition, also came down with malaria but recovered. When he died at Amphorn Sathan Residential Hall in Bangkok, he had reigned over Siam for a remarkable forty-two years. The day after the king died, the *London Mail* reported the cause of death as "uraemia" after an extended bout of "chronic nephritis".

Kidney issues were partly what motivated King Chulalongkorn's 1907 trip to Europe, during which he stayed at German resorts where treatments for kidney ailments were offered, on the advice of his European doctors. The cures at fashionable spas and resorts were a traditional part of upper-class life in the nineteenth and early twentieth centuries.

King Chulalongkorn participated in this tradition, celebrating his fifty-fourth birthday in Bad Homburg, Germany, noted for its natural hot spring spas. A spring was formally named after the king. In response, he presented the town with a Thai pavilion made in Bangkok and shipped in individual parts to Germany, where it arrived in 1910. By the time parts damaged in transit had been replaced, the Siamese Temple, as it was known to German locals, was not inaugurated until 1914, by which time Chulalongkorn was dead, so Prince Mahidol attended the ceremony.

The pavilion was placed at a prominent site in town, but not at the Chulalongkorn Spring, where the king had intended it to be. This fact may have rankled slightly over the intervening century, and in 2007, King Bhumibol and Queen Sirikit donated a second Thai pavilion to Bad Homburg on condition that it would be constructed at the Chulalongkorn Spring. So Bad Homburg possesses two Thai pavilions, all due to the persistent appreciation of the Chakri Dynasty.

Nevertheless, King Chulalongkorn's kidney issues continued, and it was considered that the cumulative stress of his ambitious reform projects may have weakened his overall health. Even years before, the 1893 Paknam Incident took its toll, as Gustave Rolin-Jaequemyns, a Belgian lawyer and diplomat who served as an advisor to Chulalongkorn on Western-style reforms, observed. Rolin-Jaequemyns, who was awarded the title of Chao Phya Abhai Raja, the highest distinction ever granted to a foreigner, was concerned by the King enduring fevers and sleepless nights, and even discussed with the King's brother Prince Devawongse what might happen if Chulalongkorn became incapacitated.

Although he did recover from this crisis, health issues presented an unpredictable impediment to his achievement of even more national accomplishments. Even so, as monarch for forty-two years, he led Siam into modernity by unifying and consolidating his rule of absolutism.

At the time, to find a Siamese ruler who rivalled his longevity and stamina, it was necessary to look back to the fifteenth century. Borommatrailokkanat or Trailok (1431–88) was the king of the Ayutthaya Kingdom from 1448 to 1488. He was one of many monarchs who was given the epithet King of White Elephants. Borommatrailokkanat's reign was also known for a massive reform of Thai bureaucracy.

His successor Chulalongkorn had solidified his rule in 1886, after the death of the last vice-king, Wichaichan, by choosing not to appoint one of his brothers as a new vice-king. Instead, Chulalongkorn appointed his eldest son Prince Vajirunhis as Crown Prince of Siam. On this occasion, Queen Victoria of the United Kingdom sent a congratulatory telegram to King Chulalongkorn and his son.

Sadly, the Crown Prince died unexpectedly of typhoid fever at age sixteen, long before he could reach the throne. King Chulalongkorn's second son, Prince Vajiravudh, was then named Crown Prince and succeeded him as Rama VI in 1910.

The king had built a European-style palace to serve as a residence for the Crown Prince, known to some as Windsor Palace, due to its partial resemblance to Windsor Castle. The building was also known to locals as *Wang Klang Thung* or *Wang Mai*. It later became part of Chulalongkorn University but was demolished to make way for the construction of Suphachalasai Stadium.

Despite these dashed hopes, King Chulalongkorn succeeded in protecting his subjects from the ordeal of Anglo-French colonialism by diplomatically abandoning claims over parts of Cambodia, Laos and Malaya.

He ensured the future of his dynasty by fathering seventy-seven children with ninety-two consorts but left behind a vast and cumbersome royal family structure.[27] By preferring the European style of royal succession through primogeniture or the right of the first-born son to succeed, King Vajiravudh became Rama VI.

By early 1912 there would be a coup attempt against King Vajiravudh, and by the reign of another son of Chulalongkorn, King Prajadhipok (Rama VII) absolute monarchy came to an end in 1932. Neither Rama VI nor Rama VII produced any male heir. So, it became clear that King Chulalongkorn's immense *barami* (reserved power or authority) of forty-two years could hardly help his successors.

Some of the thorny issues he addressed remained problems for later generations of his compatriots. For example, the protection of free speech, among other legal reforms initiated by King Chulalongkorn, was left an unclear subject. The king encouraged free speech and criticism among his legislative advisers, he also maintained a firm grip on the subject matter they were allowed to address.

There was no public freedom of speech such as is found in Western democracies. The Siamese people of King Chulalongkorn's time were scarcely permitted to criticize the official actions of judges, and fines and imprisonment awaited those who transgressed these rules.

A royal ordinance promulgated in 1899 dealt with the law of defamation. Whereas King Mongkut had proclaimed that no sanctions were necessary if attacks on the government or individuals were printed, since it would be common knowledge that any such publications would be inaccurate. Had they been well-founded, such criticisms would not need to be printed, since they could be presented before a law court or the Palace.

So, while King Mongkut believed it was unnecessary for the government to retaliate in cases of defamation, the amplified occasions during Chulalongkorn's reign for ordinary citizens to express negative opinions about the government and officials meant that some code was needed to prevent malicious attempts to destroy reputations or impede national progress.

One year before the royal ordinance on defamatory speech was enacted in 1899, a certain J.J. Lilly, a Western newspaper publisher, was deported from Siam for printing articles in his Bangkok newspaper suggesting that the Siamese government failed to ensure the personal safety and property of foreign visitors.

King Bhumibol, Rama IX, the Longest Reign of Thailand

Increasingly, late twentieth century Thais would compare King Bhumibol to his distinguished grandfather for intellectual capacity, empathy and leadership. By being diligent, talented, and humanitarian, Rama V and Rama IX came to symbolize direct care for their subjects.

Indeed, Thailand's Office of the National Cultural Commission made this comparison explicit by publishing in 1988, on the occasion of Rama IX's sixtieth birthday *Two Great Development Kings (song maharat nak phatthana)* discussing parallels between the two reigns.

During his long tenure, King Bhumibol guided Thailand through troublesome military rules of the 1950s and 1960s. He and his Queen,

Sirikit, as well as the Princess Mother (1900–95), helped put the nation on the international map while constructing a new monarchy.

Unlike other parts of Southeast Asia and East Asia, Bhumibol's Thailand escaped communism and some of the direct impact of the Vietnam War. And by the mid-1980s, his reign was labelled a royal hegemony (*phra ratcha amnat nam*). The king became the "Soul of the Nation", whose wishes were akin to commands. With over 3,000 Royal Initiated Projects (RIPs), he was seen as a hard-working king dedicated to national development and his subjects.

In this way, King Bhumibol acquired immense *barami* comparable to that of Chulalongkorn. Unlike King Chulalongkorn, Bhumibol had one Queen. But in his advanced years, the large and complex immediate royal family echoed a more modest version of the vast population of the Royal Palace during King Chulalongkorn's reign.

King Bhumibol and Queen Sirikit had four children and several official and unofficial grandchildren. HRH Prince Vajiralongkorn, born 1952, was appointed Crown Prince and heir apparent (*sayam makut ratcha kumar*) in 1972. Three princesses were born in 1951, 1955 and 1957 respectively. All four, especially the princesses, have been extremely devoted to royal social functions. The couple's second daughter, Princess Maha Chakri Sirindhorn, has demonstrated a range of intellectual and artistic interests that approach those of her father.

Known to the Thai people as Princess Angel (*Phra Thep*), HRH Princess Sirindhorn has published dozens of travel diaries with her observations about international outreach and goodwill tours, during which she always painstakingly took notes and photographic images to discuss them with her father upon her return to Thailand.

Her ceaseless energy for good works, like those of her parents, was rewarded in 1974 when the Thai constitution was altered in 1974 to allow for female succession, thus making her eligible for the throne. Her title, *Sayam Borom Ratchakumari*, has been interpreted by Western observers as signifying the equivalent of a princess royal. In the era of mass media, following King Bhumibol's path-breaking use of the radio to remain in contact with his subjects was expanded when television became omnipresent in the kingdom.

Since the mid-1960s, *News of the Palace*, a fifteen-minute news update of royal good deeds and activities on behalf of Thai subjects has been presented on all free TV channels. This is but one way in which the new monarchy embraced innovation in a way that might have been familiar to King Mongkut or his son Chulalongkorn, ever avid to learn about new world technological and cultural developments.

Progress was interrupted by the 1997 Asian financial crisis that gripped much of East Asia and Southeast Asia starting in July 1997. The problems began in Thailand (where they were known as the *Tom Yum Kung* crisis, after the popular spicy soup that induces perspiration in diners) on 2 July, with the financial collapse of the Thai baht after the Thai government was forced to float the baht due to lack of foreign currency to support its currency peg to the US dollar.

Political turmoil brought in new monied forces headed by Thaksin Shinawatra and his family, while a series of health issues continued to impact the monarchy, as the empathetic Thai people cared deeply about the health of King Bhumibol. There was equal reverence during King Chulalongkorn's reign for the physical well-being of His Majesty, but his subjects were not as overwhelmingly apprised in detail about the subject by television, radio and other media.

Ernst Kantorowicz's *The King's Two Bodies: A Study in Mediaeval Political Theology* (Princeton, 1957) was about how in the Middle Ages in the West, distinctions separated the monarch's corporeal being and the body politic. Although twentieth-century Thailand is certainly far in time and place from Kantorowicz's subject matter, the health of the ageing King Bhumibol was an influential matter on the body politic for his subjects, intensifying loyalties and long-held emotions, comparable to those of watching a beloved family member face health crises. In this sense, the portrayal of the King as the Nation's Father had been fully realized. When his health faltered after long and diligent outreach and service to his people, Thais were deeply moved and affected.

The 2006 Thai *coup d'état* in September of that year, when the Royal Thai Army overturned the elected caretaker government of Prime Minister Thaksin Shinawatra, failed to restore any sense of normalcy or equilibrium. Starting in September 2009, the king was admitted for an extended stay to Siriraj Hospital in Bangkok, named after Prince Siriraj, the infant son of his grandfather.

On increasingly rare occasions, the king continued to appear for public ceremonies, such as official visits by US President Barack Obama and Chinese Premier Wen Jiabao, both in November 2012, and Japanese Prime Minister Shinzo Abe in January 2013.

Yet private appearances continued to be reported. As a supplement to *News of the Palace* and other media venues, a story circulated during the catastrophic floods of 2011, that the king and his daughter, HRH Princess Maha Chakri Sirindhorn, had been driven out quietly one night in an unmarked vehicle to survey the damage in Bangkok. Their car was stopped at one flood-affected area by a security guard who, not at first realizing the royal occupants of the car, waved them away brusquely.

This widely circulated account suggested that even when ailing, the aged king retained an appetite for understanding and information that had fuelled the manifold accomplishments and innovations of his reign. Seconded by HRH Princess Sirindhorn, one of his more intellectual children, their fact-finding mission was apparently an attempt to experience something of what was gripping the Thai nation at that moment. This emotive and empathetic outreach to the people, beyond the palace walls, continued well into his old age.

As the king's health became more uncertain, Queen Sirikit, who was also cherished by her subjects for development projects and industries which she nurtured, was likewise admitted and hospitalized; she became less of a public presence after July 2012.

This exceptional twilight in Thailand echoed the challenge faced by Siam of Chulalongkorn's late reign, in terms of *barami*, that term meaning merit, reserved authority and power. Long and successful reigns represent accumulations of *barami*, but according to Theravada Buddhism, this is non-transferable.

King Chulalongkorn was, therefore, unable to bequeath his *barami* directly to his two son-kings, Kings Rama VI and Rama VII. Nor could King Bhumibol do so with his children, who relied instead on their relative accomplishments and abilities.

Over the long years of his reign, King Bhumibol had developed his style of the new monarchy, which was neither that of an absolute nor constitutional monarch. By the end of the 1950s, the king had emerged as occupying the heart of his nation. He was well protected and supported by the Thai military as well as by American presence in Southeast Asia. With support and friendship from the United States, the Thai king and queen were in the foreground of the Free World through the challenging years from the 1950s through the 1980s.

The Americans needed the Thai monarch for their intervention in Indochina. Likewise, during the Cold War, as a close American ally, the Thai military the governments of Sarit-Thanom to Prem, or 1980 to 1988, relied on the king for their legitimacy.

As mentioned earlier, the new monarchy actively developed in the 1960s was especially visible during two political crises, the 1973 Thai popular uprising and Black May of 1992. The latter events, also known as Bloody May, occurred from 17 to 20 May 1992 when popular protest in Bangkok broke out against the government of General Suchinda Kraprayoon, followed by military suppression.

In these cases, King Bhumibol became a balancing force ending violence and keeping the military at bay. On other tragic occasions, such as the 6 October 1976 massacre and the 2010 Thai military crackdown in April and May of that year against the United Front for Democracy Against Dictatorship (UDD) protests in central Bangkok, termed by the Thai media Cruel April and Savage May, the King was notably less interventionist.

King Chulalongkorn innovated by adopting the European tradition of primogeniture in matters of royal succession, and King Bhumibol respected this precedent. According to the Palace Law of Succession, B.E. 2467 (1924) and the Constitution of the Kingdom of Thailand, B.E. 2550 (2007), the throne is inherited by the oldest male heir.

This suggests that a female monarch can only inherit the throne in the absence of a male aspirant. Although limited confusion may have existed as the life of King Bhumibol drew to a close, the status of HRH Princess Maha Chakri Sirindhorn is closer to that of the British Princess Royal, an honorary title customarily awarded by a UK monarch to the eldest daughter, rather than crown princess, or someone likely to reign.

As King Bhumibol's health became more uncertain, Thailand's much-discussed *lèse majesté* laws were invoked more often. A French term, *lèse majesté* means to "do wrong to majesty" or otherwise offend the dignity of a reigning sovereign or state.

In Thailand, public criticism of King Bhumibol, his family, projects and ideas are not allowed. Yet as international media reported, in his December 2005 birthday speech, the king said:

> Actually, I must also be criticized. I am not afraid if the criticism concerns what I do wrong, because then I know. Because if you say the King cannot be criticized, it means that the King is not human. If the King can do no wrong, it is akin to looking down upon him because the King is not being treated as a human being. But the King can do wrong.

This extraordinary expression of personal humility and human fallibility was traditional in terms of Buddhist ideals but was also far in advance of what many of his subjects, especially the royalists were prepared to accept in terms of public discourse.

It might be added that during the seven decades of his reign, the king often gave invaluable advice about topics as varied as flood control methods and the need for civil servants to be disinterested and less avid for money. On many occasions, his wise words were not heeded by the public.

Paradoxically, with King Bhumibol's remarkable intellectual achievements and creativity, had his statements been made at the time of his grandfather, when the king's wishes were if anything, more of absolute command, Thailand would have advanced even more dramatically than it did in the postwar period.

The intellectual and artistic gifts of the Chakri dynasty was inevitably linked to devout Buddhism. In 1893, the same year as the unfortunate

Franco-Siamese War, as a result of which the Siamese agreed to cede Laos to France, King Chulalongkorn ordered the first printing ever, in thirty-nine volumes of the *Tripitaka*, the Pali canon which forms the doctrinal foundation of Theravada Buddhism, bound in Bangkok, and sent as royal gifts to 260 institutes of learning across five continents in 1896.[28]

Like his father King Mongkut, and indeed as a predecessor to the remarkably varied intellect of his grandson, Chulalongkorn demonstrated respect for study and higher learning, as well as the role of universities in continuing a supranational discourse not bound to time.

King Chulalongkorn's printed *Tripitaka* marked the twenty-fifth anniversary of his coronation and demonstrated his responsibility as protector of the Buddhist religion, a role that King Bhumibol also embraced whole-heartedly. Even if the immediate historical context for Chulalongkorn was the need to give up territories, the finest Siamese traditions would be transmitted across the world, with an outward-looking sense of communication that King Bhumibol also showed during his reign. Like his grandson would be, King Chulalongkorn was determined to incarnate a combination of traditional *Dhammaraja* or a righteous Buddhist and a modern king of the people.

Demonstrating the best and most advanced achievements of Siam, and later Thailand, both monarchs held lofty ideals and optimistic goals that if given the opportunity, their subjects would follow them in a path of Buddhist righteousness. Prizing education and technology, King Chulalongkorn did not send the *Tripitaka* to political leaders, but rather to more enduring intellectual centres, where students could benefit from them.

Over a century later, despite King Bhumibol's apparent invitation to criticism in his birthday speech of 2005, most Thai political entities have remained, at least in this specific instance, even more defensive of the monarchy than the king himself. It was as if they were following the literal meaning of still another French expression, *plus royaliste que le roi* (more royalist than the king).

And so, draconian *lèse majesté* laws remain as a legacy of Siam's era of absolute monarchy. During King Chulalongkorn's reign, in 1899 and again in 1908, *lèse majesté* laws were amended, although at the time the sanctions proposed were considerably lighter than similar laws as reintroduced and re-enforced in the 1960s and mid-1970s.

From 1993 to 2004, in the years immediately before King Bhumibol's December 2005 birthday speech, his semi-official biography *King Bhumibol: Life's Works* notes that new *lèse majesté* cases had halved from the offences prosecuted in previous years.

But as time wore on, and the ailing king grew older and more infirm, a natural bureaucratic instinct to protect him overshadowed his stated wishes. By 2009, following the most recent coup of 2006, an unprecedented 165 cases were brought to court.

These and other issues correspond between King Bhumibol's Thailand and King Chulalongkorn's Siam, although as might be expected, new and previously unimaginable problems have also arisen. Apart from aforementioned royal succession policies, the twentieth century saw rural discontent, especially in the North and Northeast; political unrest in the Malay-Muslim Deep South; rural and urban class divisions, plus underground and cyberspace activism; and related criticism, some of it harsh, from international academics and journalists as well as a sizeable overseas Thai community scattered around the globe.

These economic emigrants, or in some cases voluntary exiles, live in North America; Western Europe, especially Germany and France; Australia, New Zealand and Asia, notably in Japan and a few in the Association of Southeast Asian Nations (ASEAN) region, possibly in Laos and Cambodia. Finally, student activism in Bangkok and up-country became a growingly visible expression of popular will.

Towards the end of 2014, the year of the latest coup, the king did not appear as usual on radio or television for his 5 December birthday speech or to read a New Year message. Yet the televised *News of the Palace* still showed him performing royal activities, for example receiving General Prayut's new cabinet on 4 September, some months after the coup. Occasionally the king, but not the queen, would be televised for a minute or two, seen in his wheelchair slowly pushed around the hospital to the acclaim of emotional and devoted subjects.

On rare occasions, the royal couple were televised leaving the hospital for Klai Kangwon Palace at Hua Hin for a change of atmosphere. King Bhumibol Adulyadej died at Siriraj Hospital in Bangkok on 13 October 2016, at 15:52 local time, at the age of eighty-eight, as announced by the Royal Palace later that day.

Like Chulalongkorn, until his health failed him, King Bhumibol was a great traveller, not just overseas for diplomatic outreach, but especially within the kingdom, to make contact with his subjects.

Compared to Chulalongkorn who had travelled more than any other king in old Siam, King Bhumibol's expeditions extended down to the South and British Malaya-Singapore. Chulalongkorn never visited the heartland of Lan Na in the North, nor did he go beyond Khorat in the Northeast. So, King Bhumibol was indeed the first king to be physically present in all parts of his country. And as noted, his trips were not mere occasions for friendly waving; an avid and serious student of a great variety of subjects artistic and scientific, he would pay careful attention to lecture-demonstrations given by local authorities, and as an avid photographer (as indeed King Chulalongkorn had been), would preserve images of what he saw at each place.

Among his children, his method of study tours was most visibly emulated by Princess Maha Chakri Sirindhorn. Whereas King Chulalongkorn in an era of more arduous travel mainly focused on Western Europe for external tours, King Bhumibol covered a wider range of North Atlantic Treaty Organization (NATO) and Southeast Asia Treaty Organization (SEATO) countries.[29] Most of these nations were members of the Free World. King Bhumibol never visited Russia, including after the break-up of the Soviet Union, China, India, or Cambodia. One exception was in April 1994, when King Bhumibol and Queen Sirikit, accompanied by Princess Sirindhorn officially visited a Communist state for the first time, the Lao People's Democratic Republic. This occasion marked the opening of an Australian-built bridge across the Mekong River between Laos and Thailand.

After extensive travel during the 1950s and 1960s, he made no state visits between 1968 from the height of the Cold War until 1994, three years before the 1997 Asian financial crisis. It was as if he were concentrating during those years on his subjects, their hopes, problems and concerns. These years cemented the connections that had also been established with the university-educated Thai middle classes.

It has been calculated that from 1950 to 1997, the king presided over 490 graduations and personally handed diplomas to 470,000 graduates. For each of these students, the occasion was a landmark event in their lives and the lives of their families. So, while King Chulalongkorn, like his father before him, respected and promoted knowledge as a way of advancing his country's progress, King Bhumibol brought the love of learning to a more personal level of contact.

Both kings thereby accumulated *barami*. King Bhumibol's *barami* reached its height in the early 1990s, by which time he was a symbol of stability and a balancing force for the Thai nation. His country was officially labelled as a government and administration in the form of democracy with the great king as its head (*kan pokrong nai rabob prachathippatai an mi phra mahakasat song pen pramuk*). The King of Thailand was above politics, but at times of crisis, he was obliged to take sides.

Both kings were highly involved in literature. King Chulalongkorn was a prolific writer whose prose style in the Thai language was considered particularly elegant.

When King Chulalongkorn died in 1910, the German linguist Dr Oskar Frankfurter (1852–1922) who was sent to Siam, to work as a translator for German-Thai projects at the court of King Chulalongkorn, and later served as chief librarian of the National Library in Bangkok and president of the Siam Society, chose to recall the king as a man of letters.

In "The Late King Chulalongkorn", Frankfurter analysed "what Siam owes to this monarch from a literary point of view, especially as, encouraged by his august example, it has also tried to investigate the arts, science and literature in regard to the country over which he reigned."[30]

Apart from founding the National Library to commemorate the centenary of his highly literate father, to "make generally known and preserve the sacred, historical and profane literature of Siam," Chulalongkorn frequently wrote for a literary magazine issued by the library, which also printed several texts by King Mongkut of capital historical value.

Dr Frankfurter added: "Quite apart from the fact that King Mongkut may be said to have originated modern Siamese prose, these articles are and always will remain a norm of Siamese style, of which both in prose and verse King Chulalongkorn remained a past master."

King Chulalongkorn also had letters published which he had addressed to his daughter during his last journey to Europe. This is known as *Klai ban* or "Away from Home". As Dr Frankfurter observes, "The style in all publications of the King was straight and to the point. There was no straining after effect, and they may be considered as examples of the best Siamese style. Foreign words were only used if they were better able to convey the sense than the corresponding words in Siamese…"

If necessarily at some distance from this foundation role in modern Thai writing, King Bhumibol nonetheless was drawn to writing as well. In 1996, on the fiftieth anniversary of his coronation, King Bhumibol published *The Story of Mahajanaka* (*Mahajanaka* meaning Great Father) in Thai and English. An edition of 10,000 copies was printed, followed by a cartoon version for children in 1999, later animated and adapted for the stage in 2014.

King Bhumibol's retelling of the *Mahajanaka Jataka*, one of the traditional tales of the Buddha's former lives in Theravada Buddhism was lavishly illustrated to capture the reader's imagination. The plot tells of the exiled Prince Mahajanaka who through unyielding resolve, manages to return to his homeland and assume his rightful role in helping his subjects achieve a better life.

Traditionally, Jatakas were mainly about the accumulation of *barami* by the *bodhisatta*, or future Buddha, over successive lives. Yet King Bhumibol's revision of this account of moral authority does not refer to the *bodhisatta*, or the Buddha, or the fact that it is a tale about one of the Buddha's former lives. As Patrick Jory has observed, King Bhumibol's *Story of Mahajanaka* changes the ending of the narrative, so that "instead of renouncing the throne to live a life of solitude and asceticism in the pursuit of enlightenment, Mahajanaka chooses the more modern option of remaining on the throne in order to set up an institute of higher learning."[31]

In the original text and through dramatic adaptations, King Bhumibol is associated with the protagonist King Mahajanaka by references to former's biography, and allusions to real-life events, while even paraphrasing some of the king's public speeches and writings. By identifying King Mahajanaka with King Bhumibol, the latter's perseverance, benevolence, and virtue are emphasized, as he fulfilled the principles of a righteous king.

Such details shared between the traditional character and King Bhumibol as losing their fathers at a young age or spending time away from their homeland, only to return in adulthood, further accentuated the parallels obvious to readers and spectators. As King Mahajanaka had, so King Bhumibol worked mightily for agricultural development, while also labouring to alleviate the sufferings of their people.

The special emphasis on founding an institution of higher education, like the very act of turning to literary composition, showed that King Bhumibol was very much in the family tradition praised by Oskar Frankfurter.

A further extension of this use of literature to make moral points was found in King Bhumibol's *The Story of Tongdaeng* (2002), a short biography of a pet (1998–2015) adopted by the king in 1998 from the litter of a stray dog taken in by a medical centre he had recently dedicated. *Tongdaeng* means copper in Thai, referring to the colour of the dog's coat.

A story of manners as well as affection for pets, it informs the reader in Thai and English of Tongdaeng's respect for another stray which had nursed her before her royal adoption; Tongdaeng is, the king added, "different from many others who, after having become an important personality, might treat with contempt someone of lower status who, in fact, should be the subject of gratitude."

Polite deference to all is a byword of this text, which also praises Tongdaeng's seemly deference to her master: "Tongdaeng is a respectful dog with proper manners; she is humble and knows the protocol. She would always sit lower than the king; even when he pulls her up to embrace her, Tongdaeng would lower herself down on the floor, her ears in a respectful drooping position, as if she would say, 'I don't dare.'"

King Bhumibol's subjects, especially the middle class, were avid readers of these moral lessons about what he called a "common dog who is uncommon", and the book's first printing of 100,000 copies reportedly sold out promptly. In 2006, *Thailand Post* issued a commemorative block of four postage stamps featuring Tongdaeng.

This use of fondness for pets to touch the hearts of his subjects was repeated in the king's New Year cards, which were sent to his subjects from his personal computer from the late 1980s until 2015. They started with simple graphic forms with an annual reflection, such as in 2003, when the maxim was "One's best friend is a four-legged one". In 2004, he reminded the Thai people to unite while the world was rocked by terrorist bombings. Starting in 2006, the New Year cards became more vivid, with photos of the king seated with Tongdaeng and her offspring. These familiar images for New Year were almost unchanged from 2006 to 2014.

This personal touch was treasured by his subjects. The ultimate mystery of how monarchs such as King Chulalongkorn and King Bhumibol inspire their nations and endure in human memory was addressed in 1927 by Prince Damrong, a minister and major historian who gave a significant lecture about the Thai people and their nation, stating: "The Thai people have three important virtues that sustain Siam to the present day: love of national independence, tolerance, and the power of assimilation."

At the height of Anglo-French colonialism, King Chulalongkorn's Siam survived external threats and remained semi-independent by bending with the wind that blew from Great Britain and France. During the Second World War, the new 1932 government of Thailand compromised with the Japanese as well as Allied forces and emerged with even-handed results by again bending with the wind. When the Cold War began, Thailand became a close partner of the United States and the Free World, including Japan, fighting against external and internal Communist threats. It emerged as a leading Southeast Asian nation in terms of economic success and political stability.

The examples of King Chulalongkorn and King Bhumibol were beacons along these pathways, always cherishing higher education and learning, always valuing intellectual pursuits, creativity and originality. Few nations in the modern era can claim such sages as royals, and while Thais are taught from an early age to revere them, the full extent to which they were extraordinary when compared to most fellow world monarchs, remains to be told.

As mentioned in the Prologue by Craig J. Reynolds, King Chulalongkorn was succeeded by his son Vajiravudh, Rama VI (r. 1910–25), who was not nearly so interested in governing as his father while in comparisons I would like to add that to Vajiralongkorn, Rama X (r. 2016), who is more concerned in government administration than his father. Time and history will tell us what is happening next in Thailand.

NOTES

1. See also David Streckfuss, ed., *Modern Thai Monarchy and Cultural Politics: The Acquittal of Sulak Sivaraksa on the Charge of Lese Majeste in Siam* (Bangkok: Santi Pracha Dhamma Institute, 1966).

    The *lèse majesté* law (article 112 of the Civil Law) has become politically problematic especially at the time when first female Premier Yingluck was in power (2011–14). A group of Thammasat University law lecturers, led by Dr Worachet Phakeerat (born 1969) formed up a team called Khana Nitirat (Law for the People). They had been working for a reform of the law.

    The law is equipped with hard punishment for anyone who is proven guilty. One can be put in jail for the maximum of up to fifteen years. This is one of the hardest and the highest in the world. In late May 2012 the Khana Nitirat and their associates have formed up a group by the name of "Campaign Committee for the Amendment of Article 112" (Kho ro ko 112). It had gathered 26,968 signatures consisting of academics, social activists and the public. They staged a march to the General Assembly and handed the letters/signatures to Premier Yingluck's Pheu Thai Party. They were disappointed because Phue Thai, the majority party with the most votes, did not take it into consideration. See https://www.ilaw.or.th/node/1566?fbclid=IwAR0TO cf5NB3MgW_XR-BDINgVfjzqt0qLi-qZwCFnjCM79mcSBpNlF47C9mU (accessed 31 August 2021). See Søren Ivarsson and Lotte Isager, *Saying the Unsayable: Monarchy and Democracy in Thailand* (Copenhagen: NIAS Press, 2010).

2. In fact, when the coup occurred on 22 May, Mr Niwatthumrong Boonsongpaisan (born 1948), a businessman and politician from Chiang Mai, was the acting prime minister. Niwatthumrong was Yingluck's commerce minister. Two weeks earlier, on 7 May, Yingluck's prime ministership, along with nine senior members of her cabinet, were found guilty, once again, by the Constitutional Court of Thailand for abuse of power over the transfer of national security Chief Thawil Pliensri in 2011.

3. See two views on the coup against Thaksin by Kasian and Thongchai: Kasian Tejapira, "Toppling Thaksin", *New Left Review* 39 (May–June 2006): 5–37; and Thongchai Winichakul, "Toppling Democracy", *Journal of Contemporary Asia* 38, no. 1 (2008): 11–37. See also Eugenie Merieau, "Thailand's Deep State, Royal Power and the Constitutional Court (1997–2015)", *Journal of Contemporary Asia* 46, no. 3 (2016): 445–66.
4. The best book on the topic is probably by Aim Sinpeng, *Opposing Democracy in the Digital Age: The Yellow Shirts in Thailand* (Ann Arbor: University of Michigan Press, 2021). See also her article, "From the Yellow Shirts to the Whistle Rebels: Comparative Analysis of the People's Alliance for Democracy (PAD) and the People's Democratic Reform Committee (PDRC)", in *Routledge Handbook of Contemporary Thailand*, edited by Pavin Chachavalpongpun (London and New York: Routledge Taylor & Francis Group, 2020), pp. 145–55. See also Kanokrat Lertchoosakul, "The Paradox of the Thai Middle Class in Democratisation", published online by Cambridge University Press, 13 January 2021.
5. Somchot Ongsakul, *From King Rama V to King Rama IX: A Further Step Towards His Majesty's the King's Dignity* (Lanna Studies, Chiang Mai University, 2017).
6. For early films or cinematography on Siam at this period, see Dome Sukhawongs, *Sayam phapphayon* [Siam film], (Ho Phapphayon-Thai Film Archive, 2012), Chs 1 and 2. Here one can find out when King Chulalongkorn first saw the film in Singapore (p. 30) and detail of Prince Sappasartsupakij, the king's half-brother, who introduced films into Siam. Also, a concise presentation of early films in Siam is by Alexander Johannes Klemm, "The Beginning of European Filmmaking in Siam", *Malaysian Journal of Media Studies* 21 no. 1 (2019): 31–48.
7. See Lumière, "Berne. Arrivée du roi de Siam (1897)", https://www.youtube.com/watch?v=vM-UTH87orU (accessed 10 July 2021).
8. See Youtube, "The First Visit of King Chulalongkorn to Europe in 1897 (Old film)-SWEDEN", https://www.researchgate.net/publication/333660267_The_Beginnings_of_European_Filmmaking_in_Siam (accessed 10 July 2021). See also Maurizio Peleggi, *Lords of Things: The Fashioning of the Siamese Monarchy's Modern Image* (Honolulu: University of Hawai'i Press, 2002), especially Ch 2, "Presentation and Representation of the Royal Self".
9. Patricia Lim Pui Huen, *Through the Eyes of the King: The Travels of King Chulalongkorn to Malaya* (Singapore: Institute of Southeast Asian Studies, 2009).
10. Sachchiddanand Sahai, *India in 1872, as seen by the Siamese* (Delhi: B.R.

Pub. Corp., 2002). See a Thai translation by Kanthika Sriudom, *Ratchakan thi 5 sadet India* [The Fifth Reign Went to India] (Bangkok: Foundation for the Promotion of Social Sciences and Humanities Textbooks Project, 2003). Also, Edward Bosc Sladen, *King Chulalongkorn's Journey to India* (Bangkok: River Books Co.), 2000.

11. David K. Wyatt, *Thailand: A Short History* (New Haven and London: Yale University Press, 2003), Ch 7; see idem, "King Chulalongkorn the Great: Founder of Modern Thailand", *Studies in Thai History* (Chiang Mai: Silkworms Books, 1994), pp. 273–84. Also, idem, *The Politics of Reform in Thailand: Education in the Reign of King Chulalongkorn* (New Haven: 1969). See also a new reading into "the abolition of prostration and crawling" by Kongsatcha Suwannaphet, "Aan prawattisat phra pathom barom ratcha ongkan (mai)" [A new reading into the first proclamation], *Fah Diew Kan* 18, no. 2 (July–December 2020).

12. Ibid., *Thailand: A Short History*, Ch 7. See also Charnvit Kasetsiri, "The Front Palace: The Office of the Heir Apparent?", *Studies in Thai and Southeast Asian Histories* (Bangkok: The Social Sciences and Humanities Textbooks Foundation, 2015), pp. 256–74.

13. Tej Bunnag, *The Provincial Administration of Siam, 1892–1915: The Ministry of the Interior under Prince Damrong Rajanubhab* (Kuala Lumpur: Oxford University Press, 1977).

    It is well known that the history of King Chulalongkorn's reign and his reformation is a favourite of academics at home and abroad. Here we should get to know some of the leading ones written in English. The king's administrative reform can be found in Fred W. Riggs, *Thailand: The Modernization of a Bureaucratic Polity* (Honolulu: East-West Center Press, 1966), and along the same line about the same time is William J. Siffin, *The Thai Bureaucracy: Institutional Change and Development* (Honolulu: East-West Center Press, 1966).

    As on the military, the best one so far is the unpublished PhD dissertation by Noel A. Battye, "The Military, Government and Society in Siam, 1868–1910: Politics and Military Reform during the Reign of King Chulalongkorn" (Cornell University, 1974).

    On the aspect of law, a classic one is by David M. Engel, *Law and Kingship in Thailand During the Reign of King Chulalongkorn* (Ann Arbor: Center for Southeast Asian Studies, the University of Michigan, 1975). See also Tamara L. Loos, *Subject Siam: Family, Law, and Colonial Modernity in Thailand* (Ithaca: Cornell University Press, 2006).

For general picture on agriculture are James C. Ingram, *Economic Change in Thailand, 1850–1970* (Stanford: Stanford University Press, 1971); together with David H. Feeny, *The Political Economy of Productivity: Thai Agricultural Development, 1880–1975* (Vancouver: University of British Columbia Press, 1982); Hans ten Brummelhuis, *King of the Waters: Homan van der Heide and the Origin of Modern Irrigation in Siam* (Leiden: KITLV Press, 2005). See also these two books by Thai academics: Kullada Kesboonchoo Mead, *The Rise and Decline of Thai Absolutism* (London: RoutledgeCurzon, 2004), and Chaiyan Rajchagool, *The Rise and Fall of the Thai Absolute Monarchy: Foundation of the Modern Thai State from Feudalism to Peripheral Capitalism* (Bangkok: White Lotus, 1994). See also an unpublished PhD dissertation by Caverlee S. Cary, "Triple Gems and Double Meaning: Contested Space in the National Museum of Bangkok" (Ithaca: Cornell University, 1994). I would like to thank Thongchai Winichakul for suggesting this additional reading list.

14. It is interesting that a sort of family politics practices by King Chulalongkorn towards the Bunnag clan can be seen along this line. Polygamy had its pluses and minuses. Children of various wives could be jealous of one another, and palace intrigue was common in old Siam. But, on the other hand, at a certain time they could unite and be mutually protective for their own benefit. King Mongkut had eighty-four children (forty-three daughters and thirty-nine sons), including Chulalongkorn. King Chulalongkorn followed this practice by having almost a hundred wives and seventy-seven children (thirty-two sons and forty-four daughters).

Many of Chulalongkorn's brothers and half-brothers became instrumental for his projects of reform and absolutism. For almost thirty years, from 1871 to 1910, heads of the Finance Office were trusted members of Chulalongkorn's immediate family. Prince Krom Phraya Bamrabporapak (1819–86), his half uncle, held the office for thirteen years from 1873 to 1886. After the Prince died, the office was occupied respectively by the king's brother, half-brothers and sons. We will see that by the 1890s, when sons of Chulalongkorn started to return from higher education in Great Britain and other European countries, they would fill important administrative offices. These Thais educated abroad (the term *nakrian nok* developed for these privileged graduates, in recent years sometimes used ironically or derisively) included Vajiravudh, Rama VI and Prajadhipok, Rama VII.

On King Chulalongkorn's extensive offspring, see Jeffrey Finestone, *The Royal Family of Thailand: Descendants of King Chulalongkorn* (London: New Cavendish Books, 1989), see also a Thai version, *Chulalongkorn Ratchasantatiwong* [Chulalongkorn sons, daughters, and grandchildren].

15. See a classic work by H.G. Quaritch Wales, *Ancient Siamese Government and Administration* (London: Barnard Quaritch, Ltd., 1934), Chs 4–5. See Wyatt, *Thailand: A Short History*, Ch 7.
16. See an unpublished dissertation, Noel A. Battye, "The Military, Government and Society in Siam, 1868–1910". See also *Prawat krasuang kalahom & punyai boran* ... [History of the Defense Ministry and ancient cannons] (Bangkok: 1994). As for the case of the Finance Office, Chulalongkorn put his immediate family members in charge. Defense Ministers were as follows: Prince Naris (half-brother) 1894–99; Prince Krom Luang Prajak (half-brother) 1899–1901; Prince Phanurangsi (brother) 1909–10; and Prince Chiraprawat (son) 1910–13.
17. Constance Wilson, *Thailand: A Handbook of Historical Statistics* (Boston, Mass.: G.K. Hall, 1983), pp. 269–70.
18. D.G.E. Hall, *A History of South-East Asia*, 3rd ed. (New York: St. Martin's Press, 1968), see Ch 39. See also Nigel Brailey, ed., *Two Views of Siam on the Eve of the Chakri Reformation* (Scotland: Kiscadale Publications, 1989).
19. Martin Stuart-Fox, *A History of Laos* (Cambridge: Cambridge University Press, 1997), Ch 3.
20. Wyatt, *Thailand: A Short History*, pp. 194–96.
21. Charnvit Kasetsiri, *Pramuan sonthisanya ... lae phaen thi* [Collected Treaties-Conventions-Agreements-Memorandum of Understanding and Maps Between Siam/Thailand-Cambodia-Laos-Burma-Malaysia] (Bangkok: The Social Sciences and Humanities Textbooks Foundation, 2011), pp. 50–89.
22. See Prince Dilok Nabarath, *Siam's Rural Economy under King Chulalongkorn* (Bangkok: White Lotus, 2000).
23. See Prince Damrong's "Sadet truad ratchakan monthon Isan, monthon Udon", in *Nithan borankhadi* [Tales of old times] (Bangkok: Phra Chan Press, 1944; Aksonsamphan, 11th printing 1962), p. 376. The prince said that to centralize and transform Siam into a unified kingdom, the word *Lao* historically and traditionally applied the language and the people in the northeastern part of the country must be erased. It was a royal command and must be done. See also Kennon Breazeale, *The Writing of Prince Damrong: A Chronology with Annotations* (Bangkok: The Social Sciences and Humanities Textbooks Foundation, 2008).
24. Natthawut Sutthisongkhram, *Krom Luang Prajak phu thawai chiwit raksa phaendin isan* [Krom Luang Prajak who paid his life to preserve the Isan land], 2nd printing (Bangkok: Amarin, 2018).
25. Jeffrey Sng and Pimpraphai Bisalputra, *A History of the Thai-Chinese* (Singapore: Craft Print International Ltd., 2015), see Chs 4–6.

26. For the famous na Ranong clan, see Jennifer Cushman, Family and State: The Formation of a Sino-Thai Tin-Mining Dynasty, 1797–1932 (Singapore and New York: Oxford University Press, 1991).
27. King Chulalongkorn's long rule and reign are mostly viewed with admiration. However, his life and work were also seen with "corruption, venality, despotism and harem politics". These are by written accounts of two of his contemporaries, i.e., Prince Prisdang (1891) a grandson of Rama III and a cousin of Chulalongkorn, and Sir Robert Laurie Morant (1894), a British diplomat stationed in Bangkok. See Brailey, ed., *Two Views of Siam on the Eve of the Chakri Reformation*. As for the unusual life and work of the Monk-Prince Prisdang (1851–1935) see Tamara Loos, *Bones Around My Neck: The Life and Exile of a Prince Provocateur* (Ithaca: Cornell University Press, 2016).
28. See Oskar Frankfurter, "The Late King Chulalongkorn", *Journal of the Siam Society* 7, no. 2, and later reprinted in book form in 1911.
29. Matthew Phillips, "Re-ordering the Cold War Cosmos: King Bhumibol's 1960 US. Tour", *Diplomatic History*, 45, Issue 2 (April 2021): 253–67.
30. Frankfurter, "The Late King Chulalongkorn".
31. Patrick Jory, "Thai and Western Buddhist Scholarship in the Age of Colonialism: King Chulalongkorn Redefines the Jatakas", *Journal of Asian Studies* 61, no. 3 (August 2002): 891–918; and idem., *Thailand's Theory of Monarchy: The Vessantara Jataka and the Idea of the Perfect Man* (New York: SUNY Press, 2016). See especially his Introduction on "*Barami*: Foundation of a Theravada Buddhist Theory of Monarchy", pp. 15–22, and his Conclusion on "King Bhumibol as the Modern Vessantara", pp. 180–85.

Epilogue

There is no need to harm you, however, because no matter what, you must disappear in time. Sooner or later, all the old things will be confined to museums, one after the other ...

much time has elapsed already, and your world and mine are getting further apart. I'm the ghost that time has fashioned to scare those who live in the old world, to give nightmares to those who hold to the old ways of thinking, and nothing can comfort you, just as nothing can stop the march of time, which will produce more and more ghosts like me ...

but there's no way this can happen because the ghost is even more invulnerable than Achilles or Siegfried as he is protected by the shield of time ... We're worlds apart. Mine is the world of ordinary people.

Seinee Saowaphong, *Pheesart* (1957),
translated into English by Marcel Barang, *Ghosts* (2006)

In conclusion, as the ninth king regnant of the Chakri dynasty, HM King Bhumibol was extremely successful in constructing a neo-monarchy with extensive *barami*. However, according to Theravada Buddhist concepts, personal *barami* is untransferable. His successors must work to achieve it for themselves.

Just as HM King Chulalongkorn (Rama V), another successful absolute monarch whose *barami* vanished with him, HM King Vajiravudh, Rama VI (1910–25) and HM King Prajadhipok, Rama VII (1925–35) had to develop it on their own. Absolute monarchy ended in Siam in 1932, only twenty-two years after the death of King Rama V. King Rama IX's successor will face the same problem of how to maintain, or adapt, the new monarchy to suit new contexts.

As mentioned before, in 1927, Prince Damrong, a chief minister and historian, gave a resoundingly influential lecture about the Thai people and their nation. At one point, the prince said, "The Thai people have three important virtues that sustain Siam to the present day: one, love of national independence; two, tolerance; and three, the power of assimilation."

At the height of Anglo-French colonialism, Chulalongkorn's Siam managed to survive external threats and remain semi-independent. During the Second World War, the new 1932 government of Thailand, the People's Party or *Khana Ratsadon*, collaborated with the Japanese as well as the Allies with even-handed results. From the start of the Cold War, Thailand became a close partner of the United States of America and the Free World, including Japan, fighting external and internal communist threats. Thailand emerged as a leading Southeast Asian nation economically and politically.

Now confronted by more immediate internal, rather than external, uncertainties, will Thailand successfully cope and survive an extended crisis of proxy political conflict between the old *barami* (power-money-idea) against the new *barami*? Will the reputed Thai virtues that had good results once for Siam function again for Thailand today?[1]

The previous two coups, in 2006 and 2014, against Thaksin and Yingluck respectively, did not restore the nation to normalcy. HM the King's health slowly declined, and he died on 13 October 2016 at the age of eighty-eight. His only son, HRH Prince Vajiralongkorn, born in 1952, became King Rama X at the age of sixty-four.

On 24 March 2019, Thailand had another election, followed by the new king's coronation in early May. The question remains, *Quo Vadis?* a Latin phrase meaning "Where are you marching?" supposedly addressed by Saint Peter to the risen Christ during their encounter along the Appian Way, according to Christian tradition.

As a Thai and Southeast Asian academic, I noted with interest that during the March 2018 Association for Asian Studies conference in Washington, DC, a guest post was published on the University of California Press blog. Written by Claudio Sopranzetti, a postdoctoral research fellow at Oxford, it began:

In 1848, Karl Marx opened his manifesto with an eloquent sentence: "A specter is haunting Europe—the specter of communism."

One hundred and seventy some years later, Laos and Vietnam are among the fastest growing economies of twenty-first-century capitalism and the Chinese Communist Party somewhat abandoned the post-Mao doctrine of putting its assembly above any individual leader. Communism, which once materialized so prominently in East Asia, is little more than a faded ghost, haunting no one. Yet another specter has taken its place in Asia—the specter of authoritarianism.

Sopranzetti went on to elaborate:

Whether in terms of China's attempts to establish a life-long chairmanship, Philippines' systematic dismissal of habeas corpus or … Thailand's new forms of constitutional dictatorship, a new wind of authoritarianism is blowing over East Asia. Contrary to existing theories of the "end of history" or of "democratic transition," this wind does not waft against the wish of the middle classes, but rather with their support. And it is not a temporary breeze, destined to die out, but rather a stable wind, one that carries forward an alternative system of governance … the growing popularity of authoritarian ideology among local middle class, a popularity that finds its roots in the shifting local meaning of words like corruption, good governance, and rule of law.

As an academic, teaching and observing in and around Thailand, I tend to agree with Sopranzetti. After the general election of 2015, Myanmar had high hopes of a democratic transition. Now those hopes are quickly declining. The Tatmadaw, Myanmar's armed forces, is omnipresent with no sign of civilian good governance.

Laos and Vietnam are functioning rather well with one-party autocratic systems. In Cambodia, multiple parties and elections are more like window dressing. The exception is Malaysia, where a nice cool democratic breeze is blowing, at least for the time being. Meanwhile, Singapore is thriving singularly well. Further along the islands of Southeast Asia, the Philippines is in a troubling condition, while in Indonesia, democratic decentralization has turned out admirably.

Back to Thailand: yes, a spectre of authoritarianism is haunting us. As of now, with the passing of HM King Bhumibol, Rama IX, and the coronation of HM King Vajiralongkorn, Rama X, Thailand faces an uncertain future. After the disappointing 2006 coup, the subsequent coup of 22 May 2014 made the situation even more worrisome. Of course, coups are not novelties in Thailand, yet the ones of 2006 and 2014 were especially disruptive.

Now, Rama X's Thailand confronts many unprecedented problems. For example, royal succession from King Rama IX to King Rama X ran smoothly, but what happens next? More importantly, will HM Rama X follow the example set forth by his father of a democratic governmental regime with the king as head of state? Or he will innovate by transitioning to a non-democracy with the king as head of state? The answer remains to be seen.

And what of King Bhumibol's *barami*, the all-encompassing term for reverence, awe, and moral authority? Will it be transmitted to the newly crowned king and help him to become a force of balance and stability for Thailand?

Meanwhile, beyond Bangkok, especially in the North and Northeast, rural discontent is disquieting. The South Thailand insurgency, with political unrest in Malay-Muslim majority areas, is also worrisome.[2]

Thailand of HM King Rama X can no longer expect to routinely enjoy uncritical evaluation from international academics, human rights groups, and the international press. Students of the new generation born around the year 2000 appear to have unique individualist ideas about the nation and its destiny. Sporadic student activism in Bangkok and up-country is ubiquitous. Has change really arrived in Thailand?

In addition, innovative high-tech underground activism in cyberspace on Facebook, Twitter, YouTube, Line and Clubhouse increasingly targets the venerable establishment as well as long-revered *barami*, the monarchy and military. Electoral campaigns and proposals about republicanism and federalism, especially among Thai citizens living overseas, are seen as causes worth fighting for, to ensure the nation's future.

Will present-day Thailand manage to survive these existential crises? Only time and history may tell.[3]

NOTES

1. See Human Rights Watch, "Descent into Chaos: Thailand's 2010 Red Shirt Protests and the Government Crackdown", 3 May 2011. See also a critical view on Thai monarchy by Andrew MacGregor Marshall, *A Kingdom in Crisis: Thailand's Struggle for Democracy in the Twenty-First Century* (London: Zed Books, 2014).
2. See Patrick Jory, ed., *Ghosts of the Past in Southern Thailand: Essays on the History and Historiography of Patani* (Singapore: National University of Singapore, 2013).
3. See Paul M. Handley, "Getting into Seclusion: Can the Monarchy Survive Bhumibol?", in his *The King Never Smiles: A Biography of Thailand's Bhumibol Adulyadej* (New Haven and London: Yale University Press, 2006); also, his "Revisiting the King Never Smiles", in Pavin Chachavalpongpun, ed., *Coup King Crisis: A Critical Interregnum in Thailand*, Monograph 68 (New Haven: Yale Southeast Asia Studies, 2020). See Suchit Bunbongkarn, "Democracy and Monarchy in Thailand", and Kavi Chongkittavorn, "The Future of Thai Monarchy", in *Monarchy and Democracy in the 21st Century* (Bhutan: Bhutan Centre for Media and Democracy, 2009). See a provocative treatment on King Bhumibol in his twilight years by Serhat Unaldi, *Working Towards the Monarchy: The Politics of Space in Downtown Bangkok* (Honolulu: University of Hawai'i, 2016). See See also Peter Conradi, *The Great Survivors: How Monarchy Made It into the Twenty-First Century* (London: Alma Books, 2013).

    In addition, see Benedict Anderson's last article, published posthumous, "Riddles of Yellow and Red", *New Left Review* 97 (January–February 2016). In his last words about the contemporary Thai politics and the long conflict and fight of the last two decades. The late academic saw it as rather like the great Chinese literature of the *The Romance of the Three Kingdoms*:

    > Over the past fifty years, almost every Thai prime minister has been a *lukchin* [literally a son of a Chinese], like the monarchy itself. But this shared "Chinese ancestry" conceals bitter rivalries between the Teochew, Hokkien, Hakka and Hailamese. The positive side of this phenomenon is that Thailand has never experienced the kind of anti-Chinese mobilizations that have characterized the modern histories of Malaysia, Vietnam, Indonesia, Burma, and the Philippines. Capable, wealthy and ruthless

Sino-Thais have been able to climb upwards—on condition that their "Chineseness" remains very low-profile, especially under Rama IX. There are echoes here of the status enjoyed by wealthy Jews in Habsburg Vienna or Hanoverian London. In the last election, it turned out that 78 per cent of the seats in Thailand's parliament were occupied by ethnic Chinese, even though they accounted for just 14 per cent of the population.

Against this backdrop, the question now is who will be President of the Republic of Thailand? Nobody will say so explicitly, but that is exactly what is in their minds. With the system of petty warlords in each of the territories, that creates frustration for everybody: they can be sure of winning in one place but not in another. The Reds can't penetrate the territory of the Yellows, and the Yellows can't penetrate the territory of the Reds; the south is Yellow, and the north is Red. Another difficulty is that nobody can talk publicly about their Chinese identity because it would be absurd to declare that one is Chinese but plans to be the President of the Republic. Everyone knows that they are, but it's not considered appropriate to say so. There is no other way out, unless one of them gets killed, or something of that kind. Don't fool yourself that the political contest in Thailand is about democracy or anything like that. It's about whether the Teochews get to keep their top position, or whether it's the turn of the Hakkas or the Hailamese.

Index

1912 Rebellion, 15, 219
1932 Revolution, 26–27, 31, 35, 39–40, 45–46, 51–53, 60, 65, 79, 81, 84, 87, 92–94, 101, 104, 121, 125, 131–32, 134, 144, 150, 161, 166, 182, 188, 192, 219, 239

A

Abdu'r Rahman, Temenggong, 215
Abhisit Vejjajiva, 146–47
absolute monarchy, 6, 15, 24, 27–28, 31, 37, 39, 45–46, 48, 50, 56, 60, 64–65, 67, 75, 79, 85, 87, 92–93, 101, 121, 132, 134, 138, 141, 143, 145–46, 161, 200, 219, 224, 226, 239
Ackaratorn Chularat, 196
Across Chrysê: Being the Narrative of a Journey of Exploration Through the South China Border Lands from Canton to Mandalay, 13
Adul Wichiencharoen, 81–82, 150
Agricultural King, 101
Albritton, Errett Cyril, 159
Alfonso XII, 180
Allied Powers, 160
American air base, 99, 112

American Constitution, 21
American Presbyterian Mission, 51
Amnuay Silpa School, 109
Amphon Palace, 138
Analysis of the Ancient Tai Nation (*wikhroa ruang Muang Tai doem*), 54
Anand Panyarachun, 69–75, 84–86, 103, 109, 115, 118, 147
Ananda Mahidol Foundation Scholarship, 145–47
Ananda Mahidol, King, 57, 62, 70, 79–80, 88–89, 91–92, 93–95, 110–12, 117, 125, 141, 144, 150, 155, 157, 161–64, 188
Anderson, Benedict, 6–8, 32, 44
Angkor Thom, 109
Angkor Wat, 109
Angkorian Empire, 11
Angkorian Khmer, 1, 3, 13
Anglo-Siamese Chiang Mai Treaty, 211
Anna and the King of Siam, 77, 107–8
anthem, national, 40, 43, 47, 53, 59–61, 63, 148
anti-Chinese, 8, 43, 243
anti-Communist, 57, 124, 164, 166
Antiquarian Society, 14

245

Anusawari Thai (Thai Monument), play, 67
Arabian Nights, The, 179, 193
Arwut Srisukri, 175
Aryan race, 42
As You Like It, 18
Asia and Pacific Rim Peace Conference, 131
Asian financial crisis, 180, 187, 222, 228
Association of Southeast Asian Nations (ASEAN), 227
Asvabahu, 24
Atsani Phonlajan, 168–69
Aung San, 39, 44
authoritarianism, 241–42
Ayatiwat, 23–24, 33
Ayutthaya, 2–6, 8–11, 17–21, 26, 46, 49–50, 52, 56, 64–66, 89, 100, 105–6, 109, 135, 208, 214–15, 218
Ayutthya-Prasatthong dynasty, 29

B

Back to Siam movement, 37
Bagehot, Walter, 71, 103
Baker, Chris, 102–3
Ban Pong Fire, 152
Bang Kwang Central Prison, 166
Bangkok-Chakri Centennial, 22
Bangkok Christian College, 85
Bangkok Chronicle, 85
Bangkok Commercial Bank, 92
Bangkok Expo, 19–20
Bangkok Library, 14, 31
Bangkok Post, 80
Bangkok/Ratanakosin, 2, 9, 13, 19, 29, 34, 52
Bangkok Recorder, The, 21

Banjong Banjerdsilp, 168
Bank of Thailand, 195
barami, 71, 74, 115, 179, 186, 197, 219, 221, 223–24, 229–30, 239–40, 242
Battle of Thalang (*Suk Thalang*), play, 66
BBC, 72, 96
Bedfellow (*Phuean non*), 78
Bejaratana, Princess, 45, 94
Berne: Arrival of the King of Siam, silent movie, 202
Bernini, Gian Lorenzo, 180
Bhisadej Rajani, Prince, 195
Bhubing Palace, 171, 177
Bhumibol Adulyadej, King, 2, 57–58, 60, 67, 69–75, 80, 83–84, 88, 91–93, 95–104, 110, 115–17, 119, 121–22, 131–45, 148, 150, 152–53, 155, 157, 159, 161, 164, 171, 174, 181, 185, 188, 192, 195, 200, 218, 220–32, 239–40, 242
Bhumibol Dam, 123
Bhumibol Fund, 144–45
Bird's Nest Island, 216
Bloody May, 71, 86, 115, 146, 224
Board of Regency, 95, 104
Boedi Oetomo, 44
Border Patrol Police (BPP), 73, 164, 172, 174–78, 181–84, 189, 194–95
Borommatrailokkanat, King, 218
Bose, Subhas Chandra, 38
Boworadet, Prince, 46, 94, 169
Boworadet Rebellion, 62, 169
Bowring, John, 49
Bowring Treaty, 40, 49
Boy King, 95

Boy Scouts (*luk sua*), 16
BPP Aerial Reinforcement Unit (PARU), 176
Bradley, Dan Beach, 21, 51
Brahma, King, 10
Brando, Marlon, 78
Brief Chronicle (Phongsawadan) of Ayutthaya, A, 6
British Burma, 7, 89, 162–63, 209, 211, 217
British India, 211
British Malaya, 7, 134, 162–63, 201, 203, 206, 228
British monarchy, 71
British Raj, 203
Buddha, 13, 23–24, 26, 183, 185, 230
Buddharaja (Buddhist king), 83
Buddhism, 53, 197, 211, 225
Buddhist cosmology, 188, 197
Buddhist Era, 88, 130, 136, 152
Buddhist realm, 17
Burmese Lost Their Country, The, (*Phama sia muang*), 78
Burney, Henry, 5
Burton, Richard F., 179, 193
But Patthamasarin, 92

C

Cam Ranh Air Force Base, 99
Cambodia, 2–4, 19, 29–30, 66–67, 98–99, 109, 112, 122, 134, 152, 190, 192, 210, 212, 219, 227–28, 241
Celestial Monarchy, 15
censorship, 108, 130
Central Intelligence Agency (CIA), 175
Central Powers, 25, 160
Central Revenue Office, 205

Chaem Bunnag, 52, 64
Chai Nat, Prince, 47, 103–4
Chaipattana Foundation, 199
Chakri Dynasty, 2, 6, 20, 24, 27, 66, 69, 75, 79, 102, 137, 144, 170, 218, 225, 239
Chaleo Pratumros, 92
Chamlong Srimuang, 72, 74
Chamuen Waiwaranat, 213
Chan Ungsuchot, 183
Chanida Chitbundid, 118–19, 145
Chao Phya Devesra, 4
Chaoying Saenwi (Princess of Hsenwi), play, 66
Charan Pakdithanakul, 196
Charles VI, King, 88
Charnchai Likhitjitha, 196
Charoen Wanngam, 169
Chatichai Choonhavan, 86
Chavalit Yongchaiyudh, 186
Che Guevara, 168
Chiang Kai-shek, 164
Chiang Mai ruler, 67, 170, 191–92, 211
Chiang Mai Treaty, 211
Chiang Mai University, 147, 171, 175
Chin Yiang Sae Hao, 216
China, 1–4, 7, 9–11, 13–14, 19, 31, 42–43, 51–53, 55–56, 58–59, 65, 67–68, 77, 85–86, 90, 121, 129, 131, 156–57, 164, 167, 171, 188, 204, 212, 216, 228, 241
China's Relations with Foreigners, 55
Chinese Communist Party, 241
Chinese Mixed with Lao (*Jek Pon Lao*), 58
Chinese Repository, The, 29
Chino-Sayam Warasap, 25
Chit Singhaseni, 92

Chitralada Palace, 98
Choie bamrung chat (Help and Care for the Nation), 26
cholera pandemic, 158
chronicle (*phongsawadan*), 5–6, 16–18, 21, 23, 26, 28–29
Chronicle (Phongsawadan) of the Present Dynasty, A, 6
Chu Chukramol, 158
Chuan Leekpai, 87, 188
Chuang Bunnag, 207
Chulabhorn, Princess, 135, 153, 174
Chulalongkorn, King, 2, 4–8, 12, 14, 21, 28, 33, 34, 40, 44–45, 47, 49, 52, 57, 63–64, 76, 79, 87, 92–94, 98–100, 103, 106, 116, 121, 133, 156–58, 179–80, 191–93, 200–24, 226–30, 232–33, 235–36, 238–40
Chulalongkorn Spring, 218
Chulalongkorn University, 12, 51, 68–69, 80–81, 84, 140–44, 153, 163, 219
Chulathat Phayakharanond, 181
Chumporn Thummai, 73
City of Illusion/Hollywood (Muang maya), 78
Clarke, Andrew, 206
Clogs on Our Wheels, 8
CNN, 72
Cœdès, George, 17
Cold War, 57, 75, 77, 98–99, 117–18, 122–23, 131, 157, 176, 187, 199, 224, 228, 232, 240
colonialism, 49, 200, 209, 219, 232, 240
Colquhoun, Archibald Ross, 13, 55
communism, 98, 122, 155, 165–66, 170, 172–73, 221, 241

Communist Party of Indonesia (PKI), 166
Communist Party of Malaya, 166
Communist Party of Thailand (CPT), 61, 73, 118, 131, 156, 165–70, 186–87, 190–91, 195
Communist Party of Vietnam (CPV), 167
Communist Suppression Operation Command (CSOC), 176
Compulsory Primary Education Act, 182
Conference of the International Association of Historians of Asia (IAHA), 69
conscription, 208–9
Constitution Celebration Fair, 132
Constitution Day, 132
Constitution Drafting Assembly of Thailand, 57, 59
Constitution of the Kingdom of Thailand, 57
Constitution United Front, 130
constitution-writing, in Thailand, 126–27
Constitutional Court, 82, 233
constitutional monarchy, 28, 71, 79, 93, 224
Contested Nationalism and the 1932 Overthrow of the Absolute Monarchy in Siam, 24
Copeland, Matthew Phillip, 24–25
Council of Regency, 104
Council of State, 205
Country of Thailand (Prates Thai), article, 42
coup, 15, 26, 31, 46, 57, 68, 73, 75, 82, 85–86, 89–91, 93–94, 100, 107, 117, 123, 125–26, 128–29,

134, 147–48, 150, 153, 169, 188, 197–99, 223, 227, 240, 242
Cradle of the Shan Race, 13
Cromwell, John, 78
Crown Prince of Siam, 58
Crown Property Bureau, 89
cult of the Royal Father, 179
Cultural Revolution, 90, 156

D

Damrong, Prince, 8–11, 14, 17, 20, 29, 30–31, 52, 56, 94, 105, 109, 210, 232, 237, 240
Dao Siam, newspaper, 73
Dara Rasami, Princess, 191–92, 211
Davies, Derek, 75
de la Loubère, Simon, 50
de Lacouperie, Albert Terrien, 13, 55
defamation law, 220
Democracy Monument, 40
Democrat Party, 77, 86, 89–90, 107, 125, 130, 199
Department of Propaganda, 138
Devaraja (divine king), 83
Devawongse, Prince, 4, 218
Developer King, 101, 115
developmentalism, 122–24
Dhani, Prince, 103–5, 150, 195
dharma raja (righteous ruler), 70–71, 83, 100, 226
Dictionnaire Siamois Français Anglais (Siamese French English dictionary), 49
Dilok, Prince, 211
Din Tharab, 46, 62
Direk Chaiyanam, 90
Dit Bunnag, 105, 106
divine king (*Devaraja*), 83
Dodd, William Clifton, 54–55, 56

Dohbama Asiayone, 44
Doi Inthanon, 170, 172, 177, 192
Doi Tung Development Project (DTDP) palace, 184–87
Dominican Republic, and constitution, 126
Dulwich College, 85
Dunne, Irene, 78
Dusit Palace, 40, 180
Dutch East Indies, 201, 203
Dvaravati Mon, 13

E

Eakin, Isabella, 55
East India Company (EIC), 215
École française d'Extrême-Orient (EFEO), 14
Edison, Thomas, 201–2
Edward VIII, King, 139
Emerald Buddha, 110
Empress Dowager Cixi (*Susi thaihao*), 78, 157
English Constitution, The, 103
Englund, George, 78
Evans, Grant, 58
extraterritorial rights, 26, 211

F

farang, 5, 9, 11–13, 21–22, 24, 41–42, 48, 50
Far Eastern Economic Review, 75, 101
Father of Public Health and Modern Medicine, 160
"Father of Thai History", 8, 29
Father of Thai Nationalism, 15
Finland Charter, 196
"first nationalist", 8
First Opium War, 55

First World War, 121
flag gangs, 212
Florman, Ernest, 202
foreign-educated students (*nakrian nok*), 12, 15, 236
"Foundation of Ayuthia, The", article, 14
Four Reigns (*Si Phaendin*), 78–80, 108
Franco-Siamese War, 205, 209, 212, 226
Franco-Thai War, 77
Frankfurter, Oskar, 229–31
Frederick the Great, 134, 139
free press, 11, 15
free speech, 219–20
Free Thai movement, 62, 90, 129, 150, 162, 169, 195
French Indochina, 38, 59, 212, 214
Friday Aw Saw Band, 140
Front Palace Crisis, 206–7

G

Galyani Vadhana, Princess, 93, 95, 98, 140, 159, 161, 174, 188–89
generation Z, 35
Georgetown University, 87
German-Thai project, 229
Germany, war against, 25
Gilbert and Sullivan, 18
Glad to Oppose Party (*Khana yindi kan kadkhan*), 26
globalization, 75
God Save the Queen, 47, 63
Golden Jubilee, 70, 84, 102, 157, 187
Golden Triangle, 10, 98, 171, 184–85
Golsworthy, Arnold, 18
Gone with the Wind, 80
Goodman, Benny, 139

Gramsci, Antonio, 119–20
Grand Palace, 5, 40, 79–80, 90, 110, 117, 129, 134, 188, 192, 206, 211
Grand Princess of Siam, 57
Great Royal Treasury Department, 205
Great Scholar King, 15
Great Thai Empire, The, (*maha anachak Thai*), 42
Great War, 121, 160
Gulf of Tonkin incident, 155–56, 165

H

Habsburgs, 16
Hall of Opium Museum, 184
Harrison, Rex, 78
Harvard Medical School University, 93, 160–61
Hatta, 39, 44
Haw Wars, 212–13
Heavenly Royal Mother, 97, 133, 158
Heng Samrin, 190
hill tribe, 97, 147, 167, 172–73, 175, 178, 181–85
"His Majesty's Role in the Making of Thai History", speech, 70
"Historical Sketch of Siam", 20
History Instruction Guidelines (*Naeo son prawattisat*), 54
history textbooks, school, 6
Hitler, 38, 42
Ho Samut Samrap Phra Nakhon, 14
Hobsbawm, Eric, 98
Holy Man's Rebellion, 209
Holy Trinity, 16
Hong Xiuquan, 212
House of Representatives, 77, 128
Hsi-Nu-Lo, King, 10

Hun Sen, 190
Hussein Shah, Sultan, 215

I

IAHA (International Association of Historians of Asia), 69
Imagined Communities: Reflections on the Origin and Spread of Nationalism, 31–32, 44
Imeritinsky, Prince, 121
Imperial Indian Mail, 203
Imperial University of Tokyo, 7
Indochina War, 77
Indochinese Communist Party, 166
Inscription, Ramkhamhaeng, 16–17, 19, 32, 178–79
Internal Security Operation Command (ISOC), 176, 186
Inthanon, Prince, 170
Intharayut, 168
Irish Free State, 44
Isan MP, 130
Islamic Thai, 47, 210
ITV television network, 82

J

Japanese occupation, 62, 67, 79, 87, 163–64, 169
Jews of the Orient, The, 8, 25
Jit Phoumisak, 61, 168–69
Johnson, Lyndon Baines, 156, 165
Joint United States Military Advisory Group, Thailand (JUSMAGTHAI), 99
Jory, Patrick, 230
Journal of the Siam Society, 14, 105

K

Kabot R.S. 130, 15

Kambuja, *see* Cambodia
Kantorowicz, Ernst, 222
Kasem Watthanachai, 146–47
Kasetsart University, 140, 142, 144, 147, 153
Kat Katsongkhram, 150
Kennedy, John F., 173
Khamrob, Prince, 76
Khana Nitirat (Law for the People), 233
Khana Ratsadon (People's Party), 27–28, 35, 40, 42, 45, 62, 87, 127, 166, 240
Khana yindi kan kadkhan (Glad to Oppose Party), 26
Khaw Soo Cheang, 217
Khmer, 1, 3, 9–10, 13, 18–19, 30–31, 41, 48, 52, 59, 64, 109, 184, 190
Khmer Discussed (*Thok khamen*), 78
khon, dance-drama performance, 83
Khrong Chandawong, 166–67
Khuang Aphaiwong, 77, 89, 107, 125–26, 150, 163
Khun Sa, drug lord, 187
Khun Wichitmatra, 31, 52–53, 65
Khun Ying, 85
Khwankeo Vajarodaya, 184
Kid thung muang Thai (*Thinking of the Land of the Thai*), 37
Kimigayo, 48
King and I, The, 12, 107
King Bhumibol: Life's Works, 227
Kingdom of Nan Chao (Nanzhao), 1, 9–11, 13–14, 30–31, 51–53, 58, 65, 67
Kingdom of Siam, The, 4
Kingdom of Sukhothai, 1, 70
King of Siam Landing at Logårdstrappan, film, 202

King of Siam Speaks, The, 78
King of White Elephants, 218
kingship, duties of, 70
King's Two Bodies: A Study in Mediaeval Political Theology, The, 222
King Who Had a Hundred Thousand Bumps on His Body, The, 20
Klai Kang Won (Sanssouci) Palace, 27, 134, 176, 228
Kobkua Suwannathat-Pian, 132
Ko-lo-feng/Khun Luang Fa, 10
Ko-lo-fung, king, 30
Komol Kheemthong, 173–74
Korean War, 130–31
Kriangsak Chamanan, 191
Krom Khosanakan, 138
Krom Luang Prajak, Prince, 215
Krom Luang Sanphasit, Prince, 215
Krom Mun Prajak, Prince, 213
Krom Phraya Bamrabporapak, Prince, 236
K.S.R. Kularb, 22–24, 26, 33
Kublai Khan, 51, 67
Kukrit Pramoj, 57, 75–85, 92, 105, 108, 110, 150, 152, 181
Kulap Saipradit, 130
Kuomintang (KMT), 164, 182, 186

L
Lai chiwit (Many Lives), 78
Lak Thai (Thai Pillars), 31, 52–53, 65
"*lakhon luang wichit*" musical plays, 65–66
Land of the Thai (*Muang Thai*), 37, 44, 50–51, 56
Lao-Siamese War, 214
Laos, 3–4, 9–11, 30, 42, 47, 55–56, 58–59, 61, 64, 98–99, 109, 112, 122, 134, 167–68, 170–71, 182, 184, 186, 190–92, 194–95, 209–14, 219, 226–28, 237, 241
Laos Mission, 55
Lavanchy-Clarke, François-Henri, 202
Law of Succession, Palace, 70, 88, 95, 162, 224
Law for the People (Khana Nitirat), 233
Leonowens, Anna, 12, 77
lèse majesté, 22–23, 73, 225–27, 233
Life, Labours and Doctrines of Confucius, 55
Light, Francis, 215
Lilly, J.J., 220
London Mail, 217
London University, 146
Louis XIV, King, 180, 200
Louisiana Purchase Exposition, 4
Luad Suphan (Suphan Blood), play, 66
Luang Adul, 130
Luang Atthakaiwanwathi, 110
Luang Atthapreecha, 110
Luang Phibunsongkhram, *see* Plaek Phibunsongkhram
Luang Phromyothi, 59
Luang Saranupraphan, 59
Luang Thamrong, 89, 125, 130
Luang Wichianphaettayakom, 59
Luang Wichitwathakan, 31, 42–43, 52–54, 57, 59, 65–67
Luang Yutthasatkoson, 59

M
MacArthur, General, 54
Made in Thailand, song, 59
"madness", and opposing ideology, 23, 33

Mae Fah Luang, 97, 133, 158, 178, 181
maha anachak Thai (The Great Thai Empire), 42
Maha Chakri Sirindhorn, Princess, 57
Maha Mala, Prince, 206
Maha Thewi (The Great Queen), play, 67
Mahachon (*The Public*), newspaper, 168
Mahajanaka Jataka, 230–31
Mahajanaka, King, 231
Mahidol Adulyadej, Prince, 93, 158–61, 218
Mahidol University, 142, 146
Mahisra, Prince, 4
Malay, 48, 184, 194, 214
Malaya, 7, 38, 44, 98, 134, 163, 166, 194, 201, 203, 206
Malaysia, 59, 94, 122, 187, 241, 243
mandala, 192, 194, 209–10, 214
Manhattan Rebellion, 129
Manichaeism, 120
Manila Pact, 123
Mao Zedong, 77, 131
Maoism, 166–67
martial law, 69, 71, 123, 165
massacre, 73, 177, 187, 234
McCargo, Duncan, 120, 145
McCarthy, James Fitzroy, 212
McCormick Hospital Chiang Mai, 161
McFarland, George Bradley, 159
"Memories of My Childhood", essay, 132
Memory of the World Programme, 179
Meng Hsi-nu-lo/Khun Luang, 10–11

Merchant of Venice, The, 17
Mikado, 18
Military Assistance Program (MAP), 99
Ming Dynasty, 186
Ministry of Agriculture, 4, 147
Ministry of Commerce, 53
Ministry of Defence, 40–41, 66, 177, 208
Ministry of Education, 6, 56, 58, 161, 182–84, 189
Ministry of Finance, 76, 129, 208
Ministry of Foreign Affairs, 85–86, 98, 206
Ministry of Interior, 91, 177, 210
Ministry of Justice, 111
Ministry of National Development, 124, 186
Ministry of War, 208
Miss Siam/Miss Thailand competition, 132
Mitchell, Margaret, 80
Mom Daeng (Bunnag), 76
Mom Dusadi Na Thalang, 87
Mon-Khmer, 30
monarchy
  absolute, 6, 15, 24, 27–28, 31, 37, 39, 45–46, 48, 50, 56, 60, 64–65, 67, 75, 79, 85, 87, 92–93, 101, 121, 132, 134, 138, 141, 143, 145–46, 161, 200, 219, 224, 226, 239
  British, 71
  constitutional, 28, 71, 79, 93, 224
  fall of, 16, 121–22
  network, 120–21, 145
  power and prestige of, 57, 96
Mongkut, King, 2–5, 12, 14, 21, 27, 33, 49, 63, 77, 87, 104–6,

108, 201, 204–7, 220, 222, 226, 229–30, 236
Mongols, 1, 10, 65
Morant, Robert Laurie, 238
Mote, Frederick W., 31, 58
Mountbatten, Louis, 163
Muang maya (City of Illusion/Hollywood), 78
Muang Thai (Land of the Thai), 37, 44, 50–51, 56
Mussolini, 38
Must-Read Thai books, 80
My Friend Jarlet, 18

N

Naeo son prawattisat (*History Instruction Guidelines*), 54
Nakkhatra Mangala, Prince, 116
nakrian nok (foreign-educated students), 12, 15, 236
Nan Chao (Nanzhao), Kingdom of, 1, 9–11, 13–14, 30–31, 51–53, 58, 65, 67
Nan Chao (Nanzhao), play, 67
nangsu farang, 9
Narai, King, 2, 29, 100
Naresuan, King, 2, 100–1
Narin Phasit, 26, 33–34
Naruhito, Emperor, 139
nation-building, 1, 26, 47, 67
Nation, The, 88
national anthem, 40, 43, 47, 53, 59–61, 63, 148
National Assembly, 57, 70, 77, 88, 94, 123, 127, 166, 169
National Defense Plan, 209
National Economic and Social Development Board (NESDB), 118, 124

National Economic Development Board (NEDB), 124
National Economic Development Plan, 124
National Father's Day, 102, 133
national flag, 26
"national history", 11, 13
national identity, 47
National Library, 31, 229
National Mother Contest, 133
National Mother's Day, 102, 133
National Reform Assembly, 146
National Reform Committee, 146
National Security Agency, 165
nationalism, 1, 6–8, 14–16, 18, 24, 38–39, 41, 44–45, 47–48, 66, 160, 194
Nationalist Chinese Party, *see* Kuomintang
neo-mandala system, 209–10
network monarchy, 120–21, 145
"Network monarchy and legitimacy crises in Thailand", article, 120
New World, 44
News of the Palace, 222–23, 227
Nicholas II, Tsar, 121
Nitthra Chakrit, poem, 179, 193
Niwatthumrong Boonsongpaisan, 233
Nobel Prize, 146
Noi na Nagara, 215
Norman, E.B., 18
North Atlantic Treaty Organization (NATO), 228

O

Obama, Barack, 223
Office of the Heir Presumptive, 207
Office of the National Cultural Commission, 220

Office of the Prime Minister,
    see Prime Minister's Office
Office of the Royal Development
    Projects (RDP), 117–18
"Official Nationalism and
    Imperialism", 6
"Old Thai Empire, The", essay, 13
"On the Independence of a Country",
    essay, 23
Ong Keo, 209
opium, 176, 184–87, 195
Oscar II, King, 121, 202
Othello, 18
Ottomans, 16, 45, 121
Oxford University, 76, 87

P

Pa Sak Cholasit Dam, 148
Pacific War, 38, 67
Paknam Incident, 209, 214, 218
Pakpring Thongyai, 76
Pal Banomyong, 130
Palace Law of Succession, 70, 88, 95,
    162, 224
Palace Rebellion, 90–91, 129
Pallegoix, Jean-Baptiste, 49–50
Pang Malakul na Ayudhya, 195–96
Paramount Pictures, 108
Paribatra Sukhumbandhu, Prince, 87,
    94
Parker, Edward Harper, 13, 55
PARU (BPP Aerial Reinforcement
    Unit), 176
Peace Corps, 173
Peace Foundation of Thailand, 130
Peace Rebellion, 131
People's Alliance for Democracy, 199
People's Democratic Reform
    Committee (PDRC), 148, 198–99

People's Liberation Army, 168, 170
People's Party (*Khana Ratsadon*),
    27–28, 35, 40, 42, 45, 62, 87,
    127, 166, 240
Pepsi Cola, 92
"Persuading the Thais to Build their
    Nation", decree, 47
phad Thai, origin of, 63
Phaithūn Phongsabut, 12
Phak Kaona (Progressive Party), 77
Phama sia muang (*The Burmese Lost
    Their Country*), 78
Phao Siyanon, 91, 125, 129, 150,
    175–76, 182
Phaya Phahon, 46, 94–95, 125, 144
Phayom Chulanont, 129, 169–70, 190
Pheu Thai Party, 88, 233
Phibun, see Plaek Phibunsongkhram
Phichit Prichakon, Prince, 211
Phin Choonhavan, 57, 78, 89, 107,
    125, 128, 130, 150, 169
Phloi, 78–80
Pho Khun Phamuang (Lord
    Phamuang), play, 67
phongsawadan (chronicle), 5–6,
    16–18, 21, 23, 26, 28–29
Phongsawadan Krung Si Ayutthaya,
    17
Phongsawadan Muang Nua (The
    Annals of the North), 4–5
Phongsawadan Nua (Chronicle of the
    North), 17–18
Phongsawadan Yonok (Chronicle of
    the North), 52, 64
Phra Chon Khadi, 91–92
Phra Phinit Chon Khadi, 110
Phra Phutthaloetla Naphalai, 76
Phra Ratchathamnithet, 59
Phra Ruang, play, 18–19, 41

Phra Sarakanprasit, 110
Phra Wisetphotchanakit, 54
Phra Yannasangwon, 73
Phrachao Krung Thon (King of Thonburi), play, 66
Phraya Anuman, 11, 52
Phraya Boran, 20
Phraya Chao Phrom, 10
Phraya Mano, 28, 45–46, 94
Phraya Phahon, 39
Phraya Prachakit, 52, 64
Phraya Si Sitthisongkhram, 46, 62, 169
Phrom, King, 11
Phuean non (*Bedfellow*), 78
Phu Mi Bun religious movement, 209
Phuphan Ratchaniwet Palace, 97
Phuphing Ratchaniwet Palace, 97
P'i-lo-ko/Pilaoko, 10, 30
Pin Tat, 27
Pinklao, Vice-King, 201
Piriya Krairiksh, 32, 179
Piya Malakul na Ayudhya, 196
Plaek Phibunsongkhram, 31, 34, 37–39, 40–42, 46–48, 50, 54, 56–60, 62–63, 65–67, 78, 81, 85, 90–91, 104, 107, 110–11, 118, 123–26, 128–33, 136–38, 144, 150, 152, 162–63, 169, 176
Pleung Wannasri, 168–69
Pongsapat Pongcharoen, 88
Post-Colonial Society and Culture in Southeast Asia, conference, 38
Prajadhipok, King, 27–28, 31, 45, 53, 65, 70, 79, 85, 87–88, 93–95, 104, 121, 127–28, 131, 133–34, 141, 156, 162, 219, 224, 236, 239
Pramote Maiklad, 146–47

Pramote Nakornthap, 196
Pramuanwan, daily, 41
Praphan Yuktanond, 177
Prasert Sapsunthorn, 166
Prates Thai (*Country of Thailand*), article, 42
prawatisat, 16
Prawattisat sakon (International History), 52, 54
Prawese Wasi, 146–47
Praya Borihan Boriraksa, 64
Prayut Chan-o-cha, 35, 74, 88, 100, 198, 227
Prem Tinsulanonda, 100, 102, 118, 120, 147, 186, 191, 224
Pridi Banomyong, 39, 42–43, 57, 62, 65, 70, 81, 84, 88–90, 100, 104, 107, 110, 125–30, 144, 150, 162–63, 166, 169, 188
Prime Minister's Office, 41, 60, 118, 124, 138
primogeniture, and succession, 70, 89, 207, 219, 224
Princess Mother, 122, 145, 155–59, 162–65, 167, 170, 172, 174–78, 181–83, 185–89, 195–96, 221
Princess Mother's Medical Volunteers (PMMV), 173–75, 178, 184
Princeton University, 31, 58
print capitalism, 15, 21–22
printing press, 22, 51
Prisdang, Prince, 238
Privy Council, 82, 104, 127, 146–47, 196, 205
"Problems of Thai Prehistory", 31
Progressive Party (Phak Kaona), 77
prostration, abolition of, 203–4
Public, The, (*Mahachon*), newspaper, 168

Puey Ungphakorn, 82, 195
Puyi, Emperor, 157

Q
Qing dynasty, 16, 45, 212
Queen Mother, 116, 156

R
racism, 25
Radio Aw Saw, 138–40
Radio Coup, 128
Radio Thailand, 60, 138–39
Raffles, Stamford, 215
Rai Mae Fah Luang Orchard, 184
Rajamangalabhisek Royal Ceremony, 180
Raja of Ligor, 215
Ram Vajiravudh, 32
Rama I, 26–27, 32, 34, 43, 66, 100–1, 210
Rama II, 76
Rama III, 2, 5, 21, 49
Rama V, *see* Chulalongkorn
Rama VI, *see* Vajiravudh
Rama VII, *see* Prajadhipok
Rama VIII, *see* Ananda Mahidol
Rama IX, *see* Bhumibol Adulyadej
Rama X, *see* Vajiralongkorn
Ramayana, 32, 83, 109
Rambai Barni, Queen, 94, 162
Ramkhamhaeng *Inscription*, 16–17, 19, 32, 178–79
Ramkhamhaeng, King, 1, 3, 16–17, 19, 32, 100, 178–79
Ramkhamhaeng University, 142
Ramon Magsaysay Award, 146
ramvong, dance, 63
Rangsit, Prince Regent, 126
Rangsit University, 80

Ratana Sakunthai, 173
Ratanakosin/Bangkok, 2, 9, 13, 19, 29, 34, 52
ratchakitchanubeksa, 21
Ratmanu (Rajamanu), play, 66
ratthaniyom, 39, 40, 47–48, 60
Recalling Childhood, 132
red jar constitution, 150
Remote Area Security Development (RASD), 175
Revolutionary King, 100
Reynolds, Craig J., 11, 22–23, 233
Riera, José Grases, 180
righteous ruler (*dharma raja*), 70–71, 83, 100, 226
Rockefeller Foundation, 159–61
Rolin-Jaequemyns, Gustave, 218
Romance of the Three Kingdoms, The, 243
Romanovs, 16, 45
Romeo and Juliet, 17
Rosa, Ercole, 180
Royal Asiatic Society, 14
Royal Father, cult of, 179
Royal Gazette, 21, 203
royal graduation ceremony, 141
Royal Grandmother, 97, 133, 155, 158
Royal Infantry of the Line, 208
Royal Medical College, 161
Royal Military Academy, 208–9
Royal Pages Bodyguards, 208
Royal Printing House, 21
Royal Projects (RP), 117
Royal Railway of Siam, 134
Royal Research Society, 14
Royal Thai Armed Forces, 170
Royal Thai Army, 90, 171, 223
Royal Thai Army Radio, 82

258 • *Thailand: A Struggle for the Nation*

Royal Thai Marine Corps, 90
Royal Thai Navy, 90, 99
Royal Thai Police, 164
Royal Thai Survey Department, 213
royal train, 134–36
Royal Wish Projects (RWP), 117
royalism, 48, 84
royally initiated projects (RIPs), 102, 115–22, 137, 147, 221
Royally Patronized Projects (RPP), 118
Ruam Wongphan, 167
Ruang khong chat Thai (*Story of the Thai Nation*), 52
Ruang Thieo Muang Phra Ruang (*A Tour of the Phra Ruang Country*), 17
rubber plantation, 215

S

Saha Union Group, 86
Sahacheep (Trade Union), 130, 150
Saiyud Kerdphol, 170
Sala Chalermkrung Royal Theatre, 89
Salang Bunnag, 177
Samak Sundaravej, 82
samakkhi, concept of, 24
Sanam Chandra Palace, 15, 135
Sang Phatthanothai, 59
Sanga Kanchanakkhaphan, 52
Sangkhomsat Parithat, 57
Sangwan Talapat, 97, 155, 158, 160, 164
Sanssouci Palace (Klai Kang Won), 27, 134, 176, 228
Sanya Dharmasakti, 82
Saovabha Phongsri, Queen, 116, 156–57, 160
Saovabha Schools, 157

Sapathum Palace, 161
Sappasartsupakij, Prince, 202
Sarekat Islam, 44
Sarit Thanarat, 57–58, 60, 90, 102, 107, 118, 123–25, 129, 132–33, 136, 140, 165–66, 170, 175–77, 186, 199, 224
Sasakawa Peace Foundation, 186
Sathianraphap (Stability), newspaper, 131
Savang Vadhana. 93
Sayam Nikon (*Siamese People*), 85
Sayam praphet, journal, 22
Scandinavian Airlines System, 135
Scharnberger, Elisabeth, 104
scholarship grants, 143–46
school history textbooks, 6
Schurovsky, Pyotr, 63
Second Opium War, 55
Second World War, 38, 42, 54, 56, 62, 66, 79, 89, 104, 107, 122, 132, 150, 157, 162, 166, 169, 195, 198, 232, 240
Seksan Prasertkul, 187, 191
Senate, 128
Seni Pramoj, 76–78, 92, 110, 133, 150
Seraidaris, Cleon, 112
Seri Manangkhasila Party, 107, 136
Serm Suk PLC, 92
Sern Panyarachun, 85
Shakespeare, 17
Sheng-luo-pi, 10, 30
Shinzo Abe, 223
Si Intrathit, king, 1, 19
Si Phaendin (*Four Reigns*), 78–80, 108
Siam
    dynastic history of, 1–6

name change, and, 31, 37–44, 47–51, 56–57
symbol of, 26
see also Thailand
Siam Commercial Bank, 160
"Siam from an Historical Standpoint", 4
Siam Mapped, 2
Siam Rath, 76, 78, 82, 152, 181
Siam Repository, 21
Siam Society, 14, 104–5, 229
Siam Weekly Advertiser, 21
Siamese Crowned Royal Son, 207
Siamese-English dictionary, 159
Siamese French English dictionary (*Dictionnaire Siamois Français Anglais*), 49
Siburapha, 130
Siemlo, 4
Silapakorn University, 82, 142
Singapore Free Press, 29
Sino-French War, 212
Sino-Thai Business (*Thai Hua Siang Po*), 85
Sirichai Chiang Sen, 3
Sirikit Kittiyakorn, Queen, 80, 85, 91, 97, 104, 108, 116–17, 132–34, 141, 157, 181–82, 192, 195, 218, 221, 223, 228
Sirindhorn, Princess, 119, 135, 143, 145, 153, 184, 189, 221, 223, 225, 228
Siriraj Hospital, 158–59, 161, 188, 223, 228
Siriraj, Prince, 158, 223
slavery, abolition of, 203–5
"Sleeper and the Waker, The", poem, 179, 193
Smith, Samuel, 21

Social Action Party, 77
socialism, 48
Sodsri Chakrabandhu, 85
Somdet Chaophraya Si Suriwongse, 207
Somdet To, 33
Somdet Ya, 97, 133, 155, 158, 178, 181
Somsak Jeamthirasakul, 111
Song Nopphakhun, 169
Songkran, water festival, 133
Sonthi Boonyaratglin, 148, 198
Sopranzetti, Claudio, 240–41
Soul of the Nation, 96, 100, 221
Southeast Asia Collective Defense Treaty, 123, 165
Southeast Asian Buddhists, 59
Southeast Asia Treaty Organization (SEATO), 98–99, 123, 131, 228
Souvenir of the Siamese Kingdom Exhibition at Lumbini Park B.E. 2468, 20, 27, 34
Soviet Union, 98, 131, 167, 173
Speakers' Corner, 91
Sra Pathum Palace, 174
Sri Ayuddhya, 4
Sri Ayutthaya, battleship, 130
Srinagarindra Boromarajajonani, Princess, 97, 116–17, 120, 133, 155, 162
Srinakharinwirot Universitiy, 144
"statism", 39–40, 48, 60
Stengs, Irene, 180
Story of Mahajanaka, The, 230–31
Story of the Thai Nation (*Ruang khong chat Thai*), 52
Story of Tongdaeng, The, 231–32
student activism, 59, 69, 71–74, 77, 90, 118, 130, 141, 177, 191, 199, 227, 252

student enrolment, 142–43, 153
Suankularb College, 76
succession, and primogeniture, 70, 89, 207, 219, 224
Suchinda Kraprayoon, 72, 74, 86, 109, 115, 224
Suddha Dibyaratana, Princess, 87
sue pa (Wild Tigers Corps), 16, 18, 104
Suez Canal, 215
Sujit Wongthes, 58
Suk Thalang (*Battle of Thalang*), play, 66
Sukarno, 39, 44
Sukhothai, 3, 9, 11, 16–19, 29
Sukhothai-ism, 17
Sukhothai-Phra Ruang Dynasty, 20
Sukhumabhinan, Prince, 86–87
Sukhumbhand Paribatra, 74–75, 84, 86–88
Sukumalmarsri, Queen Consort, 87
Sulak Sivaraksa, 57, 105
Sultan of Kedah, 215
Suphanni Kanchanatthiti, 6
Suphapsatri (Lady), 85
Supreme Court, 82, 85, 92
Supreme Allied Commander South East Asia (SACSEA), 163
Supreme Patriarch of Thailand, 73
Surayuth Chulanont, 46, 63, 129, 169, 190–91, 196
Susi thaihao (Empress Dowager Cixi), 78, 157
Suthep Thuagsuban, 148, 199
Suvadhana, Princess, 94

T
Tai-Lao, 30
Tai race, 5, 54–55, 68

Tai Race: Elder Brother of the Chinese, The, 54–55
Taiping Rebellion, 212–14
Taksin, King, 26–27, 34, 66, 100–1, 210, 215–16
Talleyrand of Thailand, 54
Tarling, Nicholas, 132
Tasting, Ranting, cooking show, 82
Television Pool of Thailand (TPT), 196
Temple of Dawn, 130
Thai Airways, 134
Thai baht, devaluation, 69, 222
Thai books, Must-Read, 80
Thai Chinese, 51, 190, 217
Thai Film Censorship Board, 108
Thai Hua Siang Po (Sino-Thai Business), 85
Thai Khadi Research Institute, 83
Thai Patriotic Front, 167–68
Thai Pillars (*Lak Thai*), 31, 52–53, 65
Thai Rak Thai (Thai love Thai) party, 68, 147
Thai Red Cross Society, 156
Thaification, 63
Thailand
  capitals of, 9
  constitution-writing in, 126–27
  name change, and, 31, 37–44, 47–51, 56–57
  population, 142–43
  road construction in, 151
  universities in, 142–44, 153
  see also Siam
Thailand Post, 232
Thailand Research Fund, 80
Thais Are Here, The, (*Khon Thai Yu Thini*), 58
Thais are in Southeast Asia, The, (*Khon Thai yu nai usakhane*), 58

Thais Do Not Come from Anywhere (*Khon Thai Mai Dai Ma Chak Nai*), 58
Thaksin Ratchaniwet Palace, 97
Thaksin Shinawatra, 68, 86, 147, 153, 169, 196, 198–99, 222–23, 240
Thammasat University, 38, 53, 73, 77, 80–84, 90, 109, 111, 140–44, 153, 163, 168, 177, 188, 195, 233
Thanet Aphornsuwan, 126
Thanin Kraivichien, 85
Thanit Yupho, 109
Thanom Kittikachorn, 73, 81, 118, 123–25, 129, 133, 141, 155, 165, 173, 224
Thanphuying La-iad Phibunsongkram, 133
Thao Saenpom, play, 18, 20
Thawan Thamrongnawasawat, 89
Thawil Pliensri, 233
Theravada Buddhism, 71, 223, 226, 230
Thewathat, 24
Thianwan, 22, 26
Thinking of the Land of the Thai (*Kid thung muang Thai*), 37
Thip Keson, 211
Thirayuth Boonmee, 187, 191
Third World, 123, 131
Thok khamen (*Khmer Discussed*), 78
Thomas of Savoy, Prince, 121
Thong Jamsri, 168
Thongchai Winichakul, 2
Thongphan Sutthimat, 166
Thousand Years of the Tartars, A, 55
Three Seals Law, 21
Tia Sin Tat, 27
tin mining, 215, 217

Tod Kathin Ceremony, 54
Tojo, Hideki, 38–39, 107
Tom Yam Kung crisis, 157, 222
Tour of the Phra Ruang Country, A, (*Ruang Thieo Muang Phra Ruang*), 17
Trade Union (Sahacheep), 130, 150
Trent College, 76
Trinity College, Cambridge, 85
Tripitaka, 226
"True Nationhood", essay, 24
Twentieth Century Fox, 78, 107
Two Great Development Kings, 220

U
U Nu, 44
Udom Sisuwan, 168
Ugly American, The, 78
Umberto I, King, 121
UNESCO, 179, 188
UNICEF, 86
United Front for Democracy Against Dictatorship (UDD), 224
United Nations Security Council, 166
United States Operations Mission to Thailand, 175
Universal Pictures, 78
University College, London, 13
University of California, 147, 240
University of Chicago, 147
University of Colorado, 146
University of Hong Kong, 58
University of Lausanne, 91, 95, 112
University of Moral and Political Sciences, 53, 81
University of Tübingen, 211
Up the Yangtsze, 55
Ursuline Order, 93

USS *Maddox*, 156, 165
Uthong, King, 2, 4–6, 10, 20
U-T'ong Rama-thi-bodi, 3

V

Vajiralongkorn, Crown Prince, 73, 132–33, 153, 221, 233, 240, 242
Vajiravudh, King, 4, 6, 8, 11, 14–20, 23–25, 27–29, 31–34, 44–45, 47–49, 51, 70, 79, 89, 92, 94, 104, 106–7, 121, 141, 156, 160–62, 180, 192, 219, 224, 233, 236, 239
Vajirayana Library, 14
Vajirunhis, Prince, 57, 219, 207
Valaya, Princess, 158
vaṃsāvatāra, 28
Vella, Walter F., 20, 22, 31
Vibhavadi Rangsit, Princess, 195
Victor Emmanuel II, King, 180
Victoria, Queen, 63
Vietnam, 10–11, 42, 55–56, 98–99, 101, 112, 122–23, 156, 165–67, 190, 204, 212–13, 221, 241, 243
Vietnam War, 156, 165, 221
Village Scouts (VS), 176–77
Virulent Burmese Student Warriors, 87
Voice of the People of Thailand (VOPT), 167
Volunteer Defense Corps (VDC), 176–77

W

Wachirawut, *see* Vajiravudh
Wake the Nation and the Heart, policy, 16
wan chat (National Day), 39–40, 60–61, 132
Wan Waithayakorn, Prince, 105
Wang Na Incident, 206
War Department, 208
Wat Arun, 130
Wat Bowonniwet, 2, 73, 136
Wat Phra That Doi Suthep, 185
Wat Rakhang, 33
Wat Saket, 21
Wat Suan Dok, 192
Wen Jiabao, 223
Whittington, Richard, 104
Wichai Ketsriphongsa, 73
Wichaichan, Prince, 201, 206–7, 218
wikhroa ruang Muang Tai doem (*Analysis of the Ancient Tai Nation*), 54
Wilatwong Phongsabut, 12
Wild Tigers Corps (*sue pa*), 16, 18, 104
Wilhelm I, Kaiser, 121
Witayakorn Chiengkul, 80
Worachet Phakeerat, 233
World Bank, 123–24
Worshipping the Great Modernizer: King Chulalongkorn, Patron-Saint of the Thai Middle Class, 180
Wyatt, David K., 22, 210

X

xenophobia, 23

Y

Yangtse River, 9, 11
Yanhee Dam, 123
Yaowarat Incident, 164

Yingluck Shinawatra, 68, 86, 88, 148, 191, 198–99, 233, 240
Yong Sathiankoset, 52
Young Siam, 205
Yuan dynasty, 10
Yunnan, 1, 9, 11, 13, 42, 51–52, 55, 58, 64, 67, 167–68, 171, 182, 185–86, 212

Z

Zheng He, 186
Zhou Enlai, 77

The Author

Charnvit Kasetsiri, born 1941, is a Professor Emeritus of Thammasat University, Bangkok, Thailand. He is a prominent historian and a Thai Studies scholar. After obtaining his bachelor's degree in Diplomacy with Honours from Thammasat in 1963, he pursued his 1967 MA in Diplomacy and World Affairs at Occidental College, Los Angeles, California, under a Rockefeller scholarship and his 1972 PhD in Southeast Asian History at Cornell University, New York.

His thesis, *The Rise of Ayudhya and a History of Siam in the 14th and 15th Centuries*, was published by Oxford in Asia in 1976. He served as Lecturer of History at Thammasat from 1973 to 2001 and founded, in 2000, the Southeast Asian Studies Program. He was the President of Thammasat University in 1995–96. He has written approximately 200 articles and a few publications on Thai and Southeast Asian History. He has launched a "Siam Not Thailand" campaign to rename the country to reflect the reality about its ethnics, languages and cultural identities.

His late works deal with questions of war and peace and good ASEAN neighbour relations, especially between Thailand and Cambodia. He is a co-author with Pavin Chachavalpongpun and Pou Sothirak, *Preah Vihear: A Guide to the Thai-Cambodian Conflict and Its Solutions* (Bangkok, 2013). See also his *Studies in Thai and Southeast Asian Histories* (Bangkok, 2015).

Charnvit has been awarded a Fukuoka Academic Prize 2012, Japan, and the Distinguished Contributions to Asian Studies (DCAS) 2014 by the Association for Asian Studies, USA.

www.ingramcontent.com/pod-product-compliance
Lightning Source LLC
Chambersburg PA
CBHW052112010526
44111CB00036B/1834